# Law and Economic Order
# A Theory of Requisite Economy
### By
## Peter Gibson Friesen

PM Library

copyright © 2019 by Peter Gibson Friesen
ISBN: 978-1-7337025-1-5

All rights reserved. No part of this book may be used or reproduced in any manner whatsoever without written permission, except in the case of quotes for personal use and brief quotations embedded in critical articles or reviews.

PM Library
an imprint of Poetic Matrix Press
John Peterson, Publisher
www.poeticmatrix.com

Law and Economic Order

A Theory of Requisite Economy

# Contents

Forward     7

Preface:     14

Chapter 1: Demand and Supply     23

Chapter 2: The basis of Organization     49

Chapter 3: Wild Economy     81

Chapter 4: Control Economy     113

Chapter 5: Behavioral Economy     143

Chapter 6: Requisite Economy     173

Chapter 7: Regression and Progression     201

Postscript:     228

End Notes:     232

Appendix:     254

Author Biography

# Foreword

How is it that an engineer and a lawyer meet each other around the same issues? Why have I been asked by Peter Friesen to write this foreword? Well, neither of us have been trapped in our discipline, although both of us still are embedded in it. Where we meet is by sharing in our practice two experiences: the experience of language and the experience of organization.

For me this happened early in my career as ICT-project manager, later as manager of an IT-department for an American multinational. Although I learned what is called Information Theory, soon I discovered that the foundations of that theory (statistics and the Shannon and Weaver definition) lacked completely the concept of "meaning." I learned the hard way, working with my clients, that in communication the sender only generates noise, while the receiver is trying to make sense of it. The receiver is the most important component of communication, not the sender, because meaning is an attribution made by the receiver.

Now, in a world overwhelmed by recorded text in all its forms, this experience becomes of paramount importance, because text as the product of a sender is not that important. The hermeneutic activity of the reader is the real work. And this book—Law and Economic Order—has put me to an intense but rewarding work of interpretation. This foreword is the result of that work, and is offered in gratitude for the work that Peter Friesen has put into *Law and Economic Order: A Theory of Requisite Economy. Law and Economy,* as two ideas examined side by side, radically and grammatically, criticizes the oxymoron: economic law!

At times our world is overwhelmed with misunderstandings, because media communications are looked upon as the responsibility of the senders, while the work of the receiver is not considered. The experience of escalating written conflicts through electronic media, and through various recorded texts, is undeniable. But how is it then possible to have meaningful interchanges between human beings? And there, I come to a second focal point that Friesen and I share: organization. The context of all that text in human endeavors is human work and the way it is organized. If not, statements are made in a contextual vacuum, and hence become vacuous.

All living organisms, from the cell to a "society" are navigating a basic conflict, i.e., centrifugal forces generated by their interactions with an environment and centripetal forces designed to establish and maintain the "identity" of the system. I discovered in Law, the expression of the centripetal forces that manage or reduce conflict, and in Economy, the expression of the centrifugal forces that promote innovation and competition. Organizations adapt themselves as long as they can manage this basic conflict. The end of a living system, its death, proceeds through either explosion or implosion.

Friesen describes different types of economies, which you find in the headings of three chapters (Wild Economy, Control Economy and Behavioral Economy). Each of them has discovered another way of coping with that tension, this contradiction. Apparently, the most fragile of the economies, described by Friesen, is the Control Economy, because it is directly affected by the fallibility of human beings, who live with the illusion that there is no such contradiction. The ruler and his surrounding of yea-sayers is bound to betrayal. Hegel, talking from his experience as a teacher in an aristocratic German family, elaborated this illusion in his concept of Master-Slave relation, where the slave as laborer controls the livelihood and identity of his master.

The failure of so many large organizations in their attempt to change policy or direction can be readily found in a defective concept of implementation—the split between the thinkers (the decision makers) and the tinkers (those who "implement" based upon their understanding of the product of the thinkers). They meet conflicts, which necessarily arise, when confronted with the environment they are working in. The split between thinking and doing is the root of the fragility and downfall of Control Economies.

The immense gap between financial engineers and the economic reality of people indebting themselves on a massive scale can be seen as the major trigger of the financial crisis of 2008. And this is still going on.

Nevertheless, the question remains: why is it that after about 250 years of the emergence of what Friesen calls Requisite Economy, where Law and Economy balance each other in a better way than in Control Economy, Control Economy in business and in government is still in fact the major paradigm? Perhaps the split between thinking and doing is still so powerful because of some underlying mechanism.

Through Friesen's work, I have been able to detect that mechanism more clearly than I had previously.

Friesen reminds us of how Control Economy appeared in the Fertile Crescent. In the same part of the world where writing started on clay tablets which were prepared to record accounts In Sumer, the sum was invented. (Pun intended!)

As Friesen develops in the book, logic increases in complexity by adding values, which he expresses symbolically as a selected point (.) leading sequentially to a selected complex (O). The addition of elements (.) to a series (……..) will never lead by simple aggregation to an emerging (O). The emergence of an (O) out of the complexities working at the level of the (.) is something that can be described as an "emergence logic." A hierarchy of cumulations (concatenations) inhibit the appearance of emergence and avoids the tricky question of value, which is at the basis of emergence. Summing up lacks the complexity of what Friesen calls "parallel processing." I relate parallel processing with the capability of perceiving the interrelated network of (.)s, elements of a system. His logic is, in effect, a set of simplified drawings of logical hierarchy that the reader may, with modest effort, come to discover in his or her own experience.

Producing a batch of a thousand products is a completely different game than producing a thousand times one product. This discovery was made when great scale textile mills replaced farm craft weaving. This could only be done together with the building of canals and railway systems. Globalization and its economies of scale can only take place where every government in one or another way is subsidizing transport or allowing its costs to be externalized. Here Law and Economy relate directly with one another.

It is well known in statistics that an average, which is another form of sum, indicates a characteristic of a statistical population, and never may be used as a norm for an individual element of that population: one of the most common errors by users of statistics in all kind of disciplines. Even transforming a sum into an average is pointing to an emergent characteristic, but as such it is not the same as a principle or value that rules over the aggregate.

Values at the core (that enable and produce) of Requisite Economies, are left out of classical economic thinking, which is based primarily on aggregated quantities. Those aggregated quantities are sums derived from accounting practices. The basic mechanism maintaining the Control Economy is hiding in accounting processes, in sums, aggregations, averages and percentages. Accounting procedures are unaware of the fact that 1 x 1000 ≠ 1000 x 1, when taking real life experience into account. Using a monetary unit as a metric, which can add apples and pears, does not help to understand their difference in shape and taste. That is why price and value have a totally different meaning in practice. While many economists may concede this point in casual conversation, it does not become a plain, obvious and necessary aspect of formal conversation without a theoretical shift to Requisite Economy.

Although much lip service is given to networks—which are not sums, but complex systems of mutual relations—accounting and auditing still takes consolidation, aggregation and averages, as their basic operations to understand networks. Maybe the success of the Basque Mondragon Cooperative resides in the refusal to consolidate—to add up—the results of the 200 cooperatives as a management tool. They understand in practice that networks and sums are mutually exclusive. Headquarters are for them a means to interrelate, to network between the cooperatives, not to control them with aggregated figures.

Along with this, we see the absurdity of growing "Gross National Products," which are adding, in a valueless way, all that can be accounted for, and leaving aside the value that human work adds to products, and which cannot be accounted for, such as the work of volunteers and the work of women at home, etc. Even destruction is added to the Gross National Product: each car accident, each health accident, each war—each bomb and bullet—add to the numbers accounted for in the National Product. Nevertheless, this fetish figure, and its derivatives such as "National Debt" are still paramount in the language of economic policy makers. As if growing cancer cells is "good" because of their growth!

In his calm way, Friesen is pointing to the need to overhaul mainstream economical thinking by introducing the concept of value. Valuing as a human activity (not valueless pricing) was very present in the mind of the founders of economical thinking. Aristotle already pointed out that law and ethics should restrain the cancerous centrifugal forces of what he calls the "chrematistics" (the study of wealth or a particular theory of wealth as measured in money). And was Adam Smith himself not first an ethicist? A wealthy nation is an emergent characteristic and cannot be measured through the sum of the wealth of its inhabitants.

In a Requisite Economy the wealth of a nation is the result of healthy relations between its various players, between Law, government and Economy, and business, coping with the basic conflict they are living in and with. Society is not the sum of isolated elements but the complex network of relations between them, balancing cooperation and competition. A Requisite economy, by definition, is very much aware of the forms and patterns in which these relations organize.

Economic interest does not consist of human desire in a state of isolation but in the way at least two individuals value their relation, i.e.give meaning to it. The basic element of economical action is not the individual player, but the relation between players. And the same is true for Law. Individual rights are meaningless if they are taken out of the context of relations between people. Meaningfully theorizing about Economy and Law takes a system of relations as its basic element, and requires a human processing capacity capable of discerning the emergence of networks, and a social surround that welcomes that capacity.

I interpret Friesen's use of the symbolism of (.) and (O) to indicate emergence as a pragmatic statement about the recursive nature of human affairs. Requisite hierarchies stand in contrast to the classical way of looking at hierarchies that equate a hierarchic level or tier with the sum of the parts of a lower order. In a Requisite hierarchy, a system of a higher order is managing and integrating the emergent characteristics generated by the interaction of systems of lower order. This is why equating a corporation with a person leads to anomalies, that is, because the two entities pertain to a different recursion level, engaging different value systems, and different principles of Law and Economy. The equation of person and corporation is not only impractical, but dangerous.

All of what human beings do is by definition bound by human scale. And one of the basic characteristics of that scale stems from the Wild Economy. Through most of our history as a species we have lived socially in small tribes or extended families. They had and have a span of relations around about 200 individuals, which include the number of names and faces we are able to fit with one another, the number of people we can speak to and interact with in a "real" context. The illusion of Control Economy is that people shed their tribal natures and deal with issues beyond this scale. It is easy to imagine this when thinking and doing are theoretically separated. Reality, however, proves that this separation is delusional and hence self-destructive.

So, there is no difference between the President of the United States and the gardener of the White House. Each of them belongs to a tribe of the same size. Only their tribe is quite different. And normally they are involved in activities that belong to a different recursion level. They are dealing with a very different set of relations, though navigating the same basic conflict between centripetal and centrifugal forces, between Law and Economy.

Friesen's introduction of the notion of a Requisite hierarchy supports what is widely referred to in organizational theory as the "principle of subsidiarity." This principle, which argues that decisions should be made at the lowest level possible, can now be redefined in the following way: decisions should be taken at the level where the conflict between Law and Economy (centrifugal and centripetal force) is experienced and should not be delegated upward, where they lose their conflictive nature, and tend to get swept under the rug. The conflict doesn't go away, but people act as if it had by way of an administrative order.

Decisions are actions; otherwise they are no more than the expression of intentions. Thus, delegation as splitting a sum into its parts and delegating each part to an actor is at odds with the principle of subsidiarity.

Budgets and budgeting are another consequence of a primitive view of hierarchy, and are a typical expression of Control Economy. The best performing companies have no headquarters and surely no budgeting and budget accountability system. Dysfunctional businesses, by contrast, proceed as if management was a zero-sum game, where management participants go to war for the means, without any insight in why they are needed. In this environment, management and governance are reduced to budgets and accounting, and can function strangely as non-productive management pantomimes.

Real subsidiarity implies a recursive organization, each level involved with the interactions, and the networking of the activities on a lower recursion level. And each level, within its own value system, functions at a human scale. While organizations often diagram themselves into a sequence of tiers, each of which oversees a single tier that rests below it, that view is an oversimplification. People—that is, given individuals—are normally engaged simultaneously in three recursion levels. Bright divisions between levels is a theoretical construct, but plays out in reality in part through a blurring of those divisions. Friesen's book provides some useful tools through which to speak with clarity about this process.

It is useful in reading this work, perhaps, to know that there are many thinking about the problems created by class division and the frequent emergence of oppressive political structure. There is a shift occurring in the view of human organization from an aggregation of persons to a living system of relations between people activated by shared value.

The work that Elinor Ostrom, Nobel laureate in Economics, did on the practice of managing commons all over the world, points the way to a Requisite Economy. Her eight rules for a successful commons reveal a way in which Wild Economy transforms itself in Requisite Economy, without having to pass through an unpleasant, and even oppressive stage referred to here as "Control Economy."

Closing this foreword by mentioning these rules may help the reader to discover that Requisite Economy already is working. Adding recursivity in defining and redefining the commons is in my opinion the way forward towards a better balance between Law and Economy, towards Requisite Economy.

Ostrom's principles for the governance of commons:

1. Define clear group boundaries.
2. Match rules governing use of common goods to local needs and conditions.
3. Ensure that those affected by the rules can participate in modifying the rules.
4. Make sure the rule-making rights of community members are respected by outside authorities.
5. Develop a system, carried out by community members, for monitoring members' behavior.
6. Use graduated sanctions for rule violators.
7. Provide accessible, low-cost means for dispute resolution.
8. Build responsibility for governing the common resource in nested tiers from the lowest level up to the entire interconnected system.

In these rules the mutual game of cooperation and competition generates real value, even if it cannot completely be priced in monetary terms.

In this way I hope that reading Law and Economic Order, an elaborate thinking exercise, may resonate with the reader's own experiences in the way he or she deliberates over the Common Good (implicit or explicit in his or her social network) and its values. As an engineer, I cannot leave out applying the rich principles developed by Friesen in this work.

Luc Hoebeke

*Belgian consultant, author and lecturer in the field of self-organization, innovation processes and human activity systems; known for his book Making Work Systems Better: A Practitioner's Reflections (1994).*

# Preface

In 2003 I completed the first draft of a manuscript entitled On Freedom. It was written to explore the implications of a number of significant discoveries in the social science of human organization that had been gathered under the moniker "Requisite Organization"—so named by Elliott Jaques, its principal scientist. I submitted the manuscript to Jaques for review, only to discover that he passed away in March of that year. Sometime later, I was invited by his wife Kathryn Cason to join a board of advisors she was convening to discuss the future of Requisite Organization.

At a meeting with Kathryn and other advisors I expressed my view that Requisite might be useful in the development of a theory of economy, and that we might want as a group to consider developing something of that sort. As is often the case for those who propose that something be done, it later appeared that if such a thing were to occur, I would have to do it myself, even though my primary training is in philosophy and law. I undertook the task a few years ago, and have found it to be more interesting than I expected.

The essential hypothesis of Requisite—now subject to significant empirical verification—is that human organizations stratify in a way that mirrors human development. Human development manifesting in stages during childhood does not come to an end in the step we think of as "adulthood," but rather continues onward in the phased emergence (growth) of strategic orientations in human cooperative endeavors—human organization—and follows the same pattern regardless of the organizational context. Knowing how this works allows one to design work and institutions much more effectively.

My own contribution to that science started in 1979 and consisted of written submissions and dialogue with Jaques over several years. These focused on the logical foundation for that science and offered information processing as a metaphor suitable to the description of human development because it was context neutral and transferable. It could be used to describe a person's phased acquisition of control over social systems of any kind, and could also be adapted to the description of the abstract processes of first order logic. I am told that there were others who promoted the use of an information processing vocabulary as well. By the mid-1980s Jaques had adopted it into his description of human maturation.

By then an impressive assembly of researchers and practitioners were celebrating the emergence of real "science" due to measurable constants in organizational stratification. Social organization might be identified with a form that connects with something deep in the mind, and may therefore cohere more predictably than we had once thought. By the time of his death Jaques had completed a number of well-reasoned theoretical works, exploring the significance of his findings on subjects like organizational accountability, labor markets and fair payment, and the meaning of "time" and "life." He didn't have much to say about "law" and "economy," nor have other researchers and practitioners contributing to Requisite as a movement.

This is surprising, as the usefulness of organizational constants in the development of a field of knowledge called "Economics" is obvious. We depend, after all, on cooperation with others for the supply of our basic needs for food, shelter and clothing, and fare much better by combining with others—and purchasing from the combined efforts of others—than we fare alone. This brings into view our genetically evolved behavior as a species engaged with a harsh natural environment, and in competition with other species, where tribal organization could be viewed as one of our most important survival traits. As such, social organization is likely embedded in consciousness as deeply as language itself.

But in modern economic theory, not much is said about the structure of language as a basis for the productivity of markets. Modern theory emphasizes human behavior—both individually and in collections of individuals—as the study of exogenously related phenomena, i.e., interests in competition with other interests. Much of the science of economics falls within the rubric of a theory of complexity and of games designed for the most part to explain how one interest responds competitively to the asserted interest of another. Markets are complex because individuals develop strategies that anticipate and/or respond to perceived strategic orientation of others.

While market theory is imaginative and useful in the explanation of competitive behavior, it is nonetheless weak in explaining the kind of cooperation reflected in social organization. If there are behavioral constants governing cooperative endeavors, it may be useful to include them in a theory of economy.

Take, for instance, the modern economic reality of competitive markets. Competitive intercourse within such markets somehow evokes productive engagements without much regression into violence and predation. Why is that? We might say that it is because there are laws in place which prevent it, and that these serve as effective normative boundaries. In saying that, however, we identify an endogenous characteristic—something working within individual consciousness that promotes socially cohesive behavior. Though we tend to treat these boundaries—along with the boundary setting process—as legal considerations, they are probably more essential to providing for our needs than the markets which emerge within these boundaries. As we examine modern economy, we are not so much engaged in the study of competition, as in a form of organization that allows peaceful competition to occur.

This book is the first that I am aware of that examines economy as an organizational phenomenon, or rather, interprets the emergence of economic behavior through an organizational filter. Perhaps the reason for this is that before the emergence of Requisite, organization was treated, more or less, as a makeshift phenomenon. There were a number of organizational theories circulating in the early part of the 20th century, but none sufficiently connected to innate and defining human behavioral motives and structures as those which have emerged under Requisite as social science. I have thus been blessed with an opportunity not available before, which is to take the mechanics (laws of motion) applicable to human organization and use it to acquire a view of economy as an organizational phenomenon—a theory of law and economic order.

Part of this view includes what appears to be a theory of history, but I should offer some precautions in that regard. This book does, in fact, take us back in time, at least in the sense that we consider the emergence of law and economy as a property of language, existing where there were (or are) no kings and kingdoms, and man presumably extracts a living from the wild. But the chapter entitled "Wild Economy" is not meant to be anthropological—i.e., the study of hunter gatherer cultures, but is about the analysis of language as an organizational force. It is what the human organism brings to the world absent historical embellishments, where history itself may be regarded as only a brief interruption in the continuity of consciousness.

The history of civilization marked by the development of armies, empires, currencies, alphabets and religions might be viewed as a biological anomaly brought on by the success of language, and uncomfortable proximity between the diverse societies spawned by it. History seems to have begun with the emergence of centralized points of control—a different sense of organization that language acting on its own did not offer and which served to assemble much larger societies within dominative hierarchies. The human shifted from an egalitarian to a stratified social order, and a world full of war and conquest. Here again, from an organizational (and economic) perspective, there isn't much to history but the replay of a narrative. The logic of domination and control moves toward a predictable equilibrium, and predictable economic effects.

The point of going back in time, however, is to clarify the organizational content of modern economies conceived as markets gathered within representative democracies. This may represent another shift of consciousness, or depending on how one looks at it, a shift back to consciousness. The shift is scientific, as it reflects a state of understanding that allows human organization to form creatively and productively but intervenes intelligently in the formation of boundaries. Science thus benefits economic design in much the same way it benefits surgery. In enables selective and nuanced intervention, so that in the process, the intervention does not kill the patient. The design and implementation of interventions based on science is what we refer to as "Requisite" economy.

I suspect that a number of present day adherents to the findings and discipline of Requisite Organization will be uncomfortable with aspects of this book—if they are kind enough to read it. I feel, for example, that Jaques overemphasizes structure—at the expense of motivation—as an explanatory schema of human behavior. Related to this criticism, I take issue with the use of "trust" as an activating principle of Requisite organization. Rather, I feel that trust is a beneficial effect of the placement of value on the existence and autonomy of human consciousness.

An unfortunate tendency of these theoretical selections putting structure ahead of value is the promotion of a false sense of entitlement among business organizers—evident in the Objectivism of Ayn Rand—and the extension of underserved admiration for the narcissistic assemblies of political manipulators and monopolists. It is in keeping with the value of Requisite, in my view, to see economy more in terms of the enabling and motivating assumption of great roles than in the controlling behavior of great men and women. I don't believe I am alone in this criticism.

In Jaques' defense, it is worth noting that the Requisite movement was first conceptualized while anthropological, linguistic and literary intellectual movements of "structuralism" were very popular. And these have only recently been intelligently discredited. His lectures on Requisite have, moreover, emphasized the value and ingenuity of labor at all levels, and advocated moderation in the proposed compensation of senior executives. And on a more personal note, even as Jaques promoted "structure" and "structurers" as prime mover of organization, he was receptive to debate and criticism over the meaning of his discoveries, and addressed dissent respectfully—as a true scientist. It is fitting therefore to refer to the continuing evolution of this theory of organization as Requisite, and is an appropriate way to honor its progenitor.

Also in Jaques defense, it is worth noting that traditionally situated command and inspect hierarchies of old were the only available models into which to package Jaques' discoveries about adult maturation. There were, at the time of the formation of Jaques' theories (1960-1980) alternative management theories circulating, but these were not very accommodating to a theory of mind that acknowledges a hierarchy in the progress and emergence of human cognition. Jaques changed the world, in that regard, by making it impossible to think of organization outside the domain of human development.

It is ironic, perhaps, that Jaques' discovery made it easier to imagine a hierarchy other than that evident in the traditional military organizations designed over millennia to protect monarchs. Yet Jaques' work has by many been shaped into an orthodoxy that limits it to organizations of that nature. When Jaques' discovery is fully appreciated, management is viewed as a process of comprehension that protects, supports, teaches and leads others in subordinate roles. Jaques vision favors hierarchy conceived in terms of depth and integration more than of altitude and generalization.

After some examination, it becomes apparent that the types of organization available depend to a significant extent on contexts established by law and the balance between control and creativity that a given legal context allows. We can't, in other words, separate organizational form from the sense of order accompanying political and historical processes. This book might be viewed as an effort on my part to explain how environmental pressures created—and abated—by law might impact the kinds of hierarchies into which firms and markets organize.

There are points in this book which I believe would be useful in the advance of Requisite as "science" and thus a matter of interest to Jaques, his colleagues, and other participants in the Requisite movement. Some of these are that upon close examination:

- The logic of information processing structures reveals that they are the effect—not the cause—of the progressive integration of interests (states of motivation).

- The structure of language is a Requisite structure motivated by the value of shared experience—an endogenous rather than exogenous value.

- Law reveals structure identical in important respects to language—though law, unlike language, is easily converted from endogenous to an exogenous mandate.

- Property (right to control) is a legal structure enabled by ethically situated (Requisite) government processes that value individual existence and autonomy.

I've been told that my understanding of Requisite confuses ethical and epistemic considerations—of morality and capability. But for reasons set forth in the text of this book, the distinction is not as tidy as it might appear at first glance. The study of language reveals that even those perceptions and judgments that are normally attributed to a value neutral rationality respond to interests that are highly dependent on shared social input. Although I have felt for quite some time there is no necessary adhesion between the development of capability and moral value, moral judgment has an information processing component to it, and quite aside from that, there is within the human mind an inclination favoring their combination.

It is possible, however, to design a set of rules in which markets reward the compulsive accumulation of wealth, and accumulation may, depending on the circumstances, reflect interests that activate very limited capability. Where society is either silent or ambiguous in the kind of behavior it praises, it is apt to see a proliferation of avarice and even sociopathy, and the exclusion of persons from positions of leadership who have outgrown or overcome such proclivities. Within a Requisite economy, one might make conscious decisions affecting the level of agreement or disagreement between morality and capability in the selection of leaders.

And such decisions are within reach of our current phase of development as a civilization. We are at a point close to the effectuation of Requisite economy—both durable and just, just as we are barely removed from more primitive economic and commercial order and might slide backward.

Let me offer some comments about the organization of this book. I am generally reluctant to repeat myself, but am at the same time cognizant of the needs of readers to have difficult concepts examined from different angles.

Overall, my preference is to organize where possible in accordance with a narrative structure—not so much as a story (though there is some of that) as an account that is very conscious of how beginnings lead to endings, and is fairly common to the way attorneys learn to present their cases.

There is a need, at the start, to comprehend what it is that served to move organizational theory from descriptive typologies to what we mean when we use the term "science." I submit that such a point is reached not so much through the use of measurement, but in the identification of principles of motion that explain both simple and complex phenomena. To that end, it is useful to spend some time considering highly abstract descriptive terms that transfer easily from forms we think of as "logic" to strategic or navigational orientations found in the management of complex organizations. I endeavor to do that in the second chapter of this book entitled "The Basis of Organization" and believe I have been successful in developing a set of forms which indicate agreement between first order logic and hierarchically organized management systems. Unique in the examination of these forms is that they are behavioral, i.e., they identify states of motivation from which logic emerges as an effect. Logic, it seems, is driven by interest—and is thus not the neutral instrumentality that many rationalists suppose.

In an appendix, there is some effort to elaborate on how a descriptive calculus (logic) serves to link bureaucratic hierarchy to a theory of human development. I have also set out and explained this logic in my first published book, On Freedom. This book also has an appendix explaining the appropriation of the circle from G. Spencer Brown's work—Laws of Form—to express a "distinction" as idea, or rather, a motivated intervention. Organization is what we do with ideas, objects fashioned out of a void.

I suspect that the basis of our claim to the neutrality of logic is the imperative of language favoring shared experience. The problem with using language to discover logic is that it has evolved and is used for a number of purposes, and that the formation of objects as shared referents is only one of them. So, as I point out in the third chapter entitled "Wild Economy," language evolved in order to transition between and blend shared descriptions of the environment with socially cohesive normative principles—something much more apparent in complex social order than in logical calculus. But since we have moved logic from a neutral to an interest driven structure, a relationship between logic and social organization supported by language appears to be more plausible than previously imagined.

The rest of the book serves as a matter of illustration. What happens when the ethical presence of language is restricted, corrupted, or overwhelmed? The answer, it appears, are dominative hierarchies designed to protect those able to acquire control over populations through military organization. The separation of these civilizations from the ethical substance of shared human experience is remedied through the restoration of dialogue that simulates language. Thus, we have a chapter on "Behavioral Economy" that transfers most productive behavior to markets by removing personal interest of lawmakers in the economic effect of law—moving effectively from what we think of as corrupt to free political systems. The chapter entitled "Requisite Economy" focuses on issues involved in the implementation of a free political system.

Implementation can be quite difficult, as I point out in Chapter Seven, where international markets create confusion over the proper use of the productive surplus of a given economy. Productive surplus attracts a nation's enemies, both foreign and domestic. This confusion, if not dealt with consciously, can derail the progress we associate with modern economy, or otherwise leave us helpless to cooperatively (organizationally) address resource and environmental challenges on a global scale.

I must confess to a philosophical debt to Ludwig Wittgenstein's work. In my first book On Freedom: Organizational Science Examined Philosophically, Wittgenstein's solution to the Russell Paradox triggered my own thinking about the separation of and relationship between what we think of as "value" (as state of engagement) and "object" (as product of that engagement) and how the confusion of these two states impedes adaptation. A full appreciation of their separate roles leads us into far more dynamic hierarchies that allow us to better comprehend hierarchy as an ethical phenomenon. In this book we draw further on this idea, as well as Wittgenstein's later concerns over private language. His thesis is that a "private" language is incoherent because language, of necessity, includes social obligation (law). While the philosophical discussion of this idea seems quite abstract, its applications in the formation of institutions—of Law and Economics—are both profound and practical.

In writing this book, I have basically resumed from the place in which I ended my book on Freedom, taking some trouble to summarize and clarify points made there, while expanding considerably on the subject of applied social ethics within realities presented by market behavior. There is a reduced need here to address matters of spiritual dimension, except to indicate that evolutionary science is not—nor presents itself as—a confirmation or a refutation of an ethical substance impacting reality and transcending ordinary human experience. There is a strong suggestion in language, however, that value adheres to a collective interest in shared experience, and that the engagement of such value is something we use to distinguish human and animal existence.

Peter Friesen

# Chapter 1

# Demand and Supply

1. The Book of Kings II—part of the Bible's Old Testament—speaks of the career of Elisha, who is identified as a prophet. The scripturally celebrated lives of Prophets were important to ancient civilizations, as their acts satisfied a need in pious societies to give authority to voices emerging from the depth of human conscience. The special status of prophets was marked in part by the performance of miracles, which was the way that God bestowed authority on the lives of ordinary people. The universe, it seems, consists both of laws through which we navigate the world as physical organisms, but also of Law, which reflects an ethical impulse not bound by ordinary laws.

The story of one of Elisha's most famous miracles begins with his arrival at the house of a woman recently widowed. She speaks to Elisha in distress. Her deceased husband had incurred debt, and died leaving her unable to pay. The law of that day governing unpaid debt included the right of the creditor to confiscate and enslave her sons in lieu of payment. While explaining this to Elisha, she was careful to point out that her husband had been a devoted servant of Elisha, and God. But notwithstanding, the creditor would soon be coming to take her sons away, with all of the power of the state to support the act.

This did not seem to faze Elisha, who asked the women what she had. The woman replied that she had only a pot of oil—not nearly enough to cover the debt, but Elisha told her to gather as many empty pots from the neighbors as they could find, and to pour oil from the one pot into them. The family did so and thereafter filled many pots of the oil from the one pot she had. Elisha then told them to sell the oil and pay the debt—and their family was spared.

One might say that this event was what it appeared to be—a good deed performed by a good man having special contact with a power that transcends the normal imperatives of both nature and social obligation. Believers prefer to think Elisha acted with divinely bestowed authority, and that this separated his views from those of many thousands of persons whose opinions circulated within common discourse. More skeptical scholars who have examined the era have pointed out that the miracles attributed to Elisha were part of a diffuse folklore which had been building for quite some time and suggest that these miracles were attributed to him so that his views might carry more popular religious weight. It is significant, perhaps, that written account of Elisha's life now seen in the Bible occurred several hundred years after they are said to have occurred.

Whether the accounts about him are true is probably less important than the way these accounts were used to lend authority to a socio-religious movement which emphasized a singular and transcendent deity—the one God of Judaea. Elisha was successor to another prophet, Elijah, who, according to formal versions of history adopted within a complex political structure, chose and mentored Elisha, to whom he transferred his power and authority. According to legend, Elijah had been God's emissary in a campaign to root out pagan influences—in particular, worship of Baal—invoking God in spectacular exhibitions of power and healing.

Political adaptations to competing deities within the ancient melting pot of the Fertile Crescent were an important part of the evolution of the monotheism reflected in today's Bible. Elisha was there—whether he wanted it or not—to vindicate a version of history that included the delivery of humanity from the worship of false gods, and the authentication of government systems in power at the time when his life became official. By then, it wasn't Elisha performing miracles, but the spirit of the one God, working through him. And such affirmations were at this point in history offered to avoid argument over what their religious practices were about.

So, with this in the background, one can glimpse at the meaning of the delivery of a family from the harsh consequences of a developing economic system. Visible in this sketch of life is a marketplace, and along with it, the extension of credit with legal structures in place to enforce the collection of debt. It was more than a system, and functioned more like an evolved communications network. Within it, individuals at various social and economic strata made and influenced choices about the allocation of limited resources, strategies of collaboration, consumer preferences, and government. Whatever held it together might be referred to as its "substance." If compliance with its norms should fail in general, this substance disintegrates, and everyone starves. The system doesn't work perfectly, however, and there are numerous casualties.

From one ethical perspective, this tragedy is not really a problem, but an example of how a system was meant to work. Slavery is certainly something to be avoided, but one might argue that slavery is necessary to forcibly enlist labor at very unpleasant and burdensome tasks. Likewise, the threat of demotion to the status of the slave— "untouchables" as they are sometimes called—functions as an excellent motivator on a system of credit. The availability and cost of credit is a function of confidence in the capacities and motivations of borrowers, which in turn sustains a class of entrepreneurs. The family tragedy which Elisha confronted was, in other words, like a sacrifice being prepared on that society's commercial altar. Certainly, there was no "justice" in it, but it would help to fuel the motives of the commercial mechanisms they had in place. Such tragedies were like food for the deities which activated the network.

The moment these "reasons" reveal themselves, they are, in a manner of speaking, destroyed by a culturally celebrated intervention. This was the function of prophets of that era, i.e., to demonstrate that these deities are not real, or were at least subordinate to their ethical existence—invoking the same God which had delivered them from enslavement in Egypt many years before. Could God's messenger stay the execution of this sacrifice? According the legend, he did, but did so in a way which was barely disruptive of the commercial structures in place.

Their ethical substance was therefore validated by a mind that existed with or without human inventions, and the social inventions (markets) derived from obedience to that mind. The human animal might get distracted from that good from time to time, and assimilate into other deities, and wander into catastrophic losses brought on by a popular misinterpretation of what made these inventions good. Such distractions created a need, and opportunity—for prophets to speak. Thus, among the things Elisha was appointed to say was that this family was caught in the jaws of law that had somehow separated from their ethical core, a statement reinforced, of course, with a miracle. Whether one agrees with the veracity of this report, it is nonetheless a nice solution to a messy paradox. The message seems to be that economic systems and the laws which support them are naught but instrumentalities. There is nothing sacred or alive about them, and they should be examined, reformed, adjusted and at times overruled.

While the widow's rescue appears to provide an account of the intervention of a benevolent externality, it is not that at all. It is more of a statement about the ethical supports of their social order. Elisha did not appear from the outside of their world, but from the inside.

The question of how experimental and adaptive we should be in the reforms we make has been the center of political controversies in recent years. In our present political environment, for example, many would take issue with Elisha's miracle, which on the surface would be immune from criticism. They might argue that our commercial structures—vast integrations of marketplaces and governmental intervention—are like a living organism guided by a mind with an invisible hand of its own. Interference with these structures is an affront to this mind and leads to perdition. They might therefore criticize Elisha's miracle, focusing on the fact that the price of oil is dependent on supply, and that God's intervention in producing more oil would damage the interests of other oil producers, i.e., that God actually stole value from others to pay the widow's debt.

As ridiculous as this criticism might seem, it was the prevailing argument in the United States for keeping government out of the health care business. That is to say, the concern was that if government became a provider of more health care, by organizing providers into competitive networks and negotiating responsible pricing structures, it would harm the interests of others in the same business. The same argument is used against the use of government to develop energy resources, to provide easier access to credit, or to take an idle labor force and put it to work. If intervention were to produce more, it would offend a delicately balanced organism.

They have a point to make, however. They remind us that government and God are not one and the same, and the imperfections of government are such that it is an untrustworthy receptacle of responsibility for such matters. They, on the other hand, are not asking to be responsible for the effects of intervention, but to be left alone to do business as they choose. If we are unsure as to the natural effects of an unregulated marketplace, the better course is not to act, and allow its participants to find their own way. The market has its own mind, a mind which knows and delivers justice more effectively than the mind of a government representative.

As one examines the truth or falsity of statements such as these, it becomes steadily clearer that this disagreement is not superficial. They are embedded in the concepts we have evolved for the phenomena labeled "law" and "economy" and cannot be explained without some revision of our understanding of both of those concepts, as well as the basis of an alleged relationship between them.

Currently we are witnessing an acceleration of the development of the economies of large populations that have been dormant during the emergence of industrial cultures in Europe and North America, and they are claiming energy and water resources along with this development. At the same time, we are projecting scarcity in those resources likely to reach crisis proportions within fifty years. We are apt to be challenged to address issues of substance without the appearance of a prophet such as Elisha to render supply without limit, but not necessarily without an ethical compass.

2. As with the foregoing story, restrictions on behavior necessary to set up an economy appear as necessary evils. Such restrictions are interventions of government, from which economic behavior seems to flow. However, it also seems that the choices that government makes in the imposition of restrictions are based on a theory of supply—of how to convert natural resources into food and shelter for large assemblies of human beings. Complicating this somewhat is the need to promote cooperative behavior and avoid interference among these beings at work. In the midst of this process many lawyers and economists have discovered that they can make a living as advocates for policies affecting these activities.

Perhaps a concern at this point is whether there is even a need to refine the understanding of what the terms "law" and "economy" mean. Doing so is not all that simple, due to the fact that the terms "law" and "economy" were not meant in their original use to identify logically separate ideas, meaning, their development as fields of study overlap. This overlap, however, also indicates a relationship between the two.

One approach might be to look back in time in an effort to ascertain the origin of these terms, and then trace their development to the present. However, this would not be a suitable approach if we were to find that law and economics have, since the beginning, gone through major transformations. That exercise might be useful in determining whether we have made progress over the last ten thousand years or so, what the basis of that progress was, and what we might have to do in the future to protect it. That may be an excellent reason to seek clarity in the formation of these ideas, but we can hardly look back in time at the real or theoretical development of an idea without identifying what it is in the present—as it would be difficult to say what the "it" is that is being traced backward.

We are more interested in law and economy in the modern era because they have as fields of study become more complicated than they used to be. They have developed elaborate admissions structures—with fairly muscular gatekeepers, and are subdivided into cerebrally comprehensible units—sometimes referred to as "specialties." Law school is a challenging experience, and most that finish that course of study would prefer to get to work and start their lives as policy advocates. The same can be said of the course of study for economists upon receipt of their doctorates. But to advocate policy as a lawyer, one must be able to discuss the economic effect of such policy. To advocate policy as an economist, one must appreciate the rights and interests at stake. Given the complementarity and overlap between these two fields, perhaps the best explanation of their difference is the intellectual weight one must bear in order to be competent in either field. Thus, one would define law as "what lawyers do" and economy as "what economists do."

Such definitions, however, challenge one to engage in a more logical or functionally based definition, because it is necessary to explain what it is that lawyers and economists do. Instead of making efforts to be inclusive of all their behaviors, it might be better to take a more crabbed approach to terminology—i.e., what is the "emphasis" of law, by contrast to that of economy. But even here, one ought not to be too restrictive, as history reflects an unfolding of many different kinds of legal and economic systems, and we might get lost upon the encounter with systems with which we are not familiar.

This concern is evident in an attempt, for example, to think of the distinction in government intervention and its effects. Law would be about governmental interventions (rules), and economy would be about the effect of governmental interventions (commerce). The distinction has a simple logical resonance—cause and effect—but fails at some point in its application across a spectrum of social systems which vary in their imposition of and tolerance for control.

From the perspective of a highly controlled economy, rulemaking has much more to do with forcing things to happen, rather than anticipating what people will do if a rule is made. Whether a point of view that attempts to use force is effective is apt to be disputed, even though the proponents of control criticize modern economies for not being just in the way they distribute economic benefits. They might prefer, in other words, to treat law as the dominant function, and economy as subordinate, where the rightness of effect is mandatory—thereby confusing what seemed like a good distinction.

Nor does the distinction appear to always promote beneficial results in the more market-oriented economies to which it is suited. Lawyers and economists quarrel a good deal over who is more important. The quarrel is aggravated somewhat by the fact that their respective disciplines are becoming progressively less accessible to each other. One tends to criticize the other for not knowing enough about their well-developed and well-guarded intellectual disciplines—but find themselves criticized even more when they try to understand the other.

Nonetheless, there are moments of productive collaboration between these groups, which suggest that there is a logical complementarity to law and economy which—if articulated—might lead to more communication between groups of professionals. The first step, it seems, is to acknowledge that it is not so much about what lawyers and economists do, but about a need within both disciplines to continuously adjust between what ought to be and what is—of prescribing and describing.

Let us then contemplate a distinction between law and economics that utilizes this essential division, where law is a state of preoccupation with obligation (prescription), and economy is a state of preoccupation with the production of goods (description). As this book unfolds, we will come to understand that modern economics operates most effectively when description conforms with prescription.

This way of distinguishing law and economy suggests at least two changes in the nature of this dialogue. First, it affects the nature of the analysis of law. Despite much literature on basis of moral obligation and its impact on law, the tendency in the philosophy of law is to impose separation on the phenomena of moral and legal obligation. Only the latter of these two phenomena are, within this strategic pose, referred to as "law." This is the basic argument for a "positive" theory of law. The analysis which shall unfold hereafter departs from this strategy, and instead seeks to blur the distinction between moral and legal obligation. This would, at least theoretically, involve the placement of law as a formally sanctioned governmental mandate in a dependent and subordinate relationship to obligation generally. This book has much to say about how and why this takes place and how this affects economic realities.

Second, this way of distinguishing law and economy affects the universe of relevant discourse in the analysis of economics. In classic economic analysis, little effort is made to systematically evaluate the effect of the size of a firm(s) within an industry on the competitive productivity of that industry. Despite the fact that private entrepreneurs publicly extol the effects of competition on economic systems, their behavior tends inevitably toward collaborations that limit or eliminate competition, and to circumvent the best efforts of government to restrict anticompetitive behavior. An economic analysis which emphasizes a relationship between obligation administered by government and the formation of industries is apt to be much more interested in the architecture of the firm, the organizational capacities of its leaders, its ability to diminish its obligations through the manipulation of the political process, and what the government may do to assist in the introduction of effective competitors.

3. The present benefits from over a century of observation of the contrasting performance of market-based economies and control economies. The market-based economies are what have often been referred to as "free" societies, and "free markets"—and sometimes "capitalism." Control economies have been formed to avoid the various predations of the marketplace, and invoke centrally administered controls on the formation of cooperative production—sometimes referred to as "communism."

There is also a verdict out on this comparison—i.e., the competitive economies won and the control economies lost. This verdict is intoned with moral triumphalism, as the control economies had a poor reputation in the respect of their subjects' civil liberties, while competitive economies were more permissive. The morale of the narrative is ideologically exciting, with good prevailing over evil, a view of the free human being as productive and creative, the promotion of markets as magically self-corrective, the belief that the pursuit of rational self-interest produces opportunities for all, etc. While this self-admiration can be exhilarating, it might be useful to moderate these views by examining the motivations behind the standoff we had between two distinct economic theories.

The use of "obligation" and its "effects" as a means of distinguishing "law" and "economy" reveals errors in the fusion of distribution with economic issues. Distribution is about obligation and is the appropriate subject of input of every participant in an economic system. Since distribution may affect the motivational structures necessary to achieve productivity, there are economic implications.   When economists advocate greater distributions to the entrepreneur because of the rightness of it, he or she is engaged in law. When they describe the effect of distributional choices on productivity, they are engaged in economics.

Lawyers often claim that their training in the policies surrounding obligations of various kinds makes them more qualified to discuss moral obligation, and that is sometimes the case, but legal experience can have a corruptive influence on one's moral sensibilities as well. It is probably best not to speculate on who knows best the difference between right and wrong. The point is, we are all lawyers, and we are all economists.

Our tense experience with contrasting economic structures of the twentieth century was an economic engagement—of description, not prescription. What laid under the microscope was the motivational efficiency of market versus command-oriented economies. The world already knew that human beings responded enthusiastically to liberty, and that there were negative motivational effects in the controlling intervention of government. But it was also accepted that political liberty includes the emergence of clans, societies, political movements, military organizations, and civil war. The natural logic of competitive behavior is to kill the loser so that future risks will be avoided, along with continuous vigilance against usurpers. Thus, the natural consequence of unrestricted behavior is a militarily ordered feudal economy.

What the world had yet to discover was that it was possible to prevent the destructive consequences of self-interested behavior by preserving the loser of the contest. Doing this, however, involves the establishment of obligations. The most important of these obligations were those that prevented the military power of the state from reposing in or serving any of the firms formed within a competitive marketplace. The kinds of laws that emerged from these processes were laws designed to promote certain kinds of socially beneficial competitive behavior and prohibit predatory or anti-competitive organization.

The great victory of market over control economies—of capitalism over communism—was not about rewarding winners, but about limiting the casualties inherent in the clash of a socially and biologically competitive species. The designers of this system were engaged more as economists, predicting that productive behavior would flourish if they could protect government from being expropriated by the organizations likely to grow out of liberated pursuits. They did something that governments had for millennia considered unthinkable and allowed citizens to form into groups to acquire and develop organizational weight and economic strength sufficient to rival a government. They took a calculated risk that government would not collapse under the pressures this created, and appears to have been proven right. New economic orders made command-based systems seem very weak.

One of the problems with the use of "victory" to describe the compared performance of command and market economies is that we may not have reached the end. The danger of a system that grows private institutions to a point where they can appropriate or avoid legal processes continues. There is doubt at present over whether the legal processes necessary to promote an effective economy can withstand the pressure that private firms have brought to bear on the political process. The system was close to collapse at one point, and that it may reach that point again, especially as natural resources wane.

In the pages which follow we will, among other things, confirm the demise of command economies, but will explain how their demise is as overstated as the claimed victory of free market economies. It is less a matter of abdicating control, then in being wise in the assertion of control. An interesting question, perhaps, is at what point does the abdication of control make the use of the term "control" obsolete, and are we in the process of replacing it?

What some proponents of a free market do not recognize is that its successes are counterintuitive. Assuming, for example, there are decent and honorable social objectives to realize, and a political consensus to support those objectives, common sense favors the establishment of an institution suitable for the implementation of those objectives. So, if there is a problem with a privately-owned banking system—credit unavailable to deserving borrowers and productive entrepreneurs—the direct approach to a solution would be to create a capital fund through the government that addresses the need. The same logic might therefore apply on a larger scale, i.e., an economic system appropriated by highly concentrated private firms resulting in dysfunctional employment and income distributions—real suffering on a large scale. The direct approach is to place the government in charge of all the employment structures and ensure justice through direct intervention.

This has been the primary justification for control-oriented systems since the beginning of recorded history. There are bad kings and there are good kings, badly organized governments and well-organized governments. The problem is not about whether we should have them, but about whether they are good at what they are supposed to be doing. Most people, if asked whether they had to choose between a singular, centrally positioned king, and many kings, would choose the former. It is easier to support the luxuries of one ruler than ten, and far less confusing.

As great visionaries and reformers were to learn in repeating experiences throughout the twentieth century, the organizational task of socially engineering production with justice to vast numbers of people is very complicated, even if everyone cooperates. Cooperative failures within and between groups of persons are not only common, but likely, and cooperation becomes less likely as the system begins to fail, or is brought under stressors such as invasion, drought or the collapse of financial institutions.

One must at some point evaluate whether the complexity is such that cooperative systems on a very large scale are impossible, or if possible, whether it is realistic to expect that persons capable of managing this complexity are available. The more likely course will be an attempt to simplify the task by restricting or eliminating uncooperative behavior, which is what those who benefit from market based economic systems find offensive.

Offensive is probably too mild a term, as the process of simplification stimulates demonstrative oppositions, which are then quieted by overwhelming force—ultimating at times in systematic executions and imprisonments, manic propaganda campaigns, and a perpetual state of war. All of this may proceed merely as a strategy adopted by a leader—or group of leaders—who have come to realize that they cannot deliver justice, and have to worry about survival.

This happened in a number of different parts of the world, and will happen again, hopefully on a smaller scale. Thinking as economists, however, it is plain and obvious that the failure was not so much in intention, but in the technology of organization available to manage very complex social relationships. One might argue that it was not that control itself was wrong, but that the theory of control failed. People were not as easy to herd into cooperative systems as once expected, and when they were put there, they failed to work with the diligence and creativity observed in market based economic systems.

Command economies of the past are less apt to release their interest in controlling the development of their economies than they are to revise their plan of control—releasing pressure on civil liberties while developing incentive structures that encourage and coordinate creative talents. They have already learned that by giving up control on one level, they gain control on another. And their capacity to coordinate government resources on a large scale will be useful to them in the competitions likely to arise against market-based economies damaged by their inability to limit the consumptive behaviors of the firms born within them.

The contest is, in other words, hardly over, and the emergent sense of victory—brought on in large part by a failure to identify the real nature of the successes which have occurred—may be contributing to the reversal of those successes.

4. Our experience with this contest might have spurred examination and study of what sorts of obligation tend to best encourage the development of new and creative projects. But study doesn't seem to have much of an influence on the nature of the political debate. Free market advocates continue to argue that lower personal income taxes (obligation to share earnings with government) have a stimulative effect on the economy, even though comparative studies of countries with higher personal income tax rates fail to support that contention.

Variables that might complicate a study of this nature pertain mainly to what the government offers in the way of infrastructural benefits as a consequence of its taxation efforts. In countries like Sweden, for example, where taxation is very high, there are significant benefits offered by government which support initiative and improve the resource base of the region. Socialized health, communications, education and finance are a number of programs where taxes reduce business costs.

In the United States, the benefits of taxation are difficult to identify because a very large percentage of the tax revenues are spent on military projects. The beneficiaries of military spending are few by comparison to those of non-military spending, and which also has, by comparison, a stimulative and supportive effect on the growth of an economy. These benefits are so valuable that the debate shifts quickly from the economic benefits of providing for such things to the wrongness of spending on programs such as education, health, transportation, etc. The foundational premise of the argument is that government is evil, and the inefficiencies of governmental bureaucracy are proof that it is evil.

As a logician might indicate, the argument assumes the very fact that needs to be examined, as we do not know whether the inefficiencies of government are irremediable. Another way of stating the argument—perhaps more forcefully in the view of its proponents—is that the human experience with government bureaucracy has been so bad up until this moment, that there must be something ethically wrong with it. This argument suggests that there is something about size in organization, at the level of government, and the absence of financial incentives to motivate efficiencies, which has a corruptive effect on it. In reframing the argument, it seems that we have moved it from an ethical argument, of obligation, to an economic one, which is not where its proponents are comfortable. Their tendency is to insist on the evil of government, regardless of its efficiency—an argument which is very easily refuted.

A final revision of the argument might then be as follows. Since the experience with government bureaucracy has been so bad in the past, we are ethically bound to scrutinize proposals to expand upon the use of government to effectuate beneficial social programs. At this point, the political debate would tend to revolve around whether the application of skepticism to proposed administrative programs is rational, and whether proofs of concept have been vetted. This would be a favorable development, for at this point there is a good chance that the consensus generating mechanisms of the legislative wings of modern government will reach agreement.

In the process of examining the argument, a significant feature of a relationship between law and economy is revealed—i.e., that there may be implementational constraints on organization which preclude or interfere with the actualization of law. Is it true, in other words, that limits in the technology of organization make the administration of our sense of justice impossible? Have the prescriptive intentions of law and the descriptive realities of economy reached an impasse?

As important as the administrative effectiveness of organization is to the operation of government, and derivatively, the intervention of government in productive economies, there is very little in the way of literature which addresses the subject. There is a field of study referred to as "organizational development" that has become a program of graduate study and is increasingly viewed as a part of a curriculum of business schools. This field has not, however, integrated into legal and economic fields, and there does not appear to be much communication between them.

In modern economic theory, the behavioral dynamics of organization is regarded as idiosyncratic, and probably the result of influences which do not follow measurably predictable patterns. Even if there were behavioral constants available as far as organization is concerned, they would not likely have much of an impact on the policy issues to which the attention of economists in modern economies is directed. It is only recently that factors such as the size, motivational structures within the firm, and accountability to professional standards are being viewed as relevant topics of economic analysis.

But here, there is a real sense of caution in the field, in part due to the political opposition to regulation. This opposition believes that government might interfere where it is not welcome—the "evil" of government—and bases this belief on the absence of credible theoretical links between what governments would like to do (proposed laws) and the performance capability of government. It concludes, often without real evidence of failure, that government is inherently incompetent.

A growing receptivity of economic theory to the organizational properties of government has an interesting, and relatively brief history. It begins with Adam Smith's analysis of market behavior, and the observation that such behavior is theoretically self-correcting, as negotiated transactions of a given type that produce profits disproportionate to labor input would attract competition and thus a downward pressure on profit due to price. Real inequalities in bargaining position in a real world were not addressed theoretically, except to suggest that profits generated from inequality would attract stronger negotiators, and thus stable equilibria. The importance of government, in such a scheme, was to preserve the competitive environment, through laws that prevented the consolidation of markets into monopolies, so that government could theoretically withdraw from the control of commerce. Many, including Smith, had significant doubts over whether this could be implemented in a real world.

It was implemented, to some extent, and there has been remarkable economic growth to prove part of the theory. Others like Tomas Malthus, and later, Karl Marx, while not disputing the logic of market-based expansion, have questioned its sustainability. Malthus suggested that food resources would be a limiting factor on the expansion of such economies, and that competition over food might eventually derail them. Marx likewise imagined a system accelerating too quickly for its own good, and a painfully exploitative phase of history, where inequalities in bargaining power between entrepreneurs and laborers would result in subjugations so extreme that they would at some point overwhelm the system with rebellion and implement a plan of social justice through socially benevolent government.

The Marxian imaginings of a world developing toward an ultimate good has been rightly criticized for the confusion of prescriptive ideals with logistical restrictions—of law and economy. A failure to acknowledge that technological limitations in the efficiency of bureaucratic structures—a larger source of obstruction than the avarice of capitalists within a theory of history—might have been the principle source of damage to the great revolutionary movements in the early twentieth century.

As the social revolutions of the twentieth century unfolded, there were still some perplexing developments in the capital markets. The most noteworthy, of course, was an incident labeled "The Great Depression." There are many accomplished scholars of this event, who speak with authority about it, and there also appears to be limited consensus as to the lessons learned from it.

Apparently one of the consequences of the concentration of capital in the banking institutions of that day—accumulating due in significant part to the successes of free market capitalism—was a focused deliberation on how they might circumvent their obligation to protect the money on behalf of depositors and take the money for themselves. They could do that, it seemed, by using the money they had accumulated as collateral, and thus borrow from each other many times what they held in the way of deposit accounts for purposes of investment. Since it wasn't their money, they were well positioned to make incredible fortunes without risking much in the way of loss. This, it appeared, was a recipe for disaster. The financial system soon separated in a theoretical perception of value diluted by extraordinary risk from the real value of the available wealth, and the system broke under the stress of numerous stampedes.

There were at least two major lessons learned from the experience. First, that while a market has a number of self-corrective tendencies, correction is not magically automatic, and is dependent upon the behavior of individuals acting on the sensation of risk and the availability and interpretation of information. Bad behaviors could not be contained without piercing the veneer of banking institutions and understanding their motivational and accountability structures. The system was thereafter reformed to remove the temptation inherent in making bets with the money of bank depositors, and more importantly, to limit the allowable sense of risk permeating a system of credit by restricting the leveraging on collateral. These measures worked pretty well until they were lifted eighty years later, at which point the system promptly overheated into a crisis of equal magnitude.

A second, and possibly less obvious, lesson of the Great Depression was that government intervention in the form of spending—financed through combined use of borrowing and taxation—was necessary to restore the circulation of credit in the economic system. The opponents of this strategy argued that a government is like a person, and a government that borrows and spends will, as a person, lose its credibility—its credit. These opponents won the political debate, but ended up losing, as restrictions imposed thereafter upon government had a strangling effect on credit, as there were no mechanisms in place for coordinating the circulation of new currency with the reestablishment and formation of industries. After a temporary recovery, the system re-collapsed, and stayed that way until a war—brought on by economic stresses of the Great Depression—forced stimulative spending. [1]

These lessons serve as illustrations of the deficiencies of a policy of overreliance on the self-corrective features of a free market. But on a deeper level, they illustrate that the interventions of government are not like the will of a person imposing itself on an electorate—a king reigning over a kingdom, but more like a processing center within a self-aware information system. If one kills it or overwhelms it, the adaptive ability of a complex production network dies with it, and the result, starvation.

In a manner of speaking, the errors we associate with the financial crises of the last hundred years are similar to the errors made by rebellious promoters of command economies. Their common problem consists in the tendency to see government as a person separate and apart from the marketplace when it is nothing of the sort. It does not organize industries, but rather assumes a strategic role as a source of intelligence through which industries organize. It does not spend but provides intelligence in the shifting of obligation and the circulation of currency.

Government is a point of view. One is, at the same time "the" government, as well as the effect of government. Government is enabled by political processes that set the rules which activate markets. These markets provide the government its operating currency, while the government determines how much currency to issue. To think of this as "person" engaged in the same sort of dialogue one might have with a neighbor invites all kinds of error.

5. The sketch of perspectives offered above adheres in principle to a division of emphasis between law and economy. Command economies have in the past been defined by their emphasis on obligation and have become broken due to an effort to suppress rather than harness the creative energies of their participants. Market economies tend to defer to the productivity of emergent institutions, but they have had their own problems, seemingly the result of a failure to anticipate and correct

socially destructive behaviors. These destructive tendencies are magnified by the concentrations of resources and influence which these institutions acquire, and the use of those resources to influence the legal environment.

Marxian theorists have a point to make about all of this. Individuals acting under market incentives are not terribly free but are bound by stresses encountered within a competitive environment to accumulate wealth and gain market power. Theories of this nature struggle in the attempt to identify an ethical purpose to the historical processes at work, and as a consequence, they are impatient with the advancement of processes which are ethically neutral. Where a supposed mandate of history is eliminated or obscured—something more noticeable in contemporary market analysis—theory is more receptive to discoveries of a scientific nature. This significantly improves the likelihood of the evolution of systems in which there is an effective agreement between law and economy.

The most current description of the research in modern economics is in the use of mathematical models that attempt to comprehensively reveal systemic changes where measures of information access, bargaining power, resource limitations, and moral attitude are hypothetically inputted as variables within the model in order to make predictions. These models reflect an interest in whether anticipated patterns are apt to be stable or unstable, as stable patterns are valuable to planners, and can be more easily reinforced through the interventions of government. This has been referred to as "game theory" because games seem to tell us a great deal about the adaptive strategies of human beings operating within limitations. [2]

Take the following example offered in one of the leading contemporary works on economic behavior. For quite some time, the behavior of farmers within an Indian community was perplexing to economists. The production of their rice crop favored planting seed early in the season, but for some reason farmers planted at the latest possible time of the planting season, and as a consequence incurred a significant economic detriment. Their behavior was explained, however, by birds. Birds in that region which fed on seed were numerous, and so the first farmer to plant would lose his crop. There weren't enough birds to destroy all of the crops if the farmers all planted at the same time. So farmers waited until the time they knew everyone else would be planting—the very end of the planting season. They adopted a survival strategy based on what they expected others to do. The situation was unfortunate in the sense that the farmers failed to coordinate their behavior, and so established an unproductive equilibrium. If they could have obligated each other through an authoritative intervention of some sort, they could have increased their yield.

One can, through the examination of human behavior in the context of time, resource, and informational deficiencies, explain much about the behavior of persons acting alone, and thus for, example, the emergence of panic in capital markets. One can predict behaviors presented in extreme cases, such as fire in a crowded theater, or when someone shouts "fire" in a crowded theater. Their behavior is not terribly different than the behavior of flocks or herds of animals. One could study them as they might study mice.

A point of departure from the animal kingdom, however, is in the tendency of the human organism to develop cooperative relationships. This tendency stands out among human attributes, as well as a number of other primate species, as an effective survival mechanism. There isn't much else to claim as a species-based survival characteristic. Human beings are not strong enough individually to fend off predators, or fast enough to escape them, nor are they individually able to pursue and kill most available forms of prey. Infants and children are particularly helpless to fend for themselves and remain so for much of their development—compared to other animals with which they compete. It is therefore probably an understatement to suggest that cooperative behavior is useful to the survival of the species, as it is plainly at the core of species evolution. Cooperation is therefore not something that human beings use, but rather, what they are, and is programmed genetically into all of what they perceive, think and feel.

If cooperation is the most prominent feature of species survival, it makes perfect sense to develop an analysis of constants operating in cooperative behavior—if in fact there are any—and thereafter examine their applicability to modern problems. That is to say, assuming that productive behavior commonly associated with an ecosystem includes organization as a genetic necessity, our starting point in the theory of law and economy should begin with focused attention on the trait or traits necessary for such organization.

From this perspective, it may be more difficult to explain why organization fails to occur than why it does occur. Within an evolutionary panorama of tens of thousands of generations, the advantages to cooperation far outweigh the disadvantages of conflict. The principal reason for intra-species conflict—competition over natural resources—

would not have been nearly as important a factor in human evolution as the need to cooperate in the face of inter-species conflict.

In the case of the Indian rice farmers, it is therefore unlikely that a failure of cooperation was due to a lack of interest and/or simplicity on their part. In an attempt to explain this failure, or any other for that matter, it would be helpful to know something about the way the human organism processes information, and what kinds of information are relevant to the formation of cooperative relationships.

Under what conditions might we expect the farmers to take measures to coordinate among themselves? We would likely be considering the communication media they have available, and the trust they have that obligations can be effectively implemented. We might also consider whether there are influences present which would tend to frustrate obligation. Are there other organizational entities which have claimed this region as their own, and if so, do they care, or have they otherwise been corrupted?

Much of the economic theory emphasizing the behavior of individuals in games makes an implied statement that economic policy is directed primarily at the manipulation of self-interested behavior. This is unfortunate, given that one of the defining features of the human organism is its interest in participating in cooperative social systems. Participation does not imply passive acquiescence—typical in failed organization, but active participation in the purpose and intelligence of the organization.

This understanding may be more important to modern economic concerns than modern theories indicate. While Marxian notions of a historical imperative guiding human progress through the stresses of accelerating economic growth have become less popular, Malthusian notions of the human accelerating toward species extinction have not. As a scientific orientation, it makes sense that humans are apt to behave like most animals, i.e., pursue their appetites and multiply until the environment can no longer sustain them. And that is what Peak Oil theorists—along with others predicting very disappointing futures—seem to be contending.

This view asserts two premises. First, that the available resource base cannot sustain the rate of consumption—primarily energy and water. Second, the human organism is incapable of the kind of organization required to avert catastrophe.

They are correct in the first premise but should probably qualify it with some question over whether abundant energy is at least theoretically available. Their response to the question is that it doesn't really matter due to the truth of second premise. Even if abundant energy existed theoretically, it's too late, as the human is incapable of the coordination necessary to deploy it in time. The truth of the second premise is, however, less certain than the first.

The assertion that human beings are incapable of cordial and effective organization on a scale necessary to address approaching pressures may not be true, even though past attempts to make progress have been ineffective. It is not a productive assertion to make, in any event, as the arguments for a catastrophic conclusion to human history produce many different types of uncooperative behavior, along with a depressed self-image. The truth of the assertion at this point should be a matter of conscious deliberation.

- What success have the behavioral sciences had in the development of factual constants in human organization?
- In what way are human constants in work systems related to naturally occurring patterns in socio-economic systems?
- To what extent is the human capacity to engage organization limited by social and environmental stresses?
- How do modern economies liberate human potential without compromising the authority of government?
- What practical organizational constraints exist on the establishment of effective government regulation of markets?
- What kinds of organizational challenges are presented by national boundaries?

6. The scope of questions such as these gives rise to some concern as to the manageability of the project reflected by the collection of related essays into the form of a "book" on Law and Economic Order. This project is, however, less ambitious than it may seem, as there are already in place some promising developments in the technology of organization which appear to have reached conceptual maturity. These have greatly simplified the theoretical task at hand, and allow for productive applications of knowledge acquired about the formation of firms

(bureaucratic organization) to the understanding of the formation of economies. The point that allows us to bridge the divide between them is advancement in our understanding of law—an advancement assisted by advancements in the understanding of organization.

As indicated previously, effort is made here to blur distinctions between law as a legal obligation—positive law, and law as ethical obligation—ruling principle. Not that their distinction, both in practical and in theoretical discourse, is not useful in other contexts, but that it is important here to recognize that legal systems are engaged in something larger than what appears on the surface. They are engaged in a species of language, and the understanding of law is well served by an understanding of language. Language is essential to cooperation and may be properly characterized as the genetic solution to the puzzle which social based survival strategies present.

The use of language is obviously important in the coordination of tasks within a given social group. What is less obvious is that language and organization are the same thing, though not organization in the sense of arranging objects on a desktop, or even of assigning tasks under production schedules. We are speaking here of how the human packages mind into social organizations that glorify successful campaigns, protect and nurture the young, cherish and defend members in moments of weakness, educate and welcome youth into adult roles, and value the continuity of culture. Identities and moral values emerge within language, and through it we compare and evaluate with others our ethical core as well as external challenges. Language is like a boat within a roiling sea of currents, a boat which every member of a society must build.

There is, in fact, so much to say about language that the more difficult challenge is to stay on subject—law and economy—while we examine a phenomenon which reveals a social universe. Where we begin, therefore, is in the observation that nothing comes into being in a social universe without an expectancy experienced as Law and plays out as a social existence shared with others.

Such was the apparent meaning of a poem used as prologue to a story about the life of Jesus, an important religious figure of the New Testament of the Bible. "In the beginning was the word, and the word was with God, and the word was God. The same was in the beginning with God. All things were made by him; and without him was not made anything that was made. In him was life; and that life was the light of men. And the light shined in the darkness; and the darkness comprehended it not." The "word" was an effort in translation of the Greek "logos" which was meant at the time to signify "ruling principle" or "principle of order." The suggestion here is that language involves the introduction of value into a void, as intention, and that creation emerges as a product.

The poem suggests that God creates "the" universe out of a void with principle, just as the human constructs a social universe with principle, both of which can be translated as "word" in language. The "him" in the biblical passage appears to be a modification, so that the poem can refer to a historical figure, Jesus, though the importance of that figure was to lend credibility to a popular movement which had taken seed in a number of places.

Those familiar with the story of Jesus' life, as well as the stories of other famous lives around the world in what is now referred to as the "axial" age, know that this teaching emphasized the positive regard for others, cooperative and peaceful social relationships, and the benevolent resolution of social estrangements. These precepts have been gathered into a principle of well-being in which "value" is an existential state translated as "love." The life referred to above was about love, which views the bond that a human being has with others as derived from the bond between God and man. As the story is told, Jesus confronted a crudely fashioned society—latticed with a Roman Empire working in collaboration with a corrupted local priesthood—to say, in a manner of speaking, that their version of reality was incomplete. The story was not all that different than that described quite some time before in the life of Elisha.

The story is also attractive from the standpoint of science because it doesn't really matter if it is true or not. What matters at this point is its influence, and the fact that we have brought it close to our ethical center, and is literally identified as an historical event by which the passage of time is recorded, even though it is, as the poem suggests, timeless. It suggests as well, that logos has always been at work within us, notwithstanding that it was written down, or that it is now being read.

The word is only a starting point in language, as is the case in any endeavor governed by principle. Language has within it strategic instrumentalities designed to identify and organize information. There are times when it is necessary to be clear, but also times when it is better to be obscure, as there is much more at stake in language than the description of facts. Within language, one's relationship to others is constantly being reviewed and monitored. Such issues have over the millennia been as important to group continuity as food.

We have not yet begun to talk about how language is used to convey nuanced values important to group solidarity, or how it is used to establish and value selfhood, to tell stories of inspiration and tragedy, and to worship. We have formed kingdoms and nations through it, and legal systems which have survived many generations. Language is, in short, the product of a beautifully sophisticated information processing device driven at its center by inspired values supportive of social union and validation.

As much as one might marvel over formation of mental processes such as these, we are only drawing a highlight on the fact that they occur, and perhaps how they compare with the survival strategies of other species. The adaptations of a chicken are fairly remarkable, and we can presume that chickens have desires and feelings which reinforce their social structures as well as other behaviors which promote their continuity as a species. They communicate too, and in ways meaningful only to a chicken. Does that mean that they engage in language?

Much time is devoted in the biological sciences to the survival strategies of all kinds of species, as one can marvel at the organizing properties of rodents, fish, worms, protozoa, and bacteria. Within the scale of living organisms, the human assumes an elevated position on the one hand—as the best information processor but is diminished on the other—by failing to acknowledge how human existence and animal existences differ. It is an unsettled question, that is, whether the human species has in some respects separated itself from other organisms through a special adaptation in the way it processes information.

The question is important because our sense of what we can accomplish as a species is related to perceived limitations. While it is very likely true that language has evolved for use as an adaptive instrumentality in a natural universe typified by inter and intra species competitions and tribal affiliations, there is no natural rule that limits human endeavor to such affiliation. Human beings may have developed hands, for example, in order to climb trees as a primate, but that doesn't mean that climbing trees was the only use they could make of them.

Also, adaptations occur for a number of reasons, some of which are simply lucky inventions and others which are a result of consistent pressure in the environment. The eye, for example, evolved together with the visual cortex of the brain to see objects because the objects were there and needed to be seen. So, was language simply an invention which happened to produce effective intra-species coordination, or was the development of language an adaptation to something that exists in the universe, and which language allows us to perceive? If it responded to something—such as logos—then there may be more power in language than we have allowed ourselves to believe.

In what appears in the history of human endeavor, language has proven effective in transcending tribal limitation, though we haven't devoted much time to the evaluation of the stress this has placed on the human organism. This stress is evident in numerous corruptions of organization throughout the world, and much human casualty. While some argue that we are more comfortable now because of the beneficial impact of organization on economy, it may well be that a sense of estrangement from social relations through which our bodies and minds evolved increases rather than decreases the likelihood that organizational solutions to current problems will fail.

An examination, therefore, of the primitive functionality of language, may provide insight into the stresses likely to associate with the adaptations it appears to produce. Specifically, one must examine how language became what it is, what adaptations we have made with language to this point, what the consequences have been as a result of those adaptations, and what further adaptations it is capable of.

This reality thus provides some encouragement in the evaluation of the gloomy hypothesis offered by Malthus and many others in despair over the apparent trajectory of human existence.

Indeed, but for the presence of others, there would be no shared experiences, and one could not meaningfully distinguish a private reality from an objective one. That we see the same objects, experience the same fears, pains and sorrows, and exalt the same virtues at some point arouses a sense of the value of existence. We are, in the process, taught to value our own existence by being taught to value the existence of others. This value stands on its own as an ethical principle and is quite different than merely wanting something.

This phenomenon—i.e., the conversion of private to shared experience and the experience of an existential satisfaction over that conversion, may be regarded as foundational to organization and all its economic derivatives. We do not come together simply as a result of a calculus applied to self-interest. We do so because coming together in cooperative assemblies is part of what we are. So, to regard individual and autonomous existence as valuable is at a primitive level a requirement to collaborative social formations, and requisite to organization on a social scale.

# Chapter 2

# The Basis of Organization

1. The behavioral sciences have made credible efforts to follow disciplinary standards typical of scientific observation. But their success in the establishment of something we have come to rely on as "science" is limited. Behavioral "science" is often criticized for using a science-like methodology, while failing to produce scientifically satisfying results. While often valid, such criticism is now inapplicable to the study of human organization, where there have been some remarkable empirical and theoretical breakthroughs.

One indication of whether a given field has achieved maturity as science is the willingness of individuals and institutions to take risks based on predictions the field has to offer. Complicating the assessment of risk are ethical judgments which accompany scientific ones. As indicated in the last chapter, moral disgust for large governmental institutions is part of the distrust of the promises of beneficial outcomes made by the proponents of those institutions. Ethically based division within government is, however, a major variable affecting the difficulty of predictions about the behavior of complex social systems.

Since these ethical divisions are derived in part from divergent theories about the effect of the organizing force of government on behavior, a science that resolved such divergence would likely have a moderating impact on these divisions.

In general, the behavioral sciences are burdened by the complexity of living organisms. Any given organism must make selections, and the process of selection involves the processing of data gathered by the senses. The line of causation in understanding selection—a mental process—is therefore quite different than the line of causation in understanding a physical process.

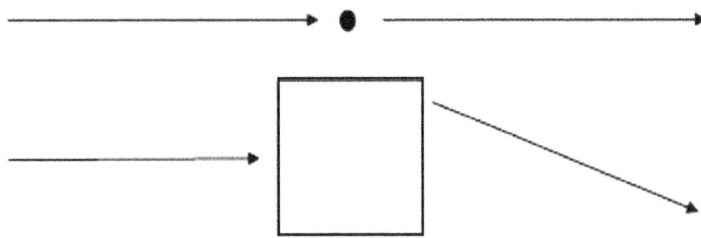

The first diagram is meant to symbolically represent a physical process, and the second, an organizational process. The first reflects the continuity of information, and science is a matter of understanding or comprehending that continuity. In the second process, science must contend with the processing characteristics of decision makers. A popular name for the box indicated above is the "black box", so called because of uncertainty typically associated with it. It is, in most important respects, a process of organization.

It can be quite complicated because our motivations are not simple. We phase in and out of different kinds of motivational states within the course of a day, and without having to try to do it. There are varieties of positive (desires) and negative (fears) operating, and at varying intensities. Fears in particular can vary in intensity and can emerge out of experiences that have been forgotten or suppressed.

We are very much aware of living within a world which is connected together physically and socially. Within this world it is often difficult on the surface to distinguish significant from insignificant changes in the environment. A slight change in the way someone says "good morning" can, depending on other circumstances, mark a significant change in social relationships.

Perhaps unique to the human as a linguistically active species is the effect of behavioral science on behavior. Hypotheses about behavior affect behavior, especially when they are assembled into a comprehensive theory about the nature of humanity. This is especially the case when theories of behavior are expressed in the form of government intervention, or law.

While many social animals care a great deal about "who" they are, no other species appears to care about "what" they are quite as much as the human. A science of organization thus accommodates numerous variables, not the least of which is a tendency of human beings to ponder and express theories about themselves. For most of recorded history, these have been expressed religiously, but more recently they have been offered under the rubric of "science." This occurs because species definition is an important tool of human organization. Science thus often functions to address a void—whether or not it is satisfying in its demonstrations.

Science in its application to social organization presents a different pair of diagrams to consider.

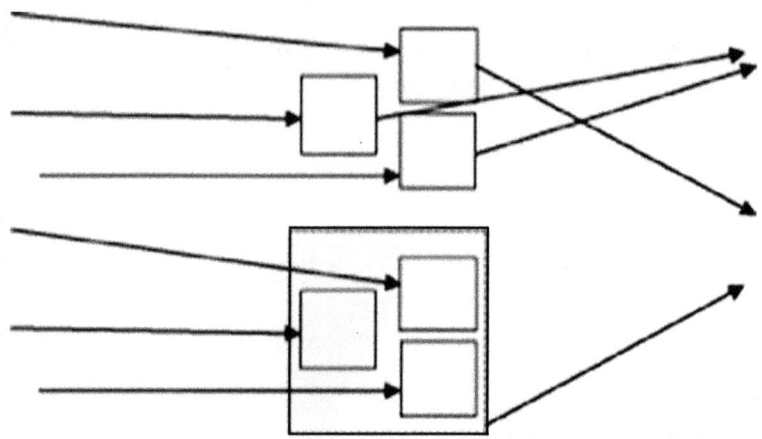

Both diagrams represent socially oriented behavior. The top diagram represents a situation where individuals are aware of others, and the awareness influences their behavior, but does not affect the individuality of the behavior. Their behavior is not consciously organized.

The bottom diagram reflects a situation of conscious organization, manifest in agreement among the group to coordinate behavior. Individuality is compromised, but is presumably more effective in that there is a far reduced likelihood of inconsistent or interferent behavior. The box which holds the other boxes exists only to the extent it is alive in the imagination of the participants. Thus, the effectiveness of organization depends on the similarity of the imagined entity among participants, and their willingness to subordinate to it.

The top diagram is more typical in a science of games and more popular among advocates of free markets because it anticipates the effect of non-interference—with social science being a matter of determining what that is. The bottom diagram represents human adaptation through organization, normally thought of as beneficial to societies—though not, perhaps, by those who perceive benefits to the preservation of competition. The bottom diagram might reflect a price-fixing cartel, for example. Overall, however, organization is something we regard as beneficial.

Is there science, therefore, applicable to the bottom diagram? If so, what effect will this have on what we prescribe (law) and how we organize production (economy)?

There are a number of intelligently conceived and useful theories of organization in circulation, but they are not "science" in the sense we have been using it here. What we are looking for as science is a set of principles which allow us to describe organizational form and behavior using formulae that transfer effectively between context. Newton's observation, for example, that gravitational force observable in the action of solid objects on earth must be related to the mass of objects—and could be used to describe the action of a number of celestial objects—brought the world from mere scientific observation to a mature science. Knowing that rules of motion were transferable greatly simplified our understanding of the world, and thus increased our confidence in many different kinds of undertakings.

Within the last 60 years, something of that nature has happened in the study of organizations. One of the more successful lines of research on human behavior has been in the area of cognitive development. A famous psychologist named Jean Piaget discovered that children acquire their perceptions of the size and volume of objects in stages. His theory was that consciousness has to work at the integration of the skills necessary to make a whole object out of diverse sensory data. The comprehension of volume was, in other words, an act of organization. [3]

  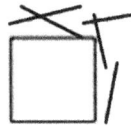 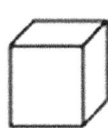

The drawings are meant to associate unatached lines with nascent experiences, i.e., the world as it might appear to the infant who has not yet learned how to integrate data, which integrated correctly, would appear as the completed three-dimensional object. There are obviously other things to learn about objects, just as there are other skills to learn, such as language. In each case, there is an incremental pattern of acquisition.

This discovery, as it turned out, allows us to understand complex bureaucratically structured organization. The study of such organization has revealed patterns in the development of stratified systems (hierarchical organization) which adhere to a pattern of cognitive development noticed in children. So, the formation of complex human institutions is like the formation of an object, except that it takes place on a different scale, and involves the integration of perceptions about the behavior of others. One's position in the hierarchy mirrors their stage of development in the understanding of that object. This discovery has made a great difference in our understanding of and control over human behavior in institutions.

2. As with most scientific advancements, this upgrade began with observation. The observation itself was illumined by the psychoanalytic movement in the personage of Eliot Jaques, a psychoanalyst who began his career in a close working relationship with the renowned child psychologist, Melanie Klein. He thereafter became co-founder of the Tavistock Institute of Social Relations, and founder of the School of Social Sciences at Brunel University. [4]

One of the foundational premises of the psychoanalytic movement was that the creations of mind reflected or projected the status of the mind as creator. Healthy internal structures—healthy mind—tend to create healthy exterior structures—organized objects. These objects can be any number of different things, i.e., bodily conditions, relationships, or hierarchically situated institutions—bureaucracies.

Among the things which stand out most to active and passive observers of bureaucracy is hierarchical organization. The best logic in support of hierarchical organization is common sense. The advantages of coordinated behavior include diversified location and the specialization of roles, along with strength in numbers. At the moment one introduces coordination as a specialized function—as in the appointment of a leader—there is hierarchy. The hierarchy is there, whether implicit as a team leader, or explicit as manager.

This tendency in human social relations seems to have its counterpart in the individual organization, where what appear to be rather trivial concerns obtain importance due to their relationship to a larger plan—a coordination of activities. Material preoccupations such as clothes, makeup, type of car, physical appearance, athletic skill, may all seem like little projects, but can be part(s) of a coordinated effort to attract a partner and thus quite important. There is hierarchy in such organization, and the importance individual behaviors are not likely to make much sense in the absence of hierarchy.

A fertile area of research, it seemed, might be aimed at the basis of individual subordination of social relationships to group objectives. The world had already seen individual subordination resulting in acquiescence to and participation in morally shocking behavior in the Second World War, and then the experimental confirmation of a strong human tendency to subordinate to the task requirements of immoral leadership in the Milgram studies of the early 1960s. Thus, a gnawing question about organization of human affairs prevailed upon organizational research. What was it about the human organism that favored the appropriation of discretion by others deemed "leader" in a bureaucratic setting? And corollary to that question is, what responsibilities, if any, do we have in the formation of such organization?

The research thus started as a psychoanalyst might begin a treatment, i.e., by asking the subject of analysis what their world was like, and to ask in such a way that would reveal placement. The question for example is really two questions: What do you do, and how does what you do fit into the coordinative structures established by the organization?

This course of study soon revealed that employees have an awareness of how their own tasks fit into time frames established by their superiors. Even if they were unable to provide clear explanations of what their superiors did, they had a good sense of how what they did was subject to supervisory constraints of time imposed upon them. The same was true of their managers. So, at an early stage of study, the research utilized "time-span-of-discretion" or "time-span" as an indicator of: (1) the complexity of the task assignments and (2) the relationship of those assignments to a coordinative hierarchy of tasks. It takes time to do something, and tasks subordinate to what needs to be done should, as a general matter, fit within the time frame of it. Workers can, without needing to know much about what their superiors do, effectively subordinate through an intuitive grasp of the temporal indicia of master and subordinate plans. In other words, one does not have to understand the plan as well as the planner to be a part of it.

It may in fact be better not to understand it, as work is hard enough as it is, without having to take responsibility for the rightness or wrongness of the plan. But someone has to take responsibility, for as might be expected, the further one goes up the chain of command, the greater the responsibility assumed as time-span-of-discretion. Did people assume greater discretion by way of arbitrary assignment, or did they assume discretion due to a demonstrable work capacity? The research—again along with common sense—supported the latter hypothesis, and moreover, that the acquisition of capability occurs in stages. There were a number of major empirical supports for this conclusion.

The first was a result of the analysis of the manager subordinate relationship. After defining manager—as one who assigns tasks, evaluates task performance, is in turn held responsible for subordinate performance, and has the power to remove from role—the time span of managers and subordinates were compared. This comparison revealed a high expected correlation. What was not expected was the discovery of ranges which excluded the formation of manager-subordinate relationships. That is to say, a given subordinate would regularly fail to identify as "manager" a superior who had failed to identify and define tasks at an identifiable threshold of time-span. The discovery strongly suggested that there are qualitative changes reflected in the emergence of larger temporal perspectives which at a given point of development enables the formation of relationships of subordination.

A second empirical finding followed sometime after the first. The points of measure for the separation of one managerial perspective and another were identical in all organizations, regardless of institutional mission, national or cultural affiliation, or industrial context. The studies of organization number in the hundreds now, and the result is the same at over ninety five percent (95%) rate of correlation. The first threshold is three months, meaning, persons functioning at time spans up to three months would almost always fail to identify as "manager" a person who had not passed three months—even if they were operating in task horizons of a week. The next horizon after three months is one year, and thereafter, 2 years, 5 years, 10 years, 20 years and onward, as institutional contexts expand. The data thus imply that persons operating as manager have had to learn to do or perceive something that their subordinates have not.

The implication that a learning process accompanies one's elevation in management hierarchy was strongly confirmed by a third major empirical finding. Longitudinal studies of the career trajectories of workers in many industries indicate that individuals progress at different rates up the management hierarchy, and that one can, by identifying age and managerial level predict what their management level will be in the future. These trajectories are not affected by career lapses or time off. At any given point in time, a person manifests a "level" of capability—where they are at a given point, and a "mode"—where they are expected to be by the end of their natural life. Something is obviously being learned, and the learning process results in phased movement, visible in bureaucracies as promotion.

A fourth source of empirical confirmation again flows from the three that preceded it. The discovery of constants in hierarchical organization has prompted a number of researchers to examine the behavioral characteristics of persons situated at various levels of work. There have also been a number of different attempts to draw very abstract conceptual boundaries, inclusive of expanding geometric diagrams and the arrangement of symbolically logical descriptions of behavior at various levels. The interplay between abstracted and sociologically nourished descriptors has become an institution, as many have now internalized a "form" to a progression of states arranged in hierarchy. It is quite alive now in the minds of a well-developed network of researchers and practitioners.

The development of these findings was only part of the work necessary to bring organization forward as a "science"—though arguably the most important part, as it has established constants applicable to human organization. The question remained as to what to do with this knowledge.

At the most obvious level, these constants are important in the development of management strategies which pivot on the selection of suitable personnel. Knowing something about the way intellectual skills progress in complex social systems is quite valuable in the establishment of task requirements for a given position, and provides an effective way to identify persons with the skills necessary to perform the tasks.

It has also revealed opportunities to make bureaucratic structures more responsible to a stated purpose. With increased confidence in the power of human capability at a given level, the primary organizational task shifts to the clarification of communication and the avoidance of influences that might interfere with or corrupt the objectives of the organization. Thus, a system of accountability that integrated a more powerful personnel selection technology together with proven accountability structures already in use throughout the world came to be called "Requisite Organization"—so called because it identified boundary conditions inhering in the nature of the human organism necessary for the existence of organization. The value offered for the establishment of systems of this nature is "trust" regarded by proponents of Requisite Organization as irreducible.

An important aspect of the union of capability and accountability structures was an interest in the universal form of organization itself. Something was governing organization as ruling principle, otherwise it would be difficult to account for the constants in the phased growth of problem solving orientations—levels of management. What was the common thread to what these workers were learning to do? Were they learning about some kind of "thing" and if they were, how might one describe the "wholeness" of the thing that was being learned?

Deliberation over these questions led to observations about how the stratification of work capability—reflected in the phased acquisition of control over a social system—also indicated or reflected an underlying order to hierarchical social structures. There were three observations made.

First, there were observations about what became known as an essential relational unit of management. That unit was not, as anticipated, the dual relation of manager to subordinate, but rather a tripartite relationship between three layers of management—i.e., subordinate, manager, to the manager's manager (manager once removed). This, it seems, was an intuitive observation that there are conflicts of interest inherent in the manager subordinate relationship that require active observation and intervention on the part of a manager once removed to assure fairness, and hence trust.

Second—and related to the first—was a high regard among practitioners in Requisite toward the importance of building organizations around durable and capable three-tiered subunits which incorporated something of the nature of a collection of operator (str.1) supervisor (str.2) and manager (str. 3). This magnified the importance of the "manager" as occupant of a central tier through which organizational subunits were gathered and upon which executive structures such as vice president (str. 4) and president (str. 5) were constructed.

Third, there appeared to be a stage of wholeness applicable to organizational formation occurring at the fifth level. Organizations at that level of management form what are regarded as complete business units functioning within a time-span of discretion of 5 years. Within a unit of this nature a director will have identified a universe of discourse—a defining purpose—suitable for the functioning of the organization. Organizations which grow beyond this point do tend to do so by gathering complete business units within them, and seeking relationships of complementarity between them.

The progress of organizational theory has thus accelerated considerably with the confidence brought on by the discovery of constants. Currently, organizational theorists are looking at organizations differently than they did fifty years ago, now as complete wholes knit together as overlapping three tiered systems of accountability. A simplified version of organization might be presented as follows—a five-tiered organizational unit bound with primary, secondary and tertiary management complexes of overlapping accountability.

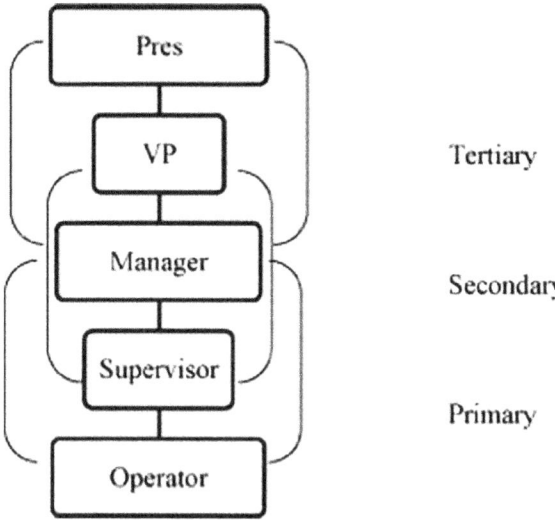

This is where organizational theory has evolved due to the efforts of adherents to Requisite Organization. The success of efforts so far is significant in that we have progressed from the view of organization as a makeshift enterprise, to a visually cohesive template against which bureaucratic structures can be compared. The results, however, while valuable and practical in their own right, have failed to identify the properties of the human organism that support these structures as a behavioral effect.

As a consequence, the application of requisite organization to issue of social organization on a broader scale, as in law and economy, is awkward. It is scientific in its methods, but it has positioned itself as a specialized application of science-like theory—an economic resource—but not as a change in the way law and economy are conceived. The ingredient necessary for the maturation of Requisite Organization as "science" required another step that connected the requisites for wholeness in organization with a theory of human development. The description of this connection shall be covered in the next two sections.

3. A common occurrence within the Requisite movement is the sudden appearance of structures in human organization of all kinds—art, politics, rhetoric, literature, history, etc.—which had passed

unnoticed previously. This occurrence is apt to be expressed in a desire to draw structured matrices on organizational phenomenon and name their elements. The phenomenon signals that at some point in the study of organization, the name-giver has conceptually internalized the pattern which inheres to bureaucratic organization and is able to use it as an observational filter for the interpretation of data in diverse organizational contexts.

Access to something of this nature was included in materials published some time ago with other theorists in stratified systems. These were prepared by logicians interested in the Requisite movement in the form of a developmental progression in the use of truth tables found in first order logic. First order logic, and the development of a propositional calculus stands out as one of the major achievements of the modern era, and has been very carefully vetted among innumerable academic articles and textbooks. If propositional logic could express the development of mind evident in bureaucratic structures, a good case could be made for the science of organization.

The use of propositional logic did, in fact, reveal a developmental progression which led from a simple distinction at the first stage—truth and falsity for a given proposition—to a complex distinction at a fifth stage—existence and non-existence within a universe of discourse. Moreover, the type of mental activity evident in the first stage of logic bore some resemblance to the type of mental activity in the first level of work in bureaucratic organization. The same was true of the second, third, fourth and fifth stages of logic. All resembled—more or less—the described problem-solving strategies of persons engaged in work in comparable bureaucratic strata.

The developmental path suggested through the arrangement of logical operations was therefore a promising place to begin a comparison of what thought is (in general) and how laborers work (in application). But there were real difficulties in the use of propositional logic. The first three levels defined in terms of dualities (1) true-false "statements", (2) conjunctive (both/and)-disjunctive (either/or) "pairs" of statements, and (3) primary-composite "types" of statements were easy to transfer to orientational states typical of problem solving activity.

At stage 4 logic, the duality offered as antisymmetric (ordered)-symmetrical (unordered) relations between "sets" of statements separated from a point of rational access to the underlying program of truth functional logic. The attempt to associate a relational calculus to truth functional logic was inaccessible except through very abstract comparison of "patterns" of propositional columns with the formative processes one tends to associate with system building in complex organizations. System formation in complex organizations is purpose driven—which is what allows one to identify pattern, but purpose was never part of the notational structure of first order logic.

This problem magnifies at stage 5 of logic, which poses a duality of predicate-term within a "universe" of discourse. It certainly appears to describe the context building behavior of level 5 managers, but the predicate calculus expressed at this logical level does not derive from or otherwise connect to the motivating substance of the operations which preceded it. Moreover, logic expressed at level 5 does not appear to provide for the description of bureaucratic problem solving at levels 6 and onward. [5]

The problem was not with the application of logic itself. The deficiency consisted in the use of a notational system which was not designed to express developmental processes. The assembly of gradually more complex logical processes suggested development, but the individual structures posed as "descriptive" of a given stage of development were not themselves formed in order to express development. They were words arranged on a developmental matrix tending to validate the matrix, but failing to explain it.

In order to logically explain development, it was necessary to utilize a notational system which more directly tracked logical development as a function of the growth of capacity. It was additionally necessary that the notational system serve a dual purpose, i.e., (1) to define a sequence of logical processes essential to first order logic of propositions, and (2) to describe work behavior of persons at different bureaucratic levels.

The response to this need was a logic using an information processing metaphor. Take a piece of information + and bury it in a field of possible locations ........, and attempt to find + with limited skills available. Start with one operative skill, and call it a capacity of 1, and move in a sequential progression, integrating other skills, identifying each integration with an increase in capacity—2[ ], 3>, 4><, and 5{}—and note the change in the form along with the efficiency of the form. The essential difference between this, and a first order logic, is the use of capacity as an independent variable.

It is like juggling. Each time the juggler adds an object to the act of keeping the objects in motion, he must adopt a new form to maintain the act. The objects here are processing strategies, and juggling is an act of integration, the form of which depends on the number of objects being integrated. A movement to a higher order of complexity is a matter of changing the size and complexity of the objects.

At each level, beginning with the first, one assumes that the available capacity is exhausted. So, at the first level, one must assume that all available capacity is consumed in an act or combination of acts which integrates that skill, and that the same is true of the others in sequence. Unless that assumption is made, in fact, it would be difficult to imagine the way in which the integration of skills occur in sequence. Movement from one level to the next thus requires an increase in available capacity, meaning either an increase in capacity, or the reduction of the capacity required by each level.

This exercise yielded four distinct forms, along with a fifth, which replicated the first and indicated a different order of complexity. These can be arranged as follows, using the sign / or ( ) as a pass.

1. (.) …....+.

   Random search—uncertain completion

   (+) equals "true."


2. [.(.)] ….+.

   Secured search—no more than 8 passes

   [.(.)] equals "conjunctive"


3. [.>. (.)>.] ..+.

   Intimative search—no more than 4 passes

   [(.)>+] equals "proof"


4. [.<(>……+<)>.]

   Ordered search—reforms to 1 pass

   [>…<] equals "ordered" relation (hierarchy)

5. {O}OOOO╬O

New ordered search where O equals >......+.<

{╬} equals higher order “true.”

These forms are modified from their original—and somewhat improved—though they are quite close in all important respects to the original. The use of terminology and the application of that terminology to the logical operations identified at each level is the subject of a completed work. Here it is important to acknowledge the availability of the forms as simple descriptors, and that the notational structure solves the problems associated with the use of propositional logic. [6]

1. The objective of information processing activity is present in the notation and remains present as organizing principle throughout the development.

2. Improvement in field navigation is a function of the introduction—incrementally—of new skills. It therefore tracks development or “growth.”

3. The transfer pictorially to the kinds of activity one sees in stratified work systems. Labor does not work in truth tables, but with objects, “.” or “O.”

4. A fifth level provides completion to sequence by lower order within a “universe” “O”, but at the same time provides means of transition to further development.

Not long after the development of this breakthrough, the Requisite movement announced that levels of work reflected information processing modalities, that there were four and only four essential descriptive forms of information processing applicable to levels of work, that an individuals interaction with a work environment takes them through these different processes in a fixed sequence, and that movement to a fifth level involve a change to a new order of complexity.

This announcement included terms which summarize the visual form of the descriptors identified above. The first level of random processing was described as “declarative” to emphasize its isolation or removal from other potential poses. The second level was described as "cumulative" in order to emphasize the use of memory as a way of accumulating knowledge, and avoiding repetition of effort. The third level is described as "serial" in order to emphasize that anticipation or implication is unidirectional when one's attention is embedded in the field. Thus, a fourth description entitled "parallel" processing, describes omni-directionality evident in the separation from the field, and the process of repackaging operations to fit within a single moment. This provides us with a descriptive panorama, with some benefits and some detriments.

| | |
|---|---|
| Order' | Declarative |
| | Cumulative |
| | Serial |
| | Parallel |
| Order'' | Declarative |
| | Cumulative |
| | Serial |
| | Parallel |
| Order''' | Declarative |

With these terms, organizational theory has a set of accessible summaries which simplify an organizational matrix, while suggesting a developmental process. The terms thus reflect a move forward in the behavioral sciences, i.e., a combined theory of social structure and individual development.

4. In the midst of setting out a logic of human development, one encounters a paradoxical trade-off between the descriptive benefits of simplification, and confusion arising from generalizations that seem far removed from any given context of work. While engaging in logic, it is wise to remember that the purpose of logic is to toss off inessential or distracting predicates, so that the form of the behaviors being described remains distinct. So, logic and a so-called "science" of mind are difficult to separate from each other, in that knowing of a rule of motion consists in formalizing it in a language, where the language both assists scientific observation and adapts to it. Various historical revisions in logic haven't been trained to gaze upon social and institutional hierarchy, and the

limits of those in the process of rising within these hierarchies. It was to this end—the description of behavior beset with cognitive limitations—that information processing was chosen as the descriptive metaphor allowing the formalization of cognitive development and its corresponding organizational hierarchies.

Indeed, the conscious recognition that the form of the observer is evident in the form of its creations is, of itself, a significant conceptual breakthrough, and allows us to make use of the logical notation of G. Spencer Brown. There is an explanation of the use of that notation in an appendix to On Freedom, where a circle that separates a space from a void stands symbolically for a motivational intervention wherein the observer selects, or distinguishes, one space where none were previously identified.

With the acknowledgment that distinction is a motivated intervention. not much is said about the intentionality of logic. What is "information" and what kinds of things are these processing modalities processing? What experience of motivation do these processes reflect? How do we know from the use of the term whether one processing modality represents an improvement over the others?

Without some elaboration on the logic of information, it is awkward to deploy these from outside of the context in which they are first adapted. Assuming that a scientific theory acquires credibility through the diversity of its applications, we should consider whether an information processing terminology now in use in the description of work systems is transferable to other contexts—as in the contexts of law and economy. The transfer of descriptive terminology from one context to another in social science has much to do with identifying the motivation of the behavior being described, and whether experience is—as a matter of intention—similar. Otherwise the description is confined to its original context as superficial—as if attempting to describe the contents of a food product by taking a picture of it.

Therefore, in order for descriptions of work systems to be useful in the description of legal and economic systems, it is necessary to add intention to them, and to a degree, substitute extrinsic descriptions with intrinsic descriptions. As extrinsic descriptions, these are more concerned with the form of the activity—the assumption being perhaps that the organism is showing exactly what it desires. Intrinsic description on the other hand identifies the intention of the organism first and describes behavior of one of possibly several manifestations of behavior. This would be quite useful in expanding a science of organization beyond the bureaucratic setting.

We could say, perhaps, that if one has simplified a descriptive matrix as much as it can be simplified, one has gone as far as possible in the scientific understanding of something. That argument is occasionally made in the physical sciences, but is far less applicable in the behavioral sciences—as the point of distinction between behavioral and physical processes is motivation and intentionality. There is no real understanding of the matrix without an understanding of the intentionality that produces it. Since the empirical discoveries here are provocative indicators of constants operating in human behavior—and reflect deeply on the human as an organizing presence in the world—they should be examined as closely as one's faculties allow.

The engagement of form (effect) before substance (intention) may well have been a fault of the designer of the information processing modalities at the start. Information was symbolically represented in terms of objects or options, and a search objective within those options, identified as "+". Navigation thus assumed or prescribed to a search device—human or not—it was to look for. There is no explanation of how "." becomes "+" within a field. That was an error, a fundamental error. [7]

The correction of the error occurs at the beginning of a developmental sequence by defining "information" in terms of the valuative state of the person whose behavior is being described—the processor. The processor brings interest to a field of possibilities by wanting something from it, and expresses interest in the context of a limited capacity to organize experience. Interest is thus tied to capacity, and the means through which capacity is expressed.

A field of data becomes information as it is broken into comprehensible pieces (pieces of limited magnitude) and fed into the maw of interest, which is itself constrained by limitation. A neutral quantum of data moves from its neutral state "." to a positive state "+" when embraced by interest "( )"—"." to "(+)". The expression "+" never really existed except as "."—data with the potential of existing in a state of agreement with "( )". The conversion of data to information thus occurs through the intervention of value. With this modification, a developmental phase begins with interest reflecting the commitment of one's entire capacity, and that commitment remains constant throughout a developmental cycle.

This represents what may appear to be a superficially nuanced change of the organizational design because it does not materially alter the forms of information processing which emerge subsequently. But it is actually a fairly radical alteration of it. By beginning with interest as an intentional posture necessary to the existence of information—the condition precedent to the emergence of "+"—intention becomes primary to organization as "organizing principle" and subsequent expansions in capacity can be viewed as intentional states deriving from that principle. The developmental model at this point has received a transfusion of value, or purpose, while retaining its exterior appearance.

Along with this modification comes a simpler link to the propositional logics that have dominated 20th century thinking. A proposition is not a thing in reality, but an expressed expectancy about reality—and expression of interest. So to say "the sky is blue" is to take "blue" as a proposed predication of the term "sky", or rather, "( )" which may be brought to "." in the form of a test—"open your eyes and look upward." Therefore, the expressions "(.)", "(+)" correspond to "false" and "true". The conversion of "." to "(+)" (agreement) or "(.)" to "." (disagreement) occurs through the distinction of agreement from disagreement with a given interest. The logical concept of "negation" thus consists in the act of distinguishing information from data. "Negation" and "distinction" are two ways of saying the same thing.

This also resolves what appeared to be a dissimilarity between propositional logic and imperative logic, where it is generally accepted that telling someone about a state of affairs and telling them what to do about a state of affairs invoke two different logical states. But in this logic, there is no distinction, because a proposition is a statement of expectation about the world, while telling someone what to do is the statement of an expectation about them (and they are part of the world). Since much of what we do in work systems is expressed in commands (imperatives), it was supposed that social systems functioned within a different system of logic. Now it is clear that there is no reason to make that distinction.

Within an interest driven logic of information processing, the development of proficiency in the navigation of the field occurs through the introduction of interests which are activated by a primary interest. An interest in remembering where one has looked within a field of data derives from an interest in finding something, and thus when distinction no longer requires conscious effort, one is able to pay attention to remembering—and become a cumulative processor (informational logic), able to extract conjunctive expressions from a disjunctive world (propositional logic).

The same is the case for movement to stages 3, 4 and 5. An acquired proficiency in remembering (to the point of being automatic) allows focus on the development of an anticipatory process. Proficiency with anticipation (serial processes) allows focused interest in ordered complexes (parallel processes). Proficiency in the development of ordered processes (now perceived as "form") allow a new order of interest to engage an expanded field. The entire process of development does not, in fact, derive from of a descriptive matrix at all, but to the contrary, is responsive to motivational states waiting their turn to express themselves.

With this understanding, it may be useful to re-examine the terminology descriptive of processing state, in order to clarify what they are, and to assist clarity in the application of these constants to other processes.

1. to (+)

    Primary interest—Declarative.

2. (.) to [......(+).]

    Interest in security—Cumulative.

3. [(.)]. to [(.)>+]

    Interest in intimation—Serial.

4. [(.)>.] to [(>......+.<)]

    Interest in order—Parallel.

5. O to {╫} New Primary interest—New Declarative.

These interests provide a mechanism for the improvement of our sense of what the descriptors mean. A declaration reflects (or is the effect of) the intervention of an interest having magnitude which acts as a defining instrumentality or container which in turn determines the size of options presented by the field—singular represented by "." or compound history represented by "O".

Standing alone as a descriptive instrument "cumulative" is vague, but vagueness is cured through the clarification of its intention. "Cumulation"—viewed as a mental act—here communicates a formal process of remembering, i.e., not only that bits and pieces of data are remembered, but that measured information complexes—"." or "O" (formations of data) become part of a list which by intention covers an entire field. Cumulation is thus about the extraction of declarative events from a field and securing them in thought, and not merely about the accumulation of experience.

Intention is useful in avoiding confusion of "information" processing with "data" processing. The use of the term "serial process" is borrowed from the data processing industry, where it actually describes a "cumulative" process—i.e., a process which encounters data one bit or enclosure at a time—avoiding repetition—until the data filter separates something responsive to a search request. If the desired information is located at a far relative distance, it will not be found until all the intermediate data are checked. Parallel processing, on the other hand, describes a partitioned data base where large groups of data can be avoided altogether. Hierarchical partitioning thus allows more efficient search by eliminating most of the data enclosures from consideration. They are referred to as "parallel" because one can move laterally from one system or group of enclosures to another without having to look inside them.

In the model that has been applied to human organization, "serial" is used to emphasize that the actor's mind is embedded in a process which has only one direction, i.e., from "here" to "there." By contrast to a "cumulative" process, it has direction in mind because "there" is included or intimated in the experience of "here." Direction is, therefore, experienced. A sense of "direction" in a cumulative process is more like looking out the back window of a train. Events conceived as "." or "O" do not acquire a fixed location in time until the observer is removed from the sequence, and asserts an interest in order—the effect of which is a "parallel" process.

Behavioral science thus uses the word "parallel" differently than it is used in data-processing. Parallel processing involves the formation and recognition of a whole composed of parts. It is similar to the difference of being preoccupied with the components of a face of another human being, without knowing it is a face, and thereafter seeing the components as gathered into a face. We know what faces are because we have a desire to know—interest and have developed a sense of the range within which face-like components can gather and still be a face—magnitude. [8]

This process is not the same thing at all as movement through partitions within an information storage system designed by data processing architects. Formation and recognition is a willful act of consciousness, guided by functional expectations.

5. These adjustments support an appreciation of the transition from one order of complexity to another, or rather, the event in which one interest is supplanted by another interest suitable to the navigation of another field. An understanding of this type of occurrence is especially useful in the development of expectancies for the regulation of systems which tend to avoid comprehension, such as industries and economies. A brief anecdote serves as introduction.

In a popular science fiction tale, a group of star travelers found themselves in a state of captivity within a city of robots, though the captivity was benign and the robots were human in appearance. The robots had been programmed to serve humans, and had somehow acquired among their governing principles that the best way to serve was to inhibit certain freedoms, such as escape from the service relationship. Humans were presumed untrustworthy in their choice over such matters.

The star travelers gained their freedom by engaging the robot leader in a dialogue of paradoxes, such as feigned agony over happiness. The coup de grace was administered through what has historically been called "the liar's paradox," which consists of the statement "everything I say is a lie." This is an impossibility because the statement itself is included in the universe of statements, which if true means he is telling the truth in that statement. The robots were unable to process this, along with other logical paradoxes, and thereafter stopped functioning. It was no problem for the humans because such a statement was a statement about a universe of possibilities and was obviously not meant to be part of it—thereby reflecting a freedom of perspective apparently unavailable to the robots.

Bertrand Russell developed a nearly identical version of this paradox as he labored over the development of his logic of propositions. The paradox, however, did not allow an implied escape rationale, as he contemplated: "The set of all sets which do not have themselves as members." This suggested impossibility because that set would, if included in the set, not belong to the set, but since not belonging to the set, should be included. The paradox was disturbing to him and a number of others, because it suggested something wrong in the use of the term "set" and that term was important to his logic.

His solution was to assert a rule of prohibition to the effect that "sets cannot have themselves as members." His justification for asserting this was that logical statements exist on a hierarchy of types, and statements about another universe of statements are automatically excluded from that universe because they are situated on a higher level of abstraction. The rule forces exclusion, even if the statement indicates intention to include itself in the set it creates. The rule, however, seemed arbitrary to a number of philosophers of the era, including Russell's protégé Ludwig Wittgenstein.

Wittgenstein offered a solution which did not require the assumption of a hierarchy external to the logic. Instead he claimed that prohibition consisted in the analysis of the terms "proposition"—statements about an object, and "set"—statements about a group of objects. He recognized that a proposition is an expression of intentionality—a proposal about it, and that a set likewise separated into an expression of intentionality—a rule of membership, and the assembled collection. To quote him directly:

> No proposition can say anything about itself, because the propositional sign cannot be contained in itself (that is the whole "theory of types"). A function cannot be its own argument, because the functional sign already contains the prototype of its own argument and it cannot contain itself. (Tractatus 3.332-3.333)

No extrinsic rule of prohibition was necessary because intention (formally referred to as "function" or "intension") was by its nature separate from the effect of intention (formally referred to as "argument" or "extension"). Intension is, in other words, an intervention within a state of affairs that becomes included in its productive effect, using the same sign to identify a state of interest as in "Predicate (Term)" or "P(T)". Its separateness as a different type of experience is already included in the logical symbols and is separate by virtue of the role it plays—the subjective state of interest it brings to an object. Once that state is objectified, it is not quite the same as what it once was.

That is to say, even though one might use the same symbol P (predicate) as the sense in which T (term) is being examined, as in "P(T)", it is not the same as a P bonded to T, as in "(PT)" to indicate a predicate bonded to and part of the object. The use of the symbols "P" and "T" are in a sense redundant, inasmuch as the symbol ( ) or { } already separates the boundary from the space within and without it. There is therefore no need to suppose an extrinsic hierarchy of logic because the intrinsic separation of interest from the object to which it is focused is presupposed.

Indeed, the Russell paradox can be reformulated in any number of different ways, such as, "this statement is a lie," "the set of members that cannot be members," "the set of objects that cannot be objects" or "the set of intensions." In each instance we identify things that cannot be made into members without changing in some fundamental sense what they are. As will be seen below, it is the basis for later reflection by Wittgenstein about the possibility of a "private" language, inasmuch as language is a process that includes a sense of public obligation that derives from, but it not identical to, a value one attributes to it.

This point is not as trivial as its technical formulations seem to suggest. It is the equivalent of stating that objects do not confer value on objects, only value can do so. There is no organizational utility, in other words, in developing a higher level of abstraction without there being a functional motivation in support of it. They are distinctions without differences. One might therefore appreciate that since institutional hierarchies are difficult to maintain, motivational factors would be quite important in their design.

Moreover, once one becomes comfortable with the separation of "intension" and "extension"—interest and object—it becomes plain and apparent that the experience of interest can be more or less focused, and that human labor moves within a continuum of relatively focused and unfocused states of interest.

We are thus encouraged to organize interests hierarchically, but this is usually more complicated than it seems, because some interests are instrumental to others, while others are merely more focused versions of other more broadly situated interests. Indeed, a common error in applied behavioral science is the confusion of methodological (logical processes) hierarchy from a purely abstractive hierarchy (progressive generalization). The example below illustrates how they may become confused.

> Two points are represented by "a" and "b" combine them into a meta-point represented by A. Two meta-points "A" and "B" combine into a meta-meta-point "aa". Meta-meta-points "aa" and "bb" combine into meta-meta-meta- point AA.

The temptation, of course, is to view this as a description of a four-level hierarchy which moves from one level to the next by combining the constituents into an abstracted whole. This combination typifies simple abstraction. Abstractive hierarchy makes no assumption about capacity and thus is available as a feature of language, which exhibits quite a lot of abstractive lability—even at low levels of functioning. The correct identification of levels for the illustration set apart above is that there are none, as there is only one skill on display—an abstractive skill, and thus no basis in which to identify a second level.

Part of the difficulty in assessing the presence of methodological "hierarchy" is that there are no assumptions made about capacity. Since every point of information "." or its newly ordered counterpart "O" represent a point within a repeating cycle of information organization, each represents the use of the full complement of navigational instrumentalities at a lower order which preceded its formation. Methodological hierarchy (also appropriately referred to as "logical" hierarchy) does not examine the relative states of generalization of its constituents, but the relative state of integration of a limited assortment of available integrative skills (instrumentalities) within an established order of complexity.

While the abstractive properties of language are important to organization for a number of reasons, they are not essential to the definition of the developmental process which is the basis of institutional hierarchy. This analysis strongly suggests that "magnitude" measured in terms of the breadth of time frames or of conceptual schemes can be misleading, and that their expansion along with an increase in capacity is an effect and not the substance of an organizing process. This reality is the basis of many ironic stories involving the intervention of higher authorities with disarmingly simple solutions to problems—made possible not so much by abstraction, but through the integration (and resultant simplification) of numerous processes.

6. Standing out more prominently in the evaluation of organization, therefore, is how an order of complexity arises. It is useful to know that an "order" of complexity emerges through a cycle, but there is some question over what a change of the "order" of interest is. In the process of an evaluation of this nature we gain a point of access toward the understanding of processes which are internal to organizational "units." We also bring within view an approach for the theoretical treatment of the organizing properties of language, and its derivative, law.

Recall earlier in this chapter that an essential part of the formation of accountability structures in bureaucracy was the insertion of a manager once removed in what had been previously conceptualized as a two-piece manager-subordinate relationship. The affirmation of a three-tiered relationship was based on intuitive notions of fairness and order—i.e., that the one being held accountable for performance must be held accountable by someone other than himself, and that the sources of accountability emerge from a different organizational tier. In concept, this produced a visual image of an organization bound within three overlapping matrices of accountability. Levels 1-3 constituted a single unit of accountability, as did levels 2-4 and levels 3-5, and all were bound within a singular business unit.

We have until this point been treating the initial phase in a cycle of development as an information processing cycle which includes declarative, cumulative, serial and parallel processes. There is an idiosyncrasy present in the declarative stage which suggests that it is either not an information processing form, or that it is a fundamentally different type of information processing form.

The essential difference consists in the nature of the intentionality involved. At a declarative level, intention is primary in that it provides the motivation for an entire sequence of development. The intentionality of subsequent processes is derivative or secondary—i.e., having value because they improve on the efficiency of an information search. There are therefore three intentional states common to each developmental cycle or order, which follow after the introduction or declaration of a unique intentional state providing the basis of a developmental cycle.

Complicating this observation is the recognition that a new primary intention is filtered through the capacity of the individual completing the developmental cycle that preceded it, of the completed parallel process. That capacity is determined by the formation of a compound singularity which was in a process of emergence—where the form "O" replaced "(>......+.<)", "><" indicating an interest in order. Within this framework, it would appear that a new primary interest "{ }" in some sense adds to the content of the processes which precede it, by taking an interest in a universe holding objects that are one order of complexity larger.

It is the same sentient creature who, while terminating growth within lower order interest, continues growth in the new cycle. Though the developmental model requires the introduction of a different order interest, it is far from clear that "interest" has changed in any respect other than as to scale of expression. In fact, an assumed continuity to "interest"—i.e., the same interest embracing a larger field of possibilities—suggests a picture in which interest retains its "character" as a core value of the organism, while undergoing adaptations brought on by circumstance.

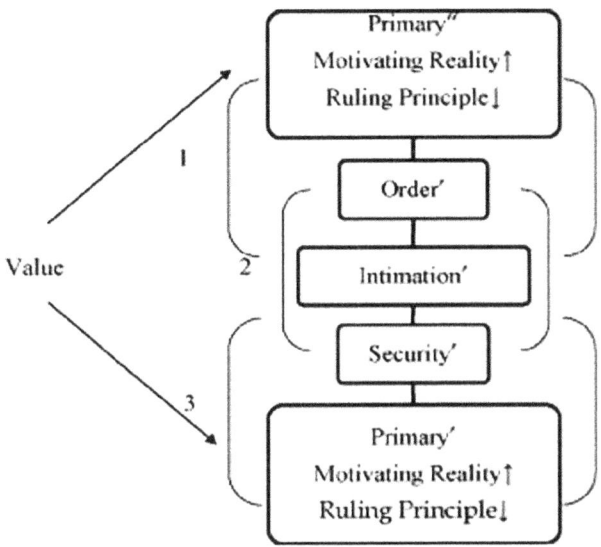

The depiction above is best treated as a working hypothesis about human development than as a fact, though its viability as a hypothesis is enabled by a logic that emphasizes a growth cycle. What stands out prominently here is the dual role of a "primary" value. On the one hand it marks a point of entry into a new and higher order of complexity, while at the same time having a consolidative effect on a lower order of complexity. It thus refers, at least theoretically, to a term used in the last chapter, to logos, because logos as "ruling principle" both activates (gives life to) and governs over (constrains) action.

Secondary or enabling sources of motivation are the sources of development and tend to act as mechanisms enabling the restless process of transition which in itself can be emotionally quite challenging. At this point, the use of the term "information processing" to describe what is happening at a Primary level of organization is problematic, as the significance of these movements is not to organize information differently, but to alter priorities within which information is organized.

Primary thus signals completion of an information processing cycle, and rests upon existing processes of order when those processes seem to occur without effort—as a tablecloth might rest upon a table to signal a time to stop building the table and to start using it. Perhaps there are four information processing states, but only three in which we are actually organizing information, and one that tells us when to stop. The idea is provocative and resonates at some level of our conscious identity as a species. [9]

Before any such considerations become available we should acknowledge that we are now at a point of transition between bureaucratic sense of organization and more general principles of organization. Discussion of logic had been in the service of organizational constants observed and recorded in institutions typical of the "firm" identified in economic models, and of the agencies which regulate economic processes. And while firms may appear to be very complicated entities, the logical structures with which we were born appear to impose limits upon them—perhaps so that we might avoid being engulfed by them. That assumes, however, that we are in a state of encounter with something that can be limited, and that is not always the case.

Social psychologists have studied the development of socially valuative states—notably Lawrence Kohlberg (stages of moral development) and Abraham Maslow (hierarchy of values). Both followed the momentum emerging some time ago within the field of developmental psychology. One might remark with interest about the appearance of similarity between their developmental matrices and those manifest in the strata of complex organizations.

| Maslow | Kohlberg |
|---|---|
| Self-Actualization | Social Contract |
| Status | Order Maintenance |
| Intimacy | Interpersonal Concord |
| Safety | Reciprocity |
| Physiological | Punishment |

But more interesting than an evident similarity between these developmental courses and the intentionality we associate with information processing modes, is the absence of a one to one relationship between cognitive capacity evident in management level and the stage of that individual's moral development. How is it that they have a similar appearance, but do not match up demographically?

This may come as somewhat of a relief to those interested in human freedom, as it seems that our ability to master relatively fixed objects—such as an organization or work systems—occurs on a different growth schedule than our ability to master more elusive objects—such as one's selfhood or identity.

The difference here may rest in the fact that one's encounter with oneself is not like an encounter with a fixed object. The growth can, in other words, be similar, while following a different course. There may well be a point of ethical completion in one's search for soul, but as a target it changes along with growth, and may not be accessible except through disciplines developed over many centuries. Persons who have no difficulty at all distinguishing and managing complex objects often become overwhelmed by the growing difficulty of placing themselves within a social universe. But this is exactly where law abides, and where one makes peace with oneself as a social being.

7. The foregoing description and analysis of the social science of organization serves not only as an inventory of empirical discoveries relevant to social organization but allows us to make defining generalizations about the appearance of "order" or "organization" in social systems.

We arrive at that point because there is a meaningful similarity between cognitive development and bureaucratic hierarchy, and this implies a strong relationship between something within the human mind and ordered social systems. This brought thought to a threshold of scientific breakthrough evident in other disciplines, where rules of organization and/or motion evident at a microscopic level are comparably manifest on a macroscopic scale.

Our confidence in these breakthroughs is strengthened significantly with the identification of intentions that match with hierarchically arranged forms, as behavioral expressions are best explained as the consequence of volitional states. It allows us to effectively separate abstracted hierarchies from a methodological hierarchy—and thus avoid confusion over terminology. Acquired skill is not so much about abstractive generalization as it is about the integration and coordination of intentions.

Probably the best way to honor Jaques' contribution to the social science of organization is to adopt his moniker "Requisite Organization" as a term inclusive of the science emerging from his research. What it covers as "science" are requirements of organization resulting from human nature, such that their presence or absence constitute the strength or weakness of organization.

Since it tends to favor organizational strength as a feature of "health," it is not ethically neutral, because it at least attempts to separate better from worse. Whether there is an ethically neutral social science is in any event questionable. A "requisite" organization or structure is whole, complete and stable due to the presence of a number of characteristics, all of which are essential to the nature of organization and can be verified through replicable observations. These characteristics are confirmed by empirical research and by the calculus of abstract logic, some of which may be enumerated.

> 1. There is a hierarchical structure to human organization constant across contexts that mirror the constancy of phased cognitive mastery over fields of data. The strata reveal methodological—not abstractive—hierarchy, in which "higher" levels appropriate and add to controls manifest in lower levels, allowing persons mastering higher level controls to manage the affairs of others at lower levels.

> 2. The methods are themselves the manifestation of volitional states (intention or interest) which bestow value on navigational improvement. Value itself separates into two categories—primary and secondary. Primary value is a state of wanting something from a real world, while secondary represents a strategy which derives value from its usefulness as a navigational orientation.

> 3. By applying and integrating navigational orientations to a field, the field changes to object. This occurs at a fifth stage through the redefinition of primary value, which operates both as activating value for a new cycle of development, and ruling principle on the old cycle. This "locates" three information processing phases within two sources of connection to a shared social environment.

> 4. The two sources of input for primary value—as both expansive and consolidative principle—are integrated through a nexus of processing instrumentalities which together form a five-level organizational unit. The process of integration involves three

overlapping management events, each of which is situated within a three-tiered complex involving manager, subordinate and manager once removed.

Conscious recognition of the intervention of value, allows one to distinguish the substance of organization from its form. They are not the same. As mentioned in the preceding chapter, organization as a human activity occurs with a purpose that brings organization from a theoretical state to a state of engagement with reality. When some individual steps into organization, he or she becomes engaged in a state of social intercourse having consequences, even as it gets overwhelmingly complicated.

Item number "4" above, for example, which describes overlapping three-tiered management events within a five-tiered hierarchy, may not describe a neat process, but it is unlikely that the evolution of human social organisms was ever consciously designed to be anything but adaptive to human interest. It reinforces the view that organization is less about the delineation or assembly of strata, than it is about the formation of objects useful to human existence, many of which are, by design, fuzzy constructs.

# Chapter 3

# Wild Economy

1. One question of a philosophical nature is whether there is such a thing as "economics" without a theory of economy. When a person within a primitive group of collaborators identifies a strategy of common survival, he or she is expressing a social theory. Since social strategies usually require some degree of specialization and coordination, it may be fair to think of the resulting activity as "economy" by virtue of the group awareness which accompanies the activity. Group awareness consists in the expression of a strategic plan to others and the expectation that the pursuit of it depends on collective acquiescence.

As this chapter develops, it will become evident that group awareness and self-awareness are closely related. This is based on a theory of language that is—in its application—a theory about the formation of identity, and the use of the organizational structures in language to promote it. So, while there are theories of survival that place the individual in wealthy isolation from a social herd, it is difficult to think of them as "economic" theories because they have not identified society as a strategic beneficiary.

Even sophisticated commercial structures driven by such assumptions can hardly be referred to as "economy" unless they are supported by a credible theory of supply to a broader social system. Economy—as a strategy of survival—may be more visible in its primitive form. Call this form "wild economy" as it derives from a thought experiment in which social instrumentalities we think of as the product of civilization—or "institutions"—are subtracted from the economic landscape.

Such economy is also commonly referred to as "hunter-gatherer." Here the term "wild" is preferred due to the emphasis on a very long period of evolution in which the human organism acquired survival traits adequate to a natural environment subject to negligible human modifications. The subject material of wild economy is the logic of evolutionary genetics, and genetically adapted human traits useful in managing environmental challenges and competitions.

It is worth mentioning, perhaps, that the human evolved to its present state of cognitive acuity around 150,000 years ago, and continued in a world to which it was adapted for close to 140,000 of those years. We haven't had time, in other words, to genetically adapt to the changes we have introduced into our own environment.

The logic of evolutionary genetics represents one of the most productive scientific discoveries in the history of the world. It is so successful that many are tempted to construct a closed system around it. A theoretical system is "closed" when influences outside the logical structure of the system are regarded "false" or "unreal" because they fail to utilize the logic of the system. The logic of evolutionary genetics has the following important components.

> 1. Biological existence consists in the organization of materials into systems, systems of systems, systems of systems of systems, etc.
>
> 2. One way for a biological system to continue through time is to replicate itself through the genetically coded reproductive subsystems.
>
> 3. Systems which are successful in handling environmental challenges and competitions will be able to replicate more than systems which are not.
>
> 4. Genetic reproduction is not and cannot be perfect or the reproduction would not be able to adapt to environmental changes.

These principles are, within the scientific community accepted as correct descriptions of the way biological organisms continue their genetic lines. There are other hypotheses derived from these which are less widely accepted. One of these is that all desires are genetically evolved.

The reasoning in support of this hypothesis is that we are more likely to advance, defend or replicate biological organizations with supportive motives in place. And there is evidence to support this hypothesis. Within reproductive systems alone there are strong desires to mate and to protect familial offspring—presumably because mating and familial protections promote survival and genetic continuity.

There are also experiments in which changes in neurological structure and composition alter motivation. We have known for thousands of years that the motivational states of breeds of animals can be manipulated—though it wasn't known that the manipulation was genetic. Mood disorders are currently treated as physiologic, with significant investments in the development of psychoactive chemicals designed to alter dysfunctional motivational states.

Where controversy seems to arise is in the qualitative dissimilarity between the physical composition of an organism and its motive—one of which we describe structurally, while the other we describe experientially. Although we acknowledge a relationship between physical structures and states of pain and pleasure, we wouldn't care about the physical structures if not for their effect on things we feel. This presents irony, almost to the point of paradox, in that there is a sentient universe of intellectual constructs, motivations, gratifications and pains—all that we have direct experience with—while there is a physical universe known only indirectly and that is now presumed to dominate the sentient one.

The controversy is aggravated somewhat by the fact that we are social creatures bonded by social motives also subject to the influence of genetically based material structures. Within the logic of evolutionary genetics, we might assume that desires impacting our relationships with others are the consequence of physical structures evolved under the pressure of a host of environmental competitions. There is apt to be some sensation of disappointment accompanying that point of view, as the promotion of nurturing social systems and the peaceful resolution of anger and estrangement are frequently associated with transcendent spiritual orientations—timeless, elevated and true.

There is, therefore, a dissonance between the experience of value that edifies social existence, and a material explanation of experience. One way of resolving the dissonance this presents is to ignore it, and allow each universe to be what it is. The universe of consciousness—call it the "ethical" universe—is deep enough to keep its students busy for quite some time without having to resolve issues of dependency on a physical universe.

However, the genetic universe—in contradistinction to the universe of consciousness—makes no ethical judgments, except to record what survived and what did not, and survival is not an ethical principle. A species may become extinct because it was too efficient, and thus devoured its available resources, or it may encounter an environmental influence to which it cannot adapt. Great dinosaurs were overwhelmed by climate change, while rodent sized mammals (of similar intelligence) fed off their rotting carcasses and other grubs and insects—and survived to become primates. Within an evolutionary logic, there is no way to determine whether a moral value will assist or kill the species until long after a moral decision is made—and yet the importance of ethical reasoning is to determine wrongness of an act before it is done.

This fact itself is not likely to discourage theorists from attempting to cross the divide between genetics and ethics, and a hope of finding a gene complex—for example—which if present results in the practice of the golden rule, and which if absent produces sociopathy. Nor will it inhibit theory in the opposite direction—mind impacting matter. The discovery of quantum phenomena that have identified transformational effects of observation on the identification and location of physical particulates suggests a link of this nature. The discovery of organizational constants in the Requisite movement suggests something similar, i.e., a universe functioning within organization, the perceptibility of which may only occur in mind.

This is the point at which those interested in the apparent division between mind and matter often find most perplexing. Does the existence of organization imply a mind that experiences organization? If so, is that organization subject to a ruling principle, or conscious interest? And if so, is that ruling principle ethical in nature?

If there were, for example, a value which—like other mental phenomenon—is experienced through evolved processes, then the value might be said to have pressured the organism to adaptations in the same way objects pressured the formation of eyes and of cerebral structures for the integration of visual information. It is there, and the organism which adapts toward the perception of it is likely to multiply. In that sense, one might argue that the experience of something such as the "love" emphasized within many religious traditions is not an invention of brain but exists as something to which brain adapts.

A difficulty with this approach is that many values are part of a response to an environmental challenge, not the challenge itself—less as a thing which must be adapted to, than as part of the adaptation. Species which develop eyes—nearly all in one form or another—aren't developing eyes because eyes are something to which we must adapt, but because eyes are needed to perceive objects. Similarly, it can be argued that species which develop cooperative values similar to humans—only a few it seems—do not evolve them because values exist somewhere outside the consciousness of an evolving organism, but because they are needed for cooperative activities.

This comparison, however, fails to make an important distinction. There may be some values which exist as adaptation to environmental challenges, and others which exist in a manner suitable for discovery. Sexual attraction and hunger, for example, functionally serve biological processes essential for survival, and may be dependent on it, but the environmental dependency of some desires does not preclude a universe of value which exists in its own right—especially if that value resonates ethically.

This argument was once used as an "ontological proof" of the existence of God. In essence, the argument proposes that the discovery of ethical value within the mind of an individual implies a "mind" in which the value exists independently of that individual. If it did not exist in its own right, it could not be discovered. And since the human appears to acquire it through a process of discovery, it must exist independently of the consciousness of a single individual. The "mind" in which that value exists would be the mind of God.

The flaw of the argument is that it does not appear to be logically necessary to assume a God entity to account for ethical experience as discovery, but rather, only that the biological organism has established a mechanism of reinforcement of cooperative behavior within the species, and that some—but not all—species members succeed in finding it. But is it more than a genetically programmed feeling of well-being triggered by cooperative behavior? To say that it exists, in other words, fails to say much about what kind of existence it is, such as an existence we share with another human being.

The ontological argument for the existence of God does not therefore refute a genetic basis of cooperative social values. But neither does the genetic argument for value prove that such value is only a genetically organized survival strategy. While it is confusing to sort out an answer, it is not philosophically clear that there is an intellectual conflict between evolutionary genetics and the notion that language evolved at some level like an organ of sense to perceive a reality of shared or social experience.

Let us attempt to examine this idea in another way. Assume a planet with no source of light but which had evolved a species in utter darkness. They have no eyes because eyes are of no use, and navigate their world with highly evolved senses of touch and smell, and are therefore built low to the ground so they can navigate with those senses more effectively. Assume also that one day they are visited by a species which evolved in a light filled planet, with excellently developed eyes—and the species brings their own light sources. A description by that species to the native species about the experience of light might be portrayed as a state of awareness, a way of experiencing the environment. In this discussion, the experience of "light" is an adaptation, but an adaptation to an illuminated universe in which objects are not only perceived, but perceived in a different way.

Similarly, the humanly evolved faculty of language not only enables social collaboration (productive organization) but includes within it a different way of experiencing reality, and thus reveals an entire universe evident only in the process of looking deeply into the experience of others.

The point is, it is not always clear that evolution occurs only because it is needed for survival, but because the content of reality stimulates an organism to develop ways of perceiving it. Although one might credibly object that if the "love" that activates social collaboration is real, then all animals would have evolved a perception of it. But that only begs the question of whether other animals have eyes to see it without first evolving language.

2. One might say that we have just engaged a paradox, of sorts. On the one hand, we have accepted natural selection into a theory of social cooperation—a materially based view of economy, but on the other hand, we have created space within this perspective for an ethical principle which is not derived from or servient to it—a spiritually based view of law. The point of the discussion above is that the paradox is more practical than logical.

A scientific theory as powerful as natural selection establishes a slope favoring material over spiritual theories of behavior. This is understandable, as the natural world makes harsh demands, and rules of frugality would tend to prohibit the evolution of values not directly responsive to those demands. The scientific proponents of natural selection would therefore prefer to evaluate whether a materially evolved brain—which has evolved desires suited to nourishment and reproduction—has developed powerful and transformative ethical experiences solely for biological survival. This would be the preferred choice of Occam's razor, a rule of theory which prefers simple and ordinary over the more complicated explanations.

Occam's rule, however, does not require that simple theories overpower contrary facts. The logic of natural selection is not predisposed for or against material or spiritual views of anything, nor is it in and of itself a closed system. This logic doesn't advocate for or against light but supports the evolution of processes which use the information which light provides. The same would apply to ethical principle which enables and illuminates cooperative social processes. Whether such a principle exists independently of or transcends species evolution depends to some extent on whether it offers non-biologic advantages.

Notwithstanding the neutrality of the logic of natural selection, the supposition that mind forms from a materially organized brain does present an obstacle to our understanding of the formation of cooperative social systems. The obstacle consists in the fact that the dominant physical mechanism of human genetic replication is individual, not collective.

This is not a problem with species that have evolved hive based reproductive systems—ants and bees, for example—where there is little or no intra-species competition for reproductive activity. Cooperative behaviors evolve without much difficulty. It is quite different for other species. The horns which decorate the male gender of a variety of grazing species have some utility in fending off predators, but it seems that they are used more as weapon against other male rivals in the pursuit of females. The best survival strategy is to run faster than the predators in pursuit, or faster than other members of the herd. Horns are an impediment to flight, and only a few males are necessary to repopulate a large herd. Thus, males grow horns, and females do not, a genetic development spurred by sexual rivalry.

It is difficult to say why the human species evolved to a point of being individually helpless, as the tendency in biological selection is to strengthen effective defenses while weakening ineffective ones. It may have been that running fast or becoming stronger would tend to separate individuals from groups where solidarity was a far more important survival function. Individual weakness may be an important part of the herding needed for the evolution of cooperative intelligence.

Or it may have been a matter of environmental change, where species evolution did not have enough time for a genetically graceful change from vegetative regions (jungles) to less congested surroundings.

What does seem clear, however, is that at some point the need for cooperation among a number of primate species became much more important than for other species, while species replication through sexual rivalry continued. This, it seems, provided an evolutionary formula sufficient for the emergence of what we now refer to as language.

In order to understand this, it is necessary to identify some of the requisites of coordinated behavior. It seems clear that language must involve the following:

> 1. An ability to identify common intention in context, i.e., an ability to identify a state of affairs along with a proposed course of action through which a group of persons can navigate or alter that state of affairs.
>
> 2. An ability to anticipate the behavior of others, accomplished through mutual comprehension of the motivational structures of others, as well as the range of likely responses to environmental and social stimuli.
>
> 3. An ability to comprehend and support the establishment of role specialization and hierarchical authoritative structure sufficient to practically address conflicting proposals over social duties and rewards.

The functions of cooperation imply their communication, and language affects the way each of the others are experienced. Because of language we learn to observe with clarity that allows us to effectively describe it to others, think empathically about the effect a proposal will have on their interests and that of the social order, and fit a proposal with an existent sense of "good" also referred to as an "ethical system."

There is quite a lot on this plate from an evolutionary standpoint. Socially nuanced communication needs to have enough sophistication to deal with environmental challenges and interspecies competition, but as these capabilities evolve, the organizational challenge becomes more complicated because the individuals engaged in organization become more complicated.

The trend is aptly described as an iterative circle prompted by a more complex set of interests and expectations, as well as continuing intra-species competition over socially conferred benefits. Getting smarter does not make the human easier to organize, but to the contrary, the organizing capabilities of men and women hurry to keep up with smarter strategies serving the instinctive aversion to being dominated by others—particularly other sexual rivals. What one would likely anticipate at this point is an accelerated development of information processing centers of the brain—the neo-cortex—both in terms of relative mass and in available surface area.

This appears, in fact, to be what happened, as the efficiency of human organization reached a point where it exceeded what was necessary to perpetuate the human species and placed human in a different category of being than other animals—possibly excepting dolphins, who we know little about because we do not understand their language. It is not merely a shift in quantity of acquired resources, but a qualitative shift in the type of world the human organism occupies. This has by some authors been referred to as a "language suffused" world, so called because of the organizing presence of language.

On the most basic level, it refers to a much more intimately shared reality than that which other species experience. Human beings live in a world that they experience individually, but which is subject to the examination and evaluation of others, so much so that it affects the content of all experience, even the experiences in which one's privacy is guarded. The partition between private and public is fuzzy, and there may be reasons for preserving its fuzziness, as we are emotionally invested both in the preservation of a private universe which others don't see, as well as validations offered by the other with whom experience is shared.

On another level, a language suffused world is not about the spoken language at all, but about numerous effects that the information processing power of language has. With only a few moments examination of the use and evolution of spoken languages, it is obvious that words are used imaginatively and organized instrumentally, as things we adapt for different purposes. But it doesn't end with spoken communication, and has adapted everything else available—rocks, sticks, trees, people, tribes, deities, etc.

Along with the capacity to organize words into stories and other linguistic devices is the ability to modify materials, structures and processes, and to discuss them with others. A world subject to language is an imaginatively constructed technological experience, where the same faculty that allows the formation of words also allows the formation of tools. That is the case, of course, because we don't make tools with our hands, but with our minds.

With the presence of language in human affairs, it is not always clear whether we are using language, or whether language is using us. Its numerous creations include the formation and influence of a culture to which mind enthusiastically subordinates. Because culture can be communicated to younger individuals it is part of an accumulating and repeating social experience. Group experience acquires history and mythic depth in the procession of events, and a wholly different sense of time than we see in the recorded memories of other species.

Along with a sense of the continuity of time, one is placed within it, because time has been bound within words, and word like inventions shared with Other. While we ponder the time it takes to become an adult in this kind of world, it should be remembered that the term "adult" is itself a concept derived from an experience already coursing with language.

It is uncertain whether information processing capability has continued to grow—as humans do not necessarily need to be smarter to survive and breed in modern economies. However, it is clear at this stage that the expansion of the neo-cortex was at some point sufficient to produce a dramatic acceleration in human presence and consumption in a very short period of time. We are at a point where concerns over species efficiency have been eclipsed by concerns over species containment and are asking questions such as those posed in this book.

3. When we examine a wild economy, we assume the completion of biological evolution to the point of what we are. Though there is much to say about social evolution over the last ten thousand years, we shift the scale of time dramatically in doing so. On the clock of evolutionary biology, the history of civilization doesn't amount to as much as a coffee break. We have, so far, contemplated the evolutionary logic of language in order to mark the point of arrival in the emergence of a social universe. Wild economy thus describes what language is apt to produce in the manner of productive social organization in a relatively uncrowded natural setting.

By "uncrowded" is meant "absent other social systems competing for natural resources," as these have important impacts on law and economy. The mere sensation of being surrounded by other individuals is not a sense of being "crowded", but is part of the liberating presence of language, and essential to the formation of a wild economy. This will require some explanation.

A credible place to begin is with developmental processes examined and clarified within the Requisite movement and summarized in the last chapter. There it is clear that the identification of object types occurs in a phased cycle, and that the cycle begins with interest. That interest is an act of intervention by an individual consciousness and ends with a similar intervention at a higher order of complexity. To this end, we contemplated an identity in isolation, as follows, with objects available as nameable singularities or "terms" "O" subject to predication "{O}". Logically speaking, an individual in isolation can discern an object as a place within a surrounding environment or field and can attribute characteristics to it depending on a state of interest. The field can be larger or smaller, depending on the capacity that one brings to it.

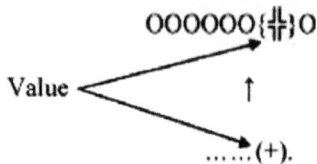

In language, however, the assumption of an individual in isolation is incoherent. This was Wittgenstein's argument regarding the possibility of a private language. The adoption of a term descriptive of an object, or of a type of object is by its nature a public offer, which if not subject to social ratification is not language. It may be something else other than language, but even the description of it as a non-linguified entity (as in animal perception) is problematic, as thought is both genetically and habitually associated with a process designed to make one's private experience of an object publicly available for others.

The notion of "value"—as that which makes objects perceptible—is embedded within a language suffused universe and is incomprehensible without a sense of obligation derived from one's existence as a social being. It is analogous to an attempt to call something a "car" which has all the exterior indicia of "car" but stands immobile because it does not have a motor. To call it a car is in a sense incoherent because it cannot do what cars do. In the case of language, the formation of a word to identify an object or any of its predicates without any sense of social obligation removes an essential defining characteristic of the "word." A word without obligation, however, represents something even more incoherent than a car without a motor, as the removal of social obligation from word removes one from a universe in which things like words and cars can be identified as such.

One might imagine a situation involving an individual with a resilient memory, and a resolute commitment to future compliance with names he or she gives to private impressions and sensations and argue that our ability to imagine such an individual discredits Wittgenstein's observation.

That argument, however, misses the point. This imaginary person has agreed to be obligated by a recollected version of his or her experience. In that sense, the individual has shifted from a private orientation to their experiences to a public one, or rather, to one that is comprehensible and accountable to other. In this case "other" is the person he or she once was. Social obligation is a matter of obligation to selves of the past, and is in that sense "public." In that sense language is of its nature bivalent, representing a processional shift from private to public (shared) orientations—occurring internally in one sense of "mind" as private, and another in a sense regarded as public.

The intuitive recognition that language represents shifting attention from internal to external points of reference is a similar observation that Wittgenstein used in the solution to the Russell paradox (discussed earlier). To recall, the paradox consists in a failure to acknowledge that the defining feature of a set—its intension—changes in a fundamental way when viewed as a set member—its extension. This is the same sort of observation prevailing in Wittgenstein's statements about language, where all experience occurs within a process that includes its objectification but is not one and the same with it.

The so called "private language argument"—something that Wittgenstein never himself called it—is better regarded as a contemplative review of language as a process that combines intension and extension and would be incomprehensible without the occurrence of both.

The argument may seem trivial in its statement about small private experiences, but all sense of the trivial vanishes when the language is directed at private experiences that are the subject of public iteration, such as "self", "soul" or "God" (deity). Law is not a product or output of language, but co-exists with language as a defining feature of language—acquired along with it.

This insight into language as a state of intercourse with social obligation deconstructs into a bivalent analysis of language and the cooperative behaviors which derive from it. Value is, on the one hand, a public offering designed and adapted for the review of other participants in language, while at the same time being subject to collective review—in real time through repetitive exchange and validation.

When one uses a word, they are in fact doing so in two different respects. They are responding to a private mandate—as if to say "I am"—

along with a public mandate—as if to say "subject to or along with Other." Every expression thus includes value emerging from "I" along with value emerging as obligation coming from "Other."

They emerge, moreover, simultaneously from the same speaker. As a person speaks he or she is also engaged as the challenger "I" and enforcer "Other" of obligation—a participant in the co-creation of shared experience. What we refer to as "conscience" is neither one nor the other, but both functioning interactively

$$\text{Value (I)} \longrightarrow \text{Interest} \longleftarrow \text{Value (Other)}$$

To view "I" and "Other" as the vantage point of two separate individuals, therefore, is to commit an error of oversimplification, inasmuch as every member of a social collective operates within kind of a "split-screen"—both affirming and socially qualifying existence, integrating individuation within collective parameters. There is an awareness within each individual, in other words, that another person represents a distinct and unique point of view—an "end"—and that they are, as individuals, sharing a social reality. The miracle of language consists in this integration of "I" and "Other" as the twin facets of shared experience. If we did not simultaneously hold a sense of Other together with the individual expression of existence, it would be difficult to imagine language, or any other kind of social organization.

Philosophical perspectives focusing on the power of human reason tend to emphasize the neutrality of "reason" in the formation of objects, along with ethical precepts which guide choices within a social universe. Indeed, the argument of rationalists proposes that if we can maintain a neutral stance in the formation of objects, the same might occur in the development of principles necessary for peaceful social relations. The foregoing analysis, however, implies that nothing of the sort occurs in the formation of objects, inasmuch as objects emerge within the domain of interest, and interest is not neutral.

The socialization of the perception of objects is more recognizable, it seems, within an information processing model of development because "interest"—as an engrossing constant within a developmental cycle—is more prominent. Since interest is essential to the perceptibility of objects, perception invokes socially regulated states of desire. These pass unnoticed in very simple perceptual acts, but the perception of complex social structures is another thing entirely, and suggests a different model.

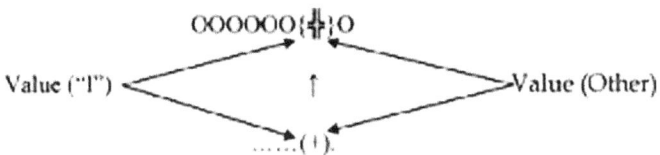

So, instead of viewing the formation of objects as the neutral product of an impassive rationality, it is more productive to view the emergence of objects—and the linguistic symbols we attach to them—as a celebration of shared experience, something "good" taken out of a void of primitive desire in isolation.

The "goodness" or "value" of existence is a social additive derived from the realization that existence is a shared experience. Without that aspect, "good" is irrelevant in the description of existence because existence without social obligation is not known except as desire. The attachment of value to a person as individuation—"I"—occurs together with the attachment of value to Other.

"Existence" becomes valuable because the existence of someone else—who represents a different terminal of desire—is included as a participant in various social formations—objects, interests, identities and institutions. Thus, one may assert that an essential Requisite principle to social organization is the principle of equality, manifest in the following two statements.

1. Human existence is valuable.
2. The value of one is equal to the value of another.

These principles bring into question the appropriateness of referring to constructs such as "person" or "government" as objects similar to "job" or "firm." The latter may be complete formations of a field of fixed complexity, while the former are in constant reformation within fields of adaptive complexity.

"Adaptive complexity"—as a term used specially here—deserves some explanation. In the course of interaction with an object of constant complexity, one will experience change in their comprehension of it, for as we described in the last chapter, the mind grows in the efficiency of its ability to navigate the data from which the object is formed. But there are objects that respond to interaction and input from those seeking to comprehend them—either because the input changes what they are, or because the objects themselves include the behavior of other beings who seek to change the object in ways that make it more complicated and difficult to navigate.

The identity of a person is something of this nature because as the endeavor to find out who we are changes who we are. Likewise, in considering the "identity" of government, what it is changes as a consequence of our efforts to assess its boundaries. Consider the following.

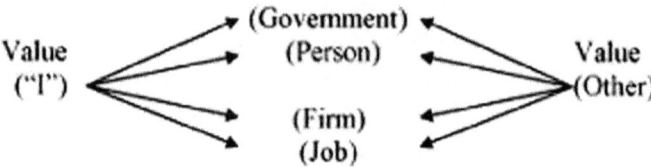

A temptation at this point is to view this proposed distinction of objects that have adaptive complexity from objects which do not as a distinction between games (competitive exchange between persons) and stationary entities. That basis falls short of what is being described here. Most games have very little adaptive complexity, even though the games' participants behave adaptively to input from other participants. In the case of competitive exchanges formed out of a set of rules, the complexity of the game is revealed through competition, though the boundaries of the game remain constant. One thus moves upward in their navigational control of the information which the game produces even though the complexity of the game is influenced by the participants.

Adaptive complexity, on the other hand, challenges us to consider situations in which the rules themselves are adapting to the input of participants. If the rules are being set by game designers, or by designers engaged in a game design process, then social value functions as a ruling principle to determine if it is a good game or not.

It is useful to bear this in mind, as there are many things we do with others to which ethical expectations are episodic—i.e., competitive exchanges bounded by rules meant to cover a transaction, or a limited series of transactions. But these episodes may produce results that are bad, even though the winner may have an ethical expectancy to the reward which the game offers. The kind of system which ethically monitors competitive exchanges in order that rules stimulate or allow productive consequences is an adaptive system—a system that brings value (law) into engagement or awareness of its effects (economy).

It is possible (and appropriate) to design games, the function of which is to evaluate and modify other games. If we as participants in a society come to rely on games of this sort to examine and improve other games, we might treat such processes with greater care than the others, and even sanctify them. It is the shift of care that marks the difference between systems—care reflecting value.

Within this standard of differentiation, there may be a continuum of data systems, some of which are relatively fixed in their complexity, and therefore comprehensible, and others which elude us because it is in their nature to elude us. Personhood—otherwise referred to as "ego" or "identity"—eludes because it was meant to elude. Government is a similar creation, though, it seems, unnecessary in primitive societies and the formation of wild economy.

4. The awareness of a value originating from Other, and its effect on the vigilance of perception—the investigation of sense data using publicly visible interest as a force of selection—is a defining feature of consciousness identified with "human." It is not so much that consciousness reels within a cloud of words—which it does also—but that the interests which give words, actions, egos and personalities their meaning are in constant collective review. We are obligated to it by design of consciousness. Law is thus revealed in a communicative exchange—language, but the question at this point is whether there is some sort of order to this sense of obligation. Is law self-organizing?

There is a way of looking at "law" which strongly suggests that it is, i.e., that the accrual of value is hierarchically organized. But as we have suggested earlier, one must be careful in the use of "hierarchy" to validate interest and intention, as the tendency is to regress into abstractive hierarchy which does little more than place smaller sets within larger sets.

Instead begin with a desire which all might regard as "primitive" but which also carries strong indicia of intra-species rivalry, like sexual desire. Within many societies, that desire is closely scrutinized by others—for a number of obvious reasons—and so becomes a matter of social interest when framed within courtship observances.

But still more is required than formal observance, as a prospective suitor is socially examined for the "value" he places on the process with which they are engaged—for her welfare, her family, and their anticipated family. Sex is a powerful motivator, but does not lend itself to "value" except through a process of socialization which legitimizes it as interest.

A wedding may thereafter celebrate such valuation as "marriage." There is thus a hierarchical division between "lust" and the value placed on it in the course of social illumination. When the value is fully embraced, "lust" changes into "love" and is thus sanctified in marriage.

Perhaps it is also useful to remember that the conversion does not occur as an artificial construct, or rather, the emergence of something out of nothing. We do not, in other words, invent love out of a void in order to placate or silence potential discord. It is more like a process of discovery in which something that we already have, and already are, is fused to an experience of instinctive interest. Social collaborators seem to know that this is what the individual really wants, and that the transformation in many ways completes and intensifies the experience of satisfaction that comes with it. We very much enjoy finding ways to love others, and affirm our existence as autonomous social beings through the expression of it.

The participants in this conversion thereby become part of a social as well as a personal covenant, where the value of the person is included in the transformation and becomes the ruling principle of an emerging family. The process is orderly, and because it has structure, can be depicted.

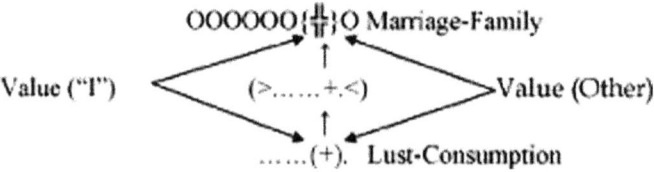

It also defines an essential economic unit common to hunter-gatherer systems—where tribes are often viewed as collections of families. One is apt to see rights associated with the productive output of a tribe, for example, identified with sanctified rites of passage, and of participatory obligations simple enough to be understood by all, and enforced intuitively as a collective manifestation of Other.

Thus, the identification of a social "interest" which comprehends the economic theory of success of a social group would be transferable and repeatable as a ruling principle applicable to a number of tribal functions. We could then see a number of transformations similar to that reflected in the establishment of the institution of marriage—all related in part to assertion of an obligatory social good (law) and the adoption of a common theory of success (economy).

| Commitment | Protection | Trust | Respect |
|---|---|---|---|
| ↑ | ↑ | ↑ | ↑ |
| Consumption | Security | Intimacy | Status |

Within the context of transformations of this nature, it becomes clear that "value" in the accommodation and affirmation of individually expressed desires is not a superficial experience. It is difficult to imagine a sense of "self" or "personhood" which does not in some sense embrace the valuative states reflected in a collectively asserted ideal. When someone is asked, for instance, "who" they are, they are apt to identify their familial commitments, their job, indicia of trustworthiness, achievements, etc., all spoken in conformity with social views. The feeling of "sin" is much like a self-imposed feeling of isolation, of losing one's identity.

There may be some utility in formulating a distinction between one's "I" and one's social identity, but an attempt to do so can be an interesting variant on Wittgenstein's private language paradox. For just as "interest" forming the basis of a proposition about existence is incoherent without socially based accountability, so too are the valuative states of a moral principle, and the "character" of a "person." They become individualized expressions of socially existent being. Each is an offering to Other.

In the absence of an offering of this sort, the "I" one associates with an identity does not disappear, but rather, loses a sense of location and confidence. It is a point of identification without attachment, a self-seeking expression without a "word", a light with nothing to reflect against, value seeking its manifestation against a void. Self is an individualized manifestation of "I exist" within a range permitted and validated by Other.

Within a social universe, therefore, there is hierarchy in the sense of a progression of more centrally situated points of view. It is hardly an abstracted arrangement of tiers, but of functionally distinct types of experience—of simple desire bonded to Object, of moral principle as social Interest, and of self as social Identity. Value integrates into experience from two different points—as the "I" of consciousness, which affirms from a point which observes but is not observed, and Other, which accepts and limits that affirmation from a point external to consciousness.

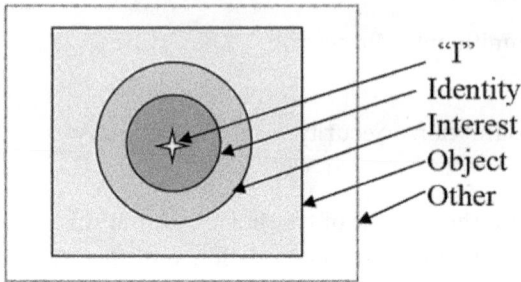

It's a map, of course, designed to discuss "mind" as a phenomenon of language, and drawn as a functional hierarchy, with three conscious experiences emerging as a single consciousness. Other represents an influence on that consciousness in which "I" participates and influences. This insight allows us to correct the depiction of language as not more than an information exchange between independent entities.

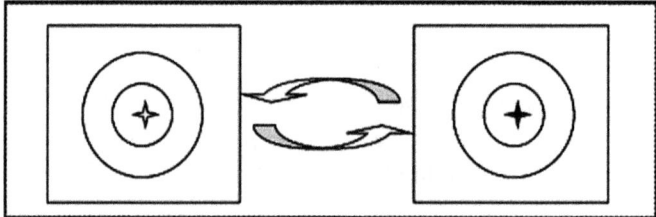

It is actually quite different altogether. Our boundaries, which within certain philosophical traditions are regarded sacred, are more porous than we typically admit in modern societies.[10]

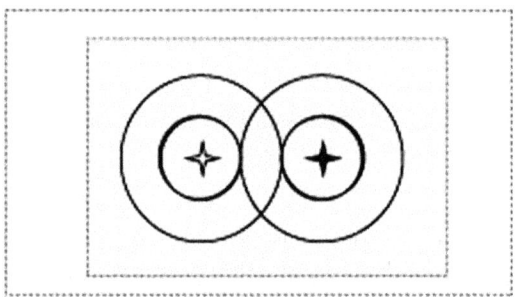

But in primitive societies, structured experiences of Object are identified and shared in fluent exchanges, while less structured experiences like Interest and Identity are nonetheless engaged through intimate observation and story-telling. In a wild economy, we are interested in each other. Reinforcement of law outside of language is uncommon, as law is embedded within language and deviance from it stands out conspicuously without the use of formal investigative structures typical of modern legal systems.

The "hunting party" is often used as a metaphor for nascent organization, as a team assembled together to build an enterprise of some sort. These are effective organizations, particularly if there is a team spokesperson or leader who brought the group together with a common purpose. The group is apt to meet informally and cooperatively, where division, if any, is focused on how to get something done, rather than on what do to. Tasks can be quite sophisticated and specialized but are marked by a common understanding of who is doing what—i.e., that cooperative design is intuitive—more or less—and comprehended in the mind of each participant.

Language, while effective toward social self-organization (organization without trying), reveals its limitations when it comes to matters of scale. There are at least two considerations of a primitive nature which pressure the wild economy to impose more organization than is present in a food gathering enterprise.

First, is the need to establish sufficient genetic diversity to avoid genetic diseases and deformities associated with intra-familial breeding. This requires geographic and cultural access to familial and/or tribal units including about 100-150 persons. This is more than is needed to form a hunting party. The second is related to the first, more or less. Pressure to organize peaceful relations on that scale begin to place a burden on the eco-system to sustain the population in the area, and thus give rise to a need for limited military organization in order to protect territories, accumulated provisions and females.

5. Upon some reflection, it appears that language itself benefits from a larger group of participants, and for reasons similar to those which render notions of "private" language incoherent. The number of participants in a language required to establish a sense of Other to which individual consciousness yields or defers as constant is unknown and may depend on more than number. But this is the point of the private language paradox—i.e., that it doesn't count as language if one does not in a meaningful sense treat it as law. How does language accomplish this?

The existentially assertive "I" of value has until this point been treated, more or less, as an abstract presence—a point on a map, and that way of presenting it may lead to certain errors. One error—repeated throughout the ages—is to treat this as a logical unity that demands consistency, and not much more. There have, in fact been at least two major ethical systems constructed on the supposition that there is a rational imperative that commands us to eliminate conflicting ideas and impulses from our behavioral universe, and that this tendency allows us to identify and explain moral behavior. [11]

This tendency has for centuries been at odds with a number of religious systems which claim the "place" from which ethical inspiration arises is more emotionally influential than human intellect standing alone. Our own examination of Requisite structures validates this view, with the observation that logic is nonsensical without the intervention of value which motivates selection—truth over error, efficient over inefficient.

The impact of a socially accountable processing orientation is more vividly apparent in the conversion of desire into socially integrated values—lust to commitment, security to contribution, intimacy to trustworthiness, and status to respectfulness—supportive of the contention that these are all states of "love" expressed by an identity that forms both individually and collectively.

There is no need, then, to separate logical from moral processes, because they are essentially the same. In most treatises on logic, so much in the way of value is removed from it that its significance as a vehicle of value passes unnoticed. Conversely, so much in the way of emotion is packed into moral narratives that their underlying logic is barely noticeable. Within the organizing power of language, we have an opportunity to examine how value is processed within a socio-logical matrix in which objective reality fuses with ethical principle. We have considered several of its features.

> 1. Value is expressed at three levels of awareness—Object, Interest, and Identity.
> 2. It seems to appear on its own as a response to stimuli from the environment and has an organizing influence on it.
> 3. Value expresses itself in the awareness of other beings—and thus validates and constrains our own behavior.
> 4. It allows us to participate in the formation of a sense of Other in a way which makes our experience of language cohere.

By definition, the existence of value as a shared social experience is the experience of Deity. It moves from the subjective sensation "I exist" to the sensation "I share in existence common to all." It comes to us as an internal presence, and thus individualizes consciousness, but individuality is shared as in "we are all different, but together in our differentiation."

It represents a range of acceptable behaviors sensed somewhat intuitively. A group of rugby players may have a different sense of the range of acceptable behaviors than a group of chess players. Though both groups are apt to play with all their energy, they are animated by different deities, and it is reflected in the environment in which they play. In the case of shared deity, however, the environment takes on a common hue.

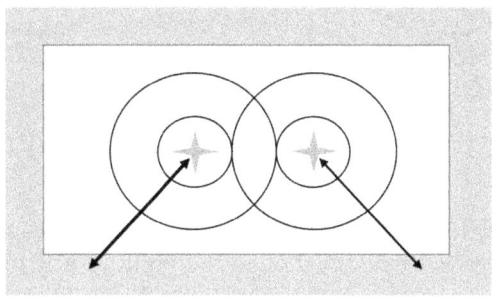

Changes in color to match a state of agreement with respect to deity are manifest in a shared reality. At this point, we are gazing upon consciousness socially bound to its environment, painting its environment with a socially unifying sense of good. Since this book is published in grey scale, the closest we can come is a grey deity that paints its environment in grey. I might be more accurate, perhaps, to identify a color, because color and value are closely related phenomena. This represents a setting capable of assimilating many individuals into a reality that is to a significant extent socially negotiated. [12]

We can do any number of things with this acquired sense of the nature of things. It can be objectified and given a name, and thus become a subject of common discourse, or it can be consciously veiled, and only referred to enigmatically. Notwithstanding, how it is put together and allowed to intervene in our lives has a significant effect on the constructs with which we are surrounded—i.e., whether they are alive or dead, quiet or rambunctious, serious or comedic. In modern societies we have some difficulty in knowing what to call it, because the primitive experience fastens on its effects, often referring to it as "pantheistic." It may be naught but a human creation, but to say so only begs the question of what the human is capable of creating.

A general claim about a supposed relationship between deity and reality is more believable as one reviews the process in which objects come into being, now using regions of consciousness as "holders" of functional intention from which logical hierarchies are created. And since logic is an interest-based process, the hierarchical structure of objects is a valuative hierarchy.

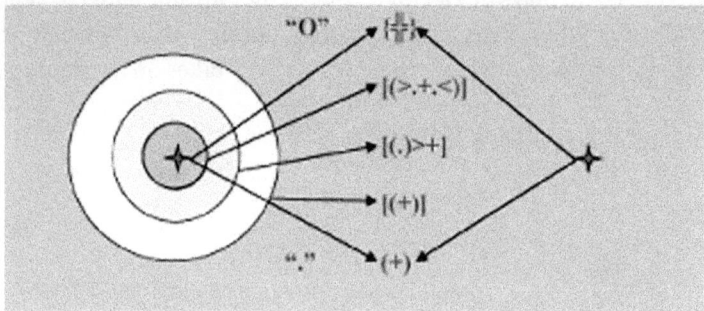

As this map is composed, it appears to support the engagement in numerous speculative exercises, though the point of it is to indicate a plausible mechanism by which agreement between an internally experienced value and an external reality might come about. Here, we examine the way in which the organization of objects replicates the organization of consciousness. In social organizations, common agreement over what arises is generally regarded as a matter of significant importance. In wild economies, social organizations formed in language are treated as live organisms animated by deity.

Whether this experience is or is not more than a psycho-social occurrence is not as important as recognizing that it is the product of a language process that converts the private experience of value into an experience that is both shared and self-activating—i.e., that emerges on its own in the universe of social intercourse and is accepted as real, less as an object than through the effect it has on objects. In this sense, the social organizations we observe in tribal societies—and occasionally marvel at—can be thought of as self-organizing, because their principle of order is not imposed upon them, and forms within a language process by which obligation emerges intuitively through social consensus.

While there is some sense of mystery in this process, it occurs nonetheless within a mind that defines, processes and selects information. There are three conscious, though not entirely separate, states of attention that bring this about, together constituting a hierarchy—thus further defining and assigning a linguistic role to Object, Interest and Identity.

The hierarchy progresses not so much toward elevation, but toward interiority, and from matters of lesser to greater importance. Since this hierarchy is co-created through social participation, there are very few covetously regarded social elites, where social importance adheres to a role rather than to a person. Economic distributions tend to occur consistent with a principle of equality.

Within a processing hierarchy of this kind, one might expect that hierarchical replications would be somewhat visible in the larger more socially participative objects in our environment, such as complex human institutions of various kinds. It is easier within this framework to perceive and to a degree "understand" a union between the organization of human consciousness and human communities, and to view this as a scientific or "requisite" state of human existence in which an ethical universe emerges within the information processing capabilities of mind functioning within a socially active game of language.

This is worthy of contemplation, as mind has evolved to handle the intervention of value from two different directions. Language manages both the receiving and giving direction in an exchange with Other. The process is linear, but iterative—i.e., it proceeds proximally from one place to the next, but direction depends on whether someone is speaking or listening. Here it is easier to draw than to say it.

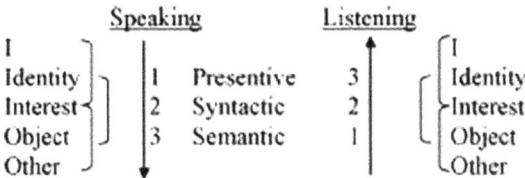

The arrow is only the direction of influence, while the number indicates the order in which the communicative event is experienced—from interior to exterior in the case of speaking, and from exterior to interior in the case of listening. This model places importance on an influence which activates an information processing region, and the proximate destination of influence. Thus, an Identity might influence or activate Interest, which attaches to or embraces Object. This would signify a Syntactic event in a direction entitled "speaking." But reverse direction to "listening" and Object activates Interest attached to Identity—likewise a syntactic event. The diagram which results from this is quite similar to the five-tiered Requisite systems bound within three interpenetrative three-tiered management units. The mind is never singularly preoccupied, but always functions within managed complexes. The power of mind to focus is therefore more aptly described as shifting states of emphasis bound within limits.

As the diagram indicates, language may unfold as a processional exchange. The encounter with Other, however, is not like the phased construction of an object out of data, but more like an adaptive process. While much can be said about language here, we have progressed sufficiently to identify and define three points of orientation. [13]

> 1. A Semantic level of language involves a preoccupation with meaning. In speaking, it is a state of engagement in Object, activated by Interest, and attaching to Other. In listening, it is engagement in Object activated by Other, and releasing to Interest.

> 2. A Syntactic level of language involves a preoccupation with structure. In speaking, it is a state of engagement in Interest, activated by Identity and attaching to Object. In listening it is engagement in Interest, activated by Object and releasing to Identity.

> 3. A Presentive level of language involves a preoccupation with personhood. In speaking, it is a state of engagement in Identity, activated by I (existence) and attaching to Interest. In listening, it is engagement in Identity, activated by Interest and releasing to I (existence).

A Presentive level of language is as indispensable to language as social organization, though not broadly discussed among theorists of language. It is, nonetheless, plainly visible in the model we have been developing of consciousness formed to express and participate in social organization. Personhood is integrated into communicative events, manifest in all the choices made in the magnitude of terms, the organization of ideas, and the irony and humor of human affairs. Indeed, unless language acts reflected against, or encountered social limitation in the form of singular "I"s comparing and refining experience, it is difficult if not impossible to imagine language at all, let alone its evolution within a biological universe.

We have equipped language for such expression because we have poured our souls into it. Because we organize around principles of this sort, as in what is good about us and how we as individuals express or reflect that goodness, a language unfolding without it would be as incoherent as the private language of analytic philosophy.

We have, in other words, discovered a theoretically plausible link between fixed and adaptive objects which allows us to understand both as Requisite organizational phenomena. In fixed objects—trees and institutions—hierarchy is discoverable in the course of a learning process, as one achieves mastery over a field of data. In adaptive objects such as "personhood" we find ourselves embedded within a hierarchy intuitively perceived as a continuum between inner and outer. The implication is that in many respects fixed objects replicate a map of consciousness in which we exist. It is plausible therefore to view complex organizations—five-tiered business units internally organized as three-tiered management events—as a copy of the organizing structure of language.

6. Within the domain of a spoken language—now identified as a Requisite phenomenon—it is appropriate to identify characteristics of societies formed within this domain. These, it seems, are empirically confirmed in archaeological and anthropological studies of hunter gatherer societies.

One characteristic would be the absence of a formalized or extrinsic government structure. Significantly, we do not equate this with the absence of government. In modern societies we use government as a processing center for the formalization and enforcement of law, and thus as foundation for economic order. But in the wild economy of so called "primitive" societies, extrinsic government is far less necessary due to the fact that social norms are embedded within spoken language and are—by evolutionary design—adequate to the collaborations necessary to extract a living from natural surroundings.

The emergent social and economic order resembles, however, the kinds of structure we strive for in modern economies. Participation is universal inasmuch as language is universal, and so there is a strong sense of public accountability manifest in visibility. Likewise, since language evolved as a processing instrumentality of shared autonomous experience—where each person represents an expression of "I" and participates in the support of "Other" to "I"—personal autonomy is not suppressed, but celebrated collectively in the passage to adulthood and the acquisition of adult names. It is not an anonymous collective, but a personalized and collaborative one which places value on individual life and of needs deriving from it.

As we have now stated a "Requisite" principle, a related characteristic of wild economy is the maintenance of an egalitarian social order. It is quite difficult, of course, within a society of interdependent participants for one individual to argue effectively to another that he or she is entitled to a greater share of the productivity of that society than another, or for that matter, that one member should assume the role as servant to another.

One might say, "My life will be more comfortable if I get what is good for me," but that is hardly an argument that will persuade the person who gets nothing. The ineffectiveness of an argument of inequality reveals value attached to the autonomy of existence, where each member of a society is regarded as an "end." If such existence is valuable and individual, then how can one experience be regarded as more valuable than another? Equality is in substance activated by the value placed on shared experience, the ruling principle of language—which cannot be shared if it is not first individualized. [14]

There may be persuasive reasons to allocate resources unequally to those engaged in wild economy, but the allocation will likely be visible, supported by a rationale, and invoke processes of endorsement deemed acceptable to a participating collective. Within such an environment, unequal distributions will be limited, but offered as a reward for individual contribution, and likely allocated without denigrating the contribution of others.

A third related characteristic is the assertion of spirituality through an intuitive and universally projected sense of good to all members of the collective in what we have previously identified with the term "deity." Primitive societies, it seems, place some importance in preserving it as an ineffable and obscure presence which manifests itself as an imperative to exist individually in such a way that this existence can be shared with others. But as we noted above, while the experience is enabled by language, it is also limited by the information processing limitations of a given language.

Terminology in a discussion of this kind is not a minor issue. One might be accused at this point of speaking disrespectfully with terms which are by their nature controversial, and likely offensive to persons with strong religious sentiments. The term deity is used sparingly, i.e., precisely because it is what comes to mind when we most need the experience of meaning in our lives.

There is a famous story about Christmas involving a man named George who had never realized a number of dreams he had as a younger man, but he had limited success in promoting a business as a lender to persons who needed loans to start businesses and build houses. As a result of his efforts, the community prospered, and he supported a lovely wife and several adorable children. But he failed in his ambitions to be rich and famous, and he was in a number of respects profoundly unhappy with himself.

An important contributor to this tale was a bad man named Potter—much older and wealthier than our friend, and who wanted to financially exploit the community, but could not because of George's lending company. He also resented George's goodness, and the local adoration which followed it. He was himself socially and physically crippled, and deeply cynical—essentially rejecting and ridiculing values in which and through which others lived happily. And thus, through some manipulation he managed to place George in a situation where it appeared as though he would lose everything he thought he had. George walked to a bridge, and prepared to commit suicide.

The story resolved beautifully by way of divine intervention of an angel, but not before George had the chance to see what the world would have been like without him—a depressed and deadly existence for all of those who he loved the most. Once he decided to live, the community he had supported for most of his life came to his rescue. Everyone gave, even those who could not afford to give, moving him from lack to abundance, as all gathered at his home to express their love and appreciation for the life he lived.

There are few who watch this story unfold who are not moved by it. The reason for this is that it brings one close to the experience of deity. It is not at all trivial, and cannot be simply defined, except through acknowledgement of the power of it. It is also very much like the experience of deity typical of wild economy, where consumptive behaviors are linked to a sense of contribution, and members seem content to trade cravings for status and power for the respectful appreciation of each other.

In wild economies, group solidarity is probably stronger, and competitions over goods and positions of authority are substantially less than were visible in George's community. Studies on hunter gatherer cultures typically marvel at the equalities achieved both in the distribution of work and the benefits of community production. Authority is neither coveted nor materially rewarded. Laws are conveyed through storytelling, and mythic narratives brimming with spirituality, and disparage ambitions which would tend to elevate one person at the expense of others. George's nemesis—Potter—defines the antithesis of good imaged in wild economies.

It is tempting, due to all the things we know now, to belittle primitive economy. We know a lot more about how the world is put together, and have seen many religious systems added to theirs, and have recorded their demise. This sense of elevation is illusory, as the loss of community may be a more primitive experience in a modern world than finding community in a primitive world. But that is not the real nature of the most common error. The error is not so much a failure to appreciate the beauty of primitive organization, but in underestimating the level of self-awareness it represents.

Cultures which function within the universe of a wild economy are usually quite aware of attitudes which interfere with peaceful social relationships. The assumption that such cultures are able to identify and root out the Potters in their midst is probably more realistic than the opposite, i.e., that they exist in a naïve state of bliss and are vulnerable to social predators. It is in fact part of the intimate vigilance of the accountability structures under which such systems operate that allows them to monitor and anticipate anti-social behavior long before it occurs.

Nor are they, as some might suggest, naively uniform in the expectancies they apply to social membership. Agreement as to the range of behaviors deemed acceptable is not the same thing as constriction in the behaviors deemed acceptable. The adoption of deity common to a group can be and is quite permissive, and it seems that what is likely to separate "free" from "oppressive" expectancies derives not from the fact of agreement, but from the type of agreement. The intuitive basis of a unified sense of value is the opposite of a coercively imposed value system. Wild economies know exactly what that is and will not allow it.

A wild economy excludes—by assumption—significant environmental pressures which would prevent intuitively derived and loving value systems from being dominant. Though sexual competition provides some basis for the evolution of social inequalities, social stratification is noticeably absent in such economies. It seems that a natural sense of "law" embedded in language solved that evolutionary paradox over many tens of thousands of years. The sexual competition typical of modern societies is better thought of as a perversion of the sociology of human sexuality.

As previously indicated, there is, in fact, an evolutionary need to preserve genetic diversification through the formation of more regionalized social exchange—but such exchange favors a more natural equilibrium between the outreach of linguistically related population, and the sharing of commerce and bloodlines. All that is necessary to avoid exploitation between tribes is the ability to make invasion more expensive than cooperation. Hence, the warrior of genetically evolved tribal societies belongs to a defensive militia—nothing like the professional soldiers in more developed civilizations.

The adaptation from diverse perspectives of value to "ruling principle" reflected in deity has been tempted by the apparent expedience of a coerced consensus, which might make social organization grow more rapidly, or allow it to engage a larger number of people. But then one would have to change the meaning of value, because in the instance of forced value, value would represent someone else's value, not theirs.

A number of scholars interested in the classification of culture by religious orientation have placed the hunter-gatherer cultures within the rubric of "Pantheism," which is ordinarily defined as the placement of deity within the material expression of existence—essentially identifying the universe with divinity. The foregoing analysis, however, suggests either that such classification should be modified, or that the definition of Pantheism should be re-examined.

What we have observed in the mapping of consciousness is not the positioning of divinity in a material other, but the acknowledgement of connection between the internal experience of value and the formation and manifestation of Other. It is, as suggested above, a conscious refusal to position divinity in Other in an effort to preserve individual access to it—a way of preserving the mystery of spirituality so that it might be experienced without external manipulation.

Pantheism, as a term descriptive of the appropriation and placement of deity in Other, does not, in other words, represent a coherent description of the religious orientation of a wild economy because language in such an economy never appropriated divinity to begin with. A sense of the divine emerged within language, not around it, and did so in such a way as to bestow value on the world, and on life, including life's discomforts.

# Chapter 4

# Control Economy

1. Perhaps the most difficult thing to grasp in the development of a science of human behavior is the perception of evil. It would be easy if "evil" meant the same thing as "bad." But "bad" is not more than an unwelcome occurrence, judged from the set of interests of a given person. Suppose a giant snake made an attempt to eat someone. That would be bad for the person, but good, perhaps, for the snake. It is likely something the snake is supposed to be doing—as it evolved to consume prey inclusive of human beings.

We typically refrain from laying fault on others for doing what they are evolved to do, even though we might have to kill them before they hurt us. Blame is another type of sentiment. "Evil" is something we say about someone who falls short of what he or she is supposed to be doing, and who in the process harms others.

The maintenance of moral neutrality is, in fact, a claimed advantage in the study of human affairs—as science—inasmuch as moral judgment tends to cloud one's understanding of a given universe of constraints, and purposes served within it. This attitude, however, seems to work better as a rule of convenience than as essential precept, because at some point in the study of human behavior, we become interested in the comparison of the effectiveness of individual and social strategies of survival, and how those become manifest in one's attempt to orient oneself through value.

Even then, the landscape can be confusing, as it is not clear what it means to be effective. Are productive and nervous people better off than relaxed and unproductive people? Is happy poverty better than miserable wealth? There are quite a number of different ways of evaluating human success, each reinforced with its own sentimental ideals. We might have been guilty of that in the last chapter, by idealizing to some degree a primitive social system in which group solidarity and cooperation developed effectively through the formation of a spoken language.

We weren't the first to do so, it seems, as one of the most famous laments of human history was expressed in a poem now canonized as scripture near the beginning of the book of Genesis—the story of Adam and Eve. It is difficult to say when the story was first told, but it appears to have been composed and adopted at a time and place where economies were shifting rapidly from the smaller more intuitively organized hunter gatherer societies to much larger agricultural economies organized as dominative hierarchies. Given that the human is at times observant and reflective, the appearance of hierarchically organized agricultural civilizations to those engaged in or comfortable with wild economies must have been quite a spectacle. It might have seemed ironic as well, as there was fair evidence available that as the human became smarter, it was also becoming much more aware of a difference between wealth and misery.

Not surprisingly, the story begins with language, with a man alone to name the various other creatures of God's creation. It is not that clear that Adam was a male figure to start with, but it was clear that being alone among numerous other species was unacceptable. A female complement to solitary existence should and did emerge from the side of Adam, and thus formed a society—Other. All of their needs were provided for in their garden, except that God placed a tree there which held the knowledge of good and evil, while warning them that eating its fruit would result in their death. A talking serpent then appeared and explained that God forbade them from eating because it would make them like God, implying that their subordination to God had been the result of God's vanity and manipulation. Eve then ate the fruit, and offered it to Adam, who ate at her request.

Their sin was then revealed to God by their shame at being naked—something they hadn't noticed before. Eve admitted to God they she had been beguiled by the serpent, and God cast them out of Eden, but not before telling Eve that women would be cursed with painful childbirth, and a servient relationship to men. Adam was told that he would toil among thorns and thistles, and have to eat the herb of the field—grains, and "in the sweat of your face shall you eat bread." God then turned to other spiritual beings apparently observing this spectacle, saying that Adam and Eve had by knowing good and evil become "like one of us," and that special care should be taken to prevent them from eating from the tree of life and live forever as gods. So, the human being was moved from pleasant ignorance to wise afflictions in a life of slavish cultivation. (Gen. 3:18-23)

There are many interpretations of this narrative, as people often wonder why our lives aren't as comfortable as we would like. The moral of the story appears at one level to suggest that we should blame ourselves for having strayed at some point in time from the lives God had in mind for us. That interpretation is superficial, as one must then ask why we were made with such a defective nature, which tends to put the blame back on a creator.

The story is more like a poetic lamentation that imagines a life of innocence and the corruption of innocence by placing the human in a world in competition with God. The story doesn't offer a contrast between good and evil, and thus the origin of evil, but a contrast between a world in which good and evil are not known, and a new world in which they are known.

The key to understanding the poem consists in the understanding of what it means to know something. The use of the word in ancient Hebrew meant more than cognitive familiarity with something, but indicated a state of manipulative engagement (control) with another through sense contact. Knowledge describes a relationship one has with objects. The state of knowledge is a state of selection, of intercourse with and influence upon an environment in which good and evil are attributed to things.

This is quite different from a wild state, consisting mostly of states to be pursued and others to be avoided. Good does not need authority to exist, nor does it need human intervention to advance or protect it. It takes care of itself, and the weakness of evil is self-destroying. All of this, as expressed in a socially cooperative economy, is a matter of trusting the essential nature of things to bring about harmonious relationships with the social and natural surround.

Before the formation of agricultural economies there was hardly any need to test instinctive organization beyond the requirements of loosely formed regionalized affiliations of language. But at some point, the human became smarter and developed technologies that made food production more efficient. Along with this came larger populations, and a host of technologies including the domestication of plants and livestock, the transportation of water, the disposal of waste and the military protection of land and human resources. Organization became much more important and essential to the maintenance of these processes and did not seem to be able to organize without the intervention of a ruling authority.

Instead of letting good look after itself, humanity became a knower of it, which meant removing value from its original position as an intimative deity—an "I" that asserts value in a universe alive with value—to an object deity subject to human description and control. The story of the fall of Adam was, in effect, an eloquent expression of regret over the visible transformations then occurring.

The account indicates change from one strategy of survival to a new one. The new strategy began what wild economies had been successful in preventing for many thousands of years—the presentation of deity as an object of knowledge. The God described in this narrative was a parody of the kind of deity that had inspired social discourse in a spiritually vibrant universe. The new God seemed more bewildered and disappointed than angry at the human choice to feel naked and ashamed, and to assume control over right and wrong. The consequence (punishment) was, among other bad things, a world where women would become servile child bearing vessels, and men would toil over a plow, eating foods made from grass.

It is almost as if the story were a criticism by a shaman of an on-looking hunter gatherer culture—told as an amusing allegory—to identify a point in the development of the human species where the organizational problem of human economy changed.

Primitive organization was designed to work within a population center that favored mobile societies with adaptive and intuitive consensus mechanisms. In the process of evaluating wild economy we did not have the occasion to ask the question that needed to be asked. What happens when the organizational capability of this type of society is, for any number of reasons, stressed, and organization needs to be forced rather than allowed or discovered?

2. The world in which we currently live has a biased view of how a need for bigger organizations came about. So much of what we consume, and the price exacted for this consumption is a matter of technological development. We are, accordingly, inclined to view the past in terms of the progressive evolution of technologies, and the ascendency of science. A modification of organization would ensue upon the development of productive technologies that require such organization.

A shift from wild to control economy is therefore usually attributed to the domestication of seed rich grasses and livestock—which allowed economies to draw much more carbohydrate and protein from a given land area than had previously been thought possible. Organization is presently viewed as a secondary adjustment to a primary innovation which relieved human societies of the expense involved in the pursuit of game and the focused maintenance of small and relatively mobile social structures.

Perhaps there were evolutionary reasons why people enjoyed things like intuitively cohesive tribes, small intimate communities, and a change of scenery. If there are, it is possible that the evolution of human beings is different than insect species which evolved toward a simpler objective of swarming and multiplying around the discovery of food sources.

Yet the prevailing explanation for the emergence of agriculturally based civilization adopts this essential predicate—i.e., that more food meant more people. A good expression of this view is offered by Jared Diamond in two interesting analyses—one explaining the emergence and predominance of industrial civilization as a lucky confluence of factors favoring the development and dissemination of technologies of domestication, and another explaining the collapse of civilization as a process following the sudden interruption of natural resources necessary to sustain productive technologies. Social organization was brought about by technology and could not do much to address the shortfall of resources. The argument is persuasive, though foreboding, as it suggests a loss of organization (civilization) at the point of resource failure—the Malthusian disaster.

There are a number of facts, however, which do not fit this view—mostly derived from the comparative study of hunter gatherer societies (wild economy) and the highly controlled societies of agriculturally supplied civilizations (control economy).

First, many ancient hunter-gatherer civilizations learned to cultivate plants and livestock long before the appearance of control economies. They did not, in other words, form spontaneously into the dominative hierarchies we associate with the Bronze Age, but instead understood and supplemented food sources with what is properly identified as agricultural technology. This continues to be true of hunter-gatherer societies of today, and that there are other preferences operating to limit the development of population centers around food production—somewhat in conflict with the human swarm theory of economy. [15]

Second, and perhaps simply confirming the first observation, it appears that the material standard of living in hunter-gatherer economies was better than what appeared later in agriculturally supplied dominative hierarchies that took their place. The studies which have been done so far indicated that except in the aristocratic classes engendered by organizationally heavy societies, the average participant in wild economy had more food to eat and more leisure time—by a significant amount. [16]

Nor did the first farming communities within the Neolithic Stone Age indicate the spontaneous formation of organizational hierarchies. They were well served by specially appointed elders, and did not appear to pass rights of control within designated families or classes. They seem to have replicated social structures common in wild economies—more or less egalitarian and intuitive in the imposition of legal obligation. [17]

Third, and perhaps most interesting in the study of organization, hunter-gather cultures under study indicate a very predictable moment of division or "branching" of social organization. That is to say, there is a point in which the natural assemblage of persons becomes too much or too many, and the tribe splits into two separate social groups. The study suggests constancy of the same convincing degree as appears in the studies of bureaucratic organizations in Requisite, and the applicability of these constants in many different cultural contexts. Wild economy, it seems, only fits within a certain social magnitude before it encounters organizational transformation. [18]

This last set of findings suggests a comfort level to community development, and a conflict-averse attitude to social formations that promote the dispersal and expansion the human species, rather than the concentration of populations around food sources. The logic of wild economy reflects a species which places high value on social harmony, and an interest in avoiding unpleasant social interactions.

The path of least resistance does not involve conquering or dominating those who do not share the same "deity" but moving to a place where differences in attitude will not be a source of conflict. This too makes more sense, as the domination of one group over another is normally quite difficult where there is ample space for the oppressed to escape oppression by moving away.

Thus, it appears that the logic of agriculturally supplied economies was really not—as many contend—about technologically supplying larger population masses. Something happened in which human populations were prevented from doing what came naturally to them, and were forced to organize differently because of pressures that genetically evolved language skills lacked. A better working hypothesis, it seems, is that more dominative economies arose as a result of pressures brought on by localized population increases, perhaps related to the success of agriculture—but not activated by it.

It was once assumed that wild economies were mobile only so that they might pursue game, but their mobility might also have had something to do with the need for diverse moral structures to live separately and to avoid dominant-submissive social structures. So, what, then, is the sort of thing which would encourage such economies to develop?

Presented now with a view of the human species which is accomplished at forming tribal units—each with its own core values—and capable of proliferating new societies activated by new deities, there is a way of accounting for human expansion. The species was successful in replication not just in the form of biological reproduction, but also in the replication of similar but not identical tribal units migrating in part for the pursuit of resources, but also to avoid social discords associated with overcrowding.

The place to look for the first emergence of control economies therefore would likely be areas bordered by uninhabitable regions—salt water oceans and deserts. This describes the areas of lying between the continents of Africa and Asia (the Middle East) and the area just to the north of the link between the Americas (Central America). The first region is also known as the "cradle of civilization" and the second is renowned for the first great civilizations of the Western Hemisphere.

"Civilization," it seems, is a name given to a number of creative adaptations to overcrowding. A number of these adaptations bear directly on the management of costs associated with the maintenance of social order and are, in effect, legal and economic in nature. But they are also presented in ideological packages that engage social participation in ways which invented an entirely different sense of human identity.

The point, however, is that resource limitations related to the propagation of the species have at least one point in history forced a revision in the nature of human identity. This revision was not gentle and persuasive, but startlingly violent, and at times perverse. This and other changes should be examined as part of managing species success. A troubling implication of this phenomenon is the possibility that humanity has to remake itself in order to successfully address organizational problems of a similar magnitude in the current era.

The analysis of this adjustment contemplates a change of motivation when tribal offsprings have no place to go. Instead of moving away from or creating comfortable distances between tribes, there is a perceived need to develop political affiliations adequate to dominate the group. The social stressors occasioned by this need have no outlet except through unnaturally competitive intra-species interactions.

These interactions tend to place value on genetically acquired capabilities that had not been prominent in competitions with other species in a wild economy. The task of dominating others within a social setting is much more complicated than dominating other species. It is, additionally, fraught with time related stressors, as failure to act promptly and with lethally directed focus places one and one's group in peril.

The situation is apt to unfold as a paramilitary campaign, where a few subtle and strategically minded individuals enlist the most physically dominant members of the social group, and act within the nervous expectancy that invasion by another group is imminent. Leaders within a game setting of this nature are particularly vulnerable, as they are targeted for assassination, while the physically imposing tribal members are regarded as interchangeable resources. The organizing principle emphasizes physically dominant expression (male over female) and machinatively nuanced (serpent like) sense of social order.

It isn't necessary to be a game theorist to appreciate the aggressive dynamism of this situation. A brief visit to a gymnasium with limited playing space to play a popular game such as basketball, with continuity of play awarded only to the victorious team. As the space fills with teams waiting to play, the tenor of the game changes dramatically. One or two teams waiting has little effect, as players seem to need the rest, but add two or three more teams, the level of aggression increases dramatically. Fights break out, along with accusations of cheating, and efforts to infiltrate the talent pool of other teams. It is almost as if a satanic presence entered the field of play, which is, in a sense, what happens.

Given the dangerousness of a game of survival in intraspecies competition within a crowded environment, there is a logic that flows directly from it upon the formation of a military unit. First is the avoidance or defeat of potential invasion from other locations, and the second—equal to the first—is the avoidance or defeat of rebellion within the unit. Since everything is at stake, and at all times, socially dominant individuals subordinate all other social interests to this logic and achieve success through the combined enlargement of and control over the military unit. The logic may not be attractive, but is simple, elegant and persuasive.

3. The principal obstacle to the achievement of the objectives of a competition of this kind is human nature. There are only a few real

players in a game of this sort, while those remaining participate are minions—which is not how people like to see themselves. As we sought to explain previously, the conscious organism we refer to as "human" moves within a sense of law that is self-affirming, accountable and cooperative. When asked to assume roles that are self-negating and subservient, the task of persuasion is formidable.

This is accomplished first through the widespread communication of a threat of invasion that will result in the death or enslavement of everyone. Persuasion is also accomplished through religious manipulation, or more specifically, as the removal of the "I" of existence from a position interior and its relocation to one exterior to consciousness. This may also be referred to as the "extraction" of law as a self-existent presence, and its repositioning as an anthropomorphically conceived object deity.

Extraction is not the same thing as objectification, though they may seem similar. Extraction involves the removal of deity from an iterative dialogue, where its emergence as a socially participative experience is limited or eliminated. The deity that emerges in the presentive event of language may or may not be objectified, though the objectification of it isn't taken very seriously. Not so for an extracted deity. Since it is always introduced externally, it is by its essential nature, object, and is submitted to a population of consumers through the various media of persuasion. Notwithstanding, as an instrumentality of control, it is usually stationary and inflexible.

Marketing is marketing, however, and an extracted deity uses whatever persuasive devices that seem to be effective, including ceremonies, incense, incantations, rituals, graven images, hymns that rhyme and theologies embroidered by myth—cast in enigmatic terms and phrases. The religious formations frequently manage to survive their makers, but they seek a political authority to become attached to, as political endorsement is their purpose. In return for the assured financing of their priesthood, they vouch for the authority and dignity of a sovereign ruler—at times in many ancient civilizations identifying that ruler as deity.

The achievement of universal consensus is not only unnecessary, but it is unimportant. The logic of control is not about ethical discernment, but about obedience to sovereign authority, and so the point of religious appropriation is to soften the resistance of human beings who by their nature make their existence in a moral universe.

The name often given for the logic of a system of this nature is "positive law." Ethical principle is something that the sovereign has appropriated through agreement with religious clergy and a servient religious theology. The claim of the theoretical tradition of positive law is that one can effectively study law by treating ethical obligation as a subset of a larger set of obligatory sentiments placed into effect by a ruling authority.

Other ways of creating a sense of obligation consist of various material rewards and punishments, which are numerous and inventive. Among the challenges in articulating a theory of law applicable to control economies generally is sorting out the essential from the superficial mechanisms through which sovereignty expresses its will. Under certain formulations of positive law, the ethical means of persuasion is treated as an inessential ingredient of law, and hence that law is essentially the "position" of a ruler—an expression of sovereign will. But the analysis presented here strongly suggests that positive law is itself an adaptation to an environment in which ethically based obligation is organizationally ineffective.

The persistent efforts of rulers in control economies to establish their laws on an ethical platform implies awareness that law is, in fact, an ethical phenomenon. It stands out as a proof, of sorts, that this ethical structure, however, was unable to override the stressors—and resultant paranoia—created in inescapably crowded regions. Positive law is therefore not an analysis reaching at the essence of law, but is descriptive of a legal adaptation brought on by necessity.

There are other characteristics of positive law, which in their absence reduce it to a nullity. In wild economy there was an assumed regularity of the expression and ratification of normative expectancies such that their clarity was part of the clarity of language. But government in a control economy—without the motivating effect of ethically based obligation—does not have common spoken language working with it in the same way.

Thus, an essential element of positive law is the formation of language-type processing instrumentalities, i.e., processes which do in a formal bureaucratic setting what the spoken language did intuitively. Positive law manifests these essentials on levels comparable to semantic and syntactic structures we examined in spoken language. These levels are, in the context of positive law commonly referred to as "substantive" and "procedural."

Substantive law is the sovereign's effort to identify obligations that adhere to membership in the state—as well as the identification of consequence of a breach of obligation. When someone makes a statement about the world, they express an expectation tested in large part by the acquiescence of others. In this respect, substantive law is not different. It is a state of expectancy about what behavior will be, except that acquiescence is obligatory.

Syntax is a set of devices—together with rules of application—which allow us to clarify the intended use of words. Likewise, the will of sovereignty loses its effect without means of clarifying what is expected, and thus the establishment of strategic approaches to the resolution of conflict over what the will of the sovereign is—thus applicable to conflicts over the facts, laws, and the authority of sovereign agents. There is thus a functional similarity between language and positive law, suggesting that positive law is set up as a species of language, but under focused sovereign regulation.

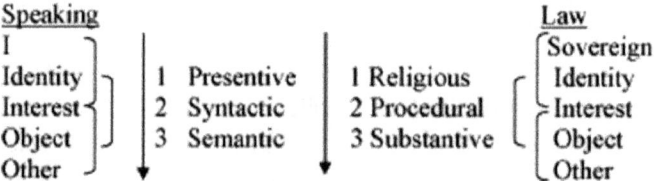

The change to the "language" represented in law is the transformation of a "presentive" event in which one speaker makes an intuitively based self-affirmation based on feedback evident in the responsive communication of others, to an event which effectively displaces the personalized expression of ethical substance with the individual will of a sovereign ruler. This kind of picture indicates limited accountability to others evident, if at all, in meekly expressed discomfort by those subject to rule. Law becomes much like a one-sided language game of speaking with a limited capacity to hear the responses of those to whom the messages are conveyed.

This perversion on language is evident in a dysphoria common in kingly rulers, who throughout history have suffered from loneliness and megalomania—abnormal to the human species. Such experience, when combined with real threats of assassination occasioned by external invasion or interior rebellion suggest a form of rule frequently afflicted with mental illnesses as mental "health" is highly dependent on social interactions presenting boundaries that both restrict and validate one's personhood.

A recurring historical irony, therefore, is the juxtaposition of state-imposed law against personally experienced autonomy and the security of a given ruler. This tendency adapts through a number of devices by which a king might engage in the kind of social intercourse on which his sanity depends. He might therefore entertain certain kinds of priests and "prophets" that have special permission to privately criticize him.

The disappearance of a presentive aspect to law—as embedded in ordinary language—is actually a bit more complicated, therefore, than the appropriation of authority by a singular leader. The nature of law requires the establishment of a social setting in which a central group can nurture the mind of the king. The unitary ruler of a control economy is more apt to have a central group of friends with special entrustments and benefits, and who serve not only as functional advisors, but as a social support in the formation of conscience—as the human organism cannot organize selfhood without it.

Despite the common fantasy of being king or queen over a realm of obedient subjects, there are a number of reasons to avoid the experience. It is extremely dangerous work, due to the accumulation of wealth—coveted both by external and internal rivals. And it is necessary to accumulate wealth to secure loyalty and commitment in those on whom rulers depend. And if not physically dangerous, there is serious danger to the mental health of a ruling agency that has not been successful in creating a sanity inducing surrounding social structure—more difficult than it seems.

The treatment of positive law, therefore, as a way of either defining or understanding law is deaf, more or less, to the behavioral features of the organizing power of language. This power, rather than casting off the ethical dimension to a language suffused consciousness, demands the construction of effective surrogates that serve to protect the ruler on a number of different fronts—i.e., the institutionalization of deity in religion, and the institutionalization of syntactic and semantic structures along with a class of servants for those structures. All of this is to repair the damage associated with the expropriation of functions which had in normal language been functioning effectively on their own in tribal societies.

4. In a wild economy, society and law exist in unity—society is the experience of Law as ruling ethical principle. Disunity activates social separation, and the species moves outward. There is no essential disruption of the tribal model, but if for some reason movement is inhibited, then disruption is overcome through the repositioning of Law to a point of human control—the extraction of law.

This process signals that other forms of disruption are possible, such as the formation of classes of people, and economic inequality between them. That is, if the artifice of positive law can be extracted from Law, then the artifice of hierarchically designed social organizations may be extracted from a social consciousness which is by its nature egalitarian.

People can be induced to follow the announced purposes of other human beings, and thus be subordinated to the designs of a single as opposed to a collective Other. This is an important economic transformation.

While "economy" as a term is more meaningful in modern economies, it is in wide use among scholars committed toward the understanding of societies first established upon technologies of agriculture. Aside from the development of agricultural technologies themselves, the question which seems to attract the most interest is the formation and stratification of social class. What is puzzling to many scholars is that archaeological evidence of Neolithic societies strongly suggests that despite well-developed agricultural technologies, significant indicia of stratification did not appear until thousands of years later in the Bronze Age.

In agrarian Neolithic (pre-bronze) societies, there is a relatively small amount of social hierarchy, as well as small fortifications to discourage marauding tribes, and the unequal accumulation of livestock and goods in certain households. But houses were built collectively, and were equal in size and apparent luxury, suggesting again that the change of productive technology was not the driving force of social change—not enough to dislodge law from its central location in consciousness. Since the change to hierarchical management structures, and social classes seems to have been a characteristic of Bronze-age societies, we ought to consider whether there was something about bronze that made a difference.

Bronze was produced by heating copper and tin to their melting point and mixing them together. The importance of bronze had little to do with farming, as it represented a very modest improvement over stone-based plows and harvesting equipment. It had a remarkable effect, however, on weaponry, which could be made more lethal—armor piercing axes and arrows, and in high quantity—of uniform quality. The importance of these innovations is that one could build armies with weapons of this nature, and coordinate attacks in phalanxes utilizing specially adapted and plentifully available bronze weapons. It suddenly became much easier for one group to appropriate the land of another, and the human sense of exposure multiplied.

As to the exact order of events, there is much to speculate about. There is a line of thinking, for example, which argues that social inequalities emerged as a consequence of an intuitive trade between a small group of managers and a larger group of laborers, where laborers sensed value in ceding control and earned surplus to managers, in exchange for the benefits of hierarchical management.

Opposing this argument is a more cynical view, contending that the threat of violence probably had more to do with popular acquiescence to the creation of a privileged class than the provision of organizational service. That social inequality followed after some revision in the technology and scale of war, tends to favor a version of history crowded with aggressive and well-armed rulers playing out a version of social Darwinism. If the nice guys all get slaughtered, the rest set standards that may take some getting used to.

What really happened is the subject of lively discussion among archaeologists and historians and is in good hands. The importance of considering in the context of a more theoretical discussion of economy is to emphasize the magnitude of the transformation which occurred—such as to move organization from its position as social assertion in language, to the position as a social instrumentality to which a region's inhabitants were subject. This, when coupled with a game of survival determined by the most powerful armies resulted in a proliferation of institutions which supported a military complex which answered to a concentrated elite—a centrally positioned ruler, their family, and other essential points of control and their families. Such would be the logical basis for the formation of an aristocracy. [19]

It is also the basis for the formation of an economy. In order to build an army, there must be a surplus of essential living resources. Without that, the ruling elite face rebellion. But the surplus must constitute a reserve large enough to afford cyclic fluctuation in productivity and a capacity to afford invasion—either as defender or aggressor. In other words, there is really no limit to how wealthy a ruler would prefer to be, but this wealth is dependent on the wealth generated by agricultural labor, and the extent to which they are able to maintain a surplus. But surplus depends on what labor will accept above and beyond subsistence; the politics of that negotiation can be complicated.

As this suggests, there may be considerable variation in the way the ruler's negotiations with his or her producers, artisans, soldiers and administrators proceed, but none of this changes the essential nature of the economy. The rulers' most important and ultimate recourse is violence because they—in the end—face violence should the rule fail. They hold others similarly accountable if they fail to discharge their obligations effectively, and they work as directors of hierarchical organizations which are centrally accountable.

In the year 2300 B.C., a region now known as Iraq developed the first great Bronze Age civilization. It came under the rule of Sargon the Great after over one thousand seven hundred years of warfare between city-states in the area. The wars were fought with cast bronze weapons, with a force of about five thousand soldiers in a region then able to support about thirty thousand persons. The Great Egypt we all know of as an impenetrable dynasty similarly emerged out of a history of war, and was twice conquered over a thousand years by opportunistic rivals that had investigated its weaknesses. These battles were fought with armies of around twenty thousand soldiers—the largest the world had yet seen.

But these were small compared to the armies assembled in the Iron Age, each army numbering in the hundreds of thousands of soldiers from Greece, Persia, Macedonia and a newly formed Egypt. The Iron Age received its name again as a consequence of the technologies of war, allowing them to replace bronze armaments with much cheaper metal alloys of iron. The competition demanded bigger armies, protecting and promoting bigger dynasties, which required the accumulation of greater surpluses from farming activities, and larger bureaucracies to manage these activities.

Iron was quite a remarkable innovation, but it had no effect on law or on economy, except to increase the size and scale of armies and the various structures needed to support them.

It was a process of evolution similar to the dinosaur, except developing thousands of times faster. Processes of evolution prompted many species of dinosaur to competitively evolve by becoming bigger, and they got so big that they were not good at responding to idiosyncratic environmental challenges—like climate change. Riven by constant war, control economies have throughout the ages evolved as if the only major environmental challenge was invasion. The Bronze Age civilizations were doing well until a series of earthquakes, and a draught lasting several years destabilized the entire Mediterranean region. Many great civilizations lost their control, and were overrun by invasion. Egypt held on by the skin of its teeth.

Until the development of control economies, the notion of "property" was a fiction designed to apply to personal items accumulated through an individual's work, and through affectionate relationships with others. It was not applicable to the land from which economic productivity derived. Hunter gatherers laughed at the accumulation of property—too much to carry, and Neolithic stone farmers regarded land as a community asset. But that all changed with the emergence of armies. Land was the source of the surpluses that fed armies, and thus had to be controlled. Dominion became the military predication of real estate as a property—property controlled by armies in order to feed armies.

The central control of real property, and the use of its surplus to support the other functions of state—the army being the "soul" of control—has been the essential rationale for control economy since its inception. It favors and encourages a circular argument. If someone is able to control something, they own it. If they own it, it is wrong to steal it, or otherwise interfere with the use of it. Trespass thus became a moral issue deriving at some point from an act of violence through which control was asserted over a given area of real estate by a ruler.

It is therefore not uncommon for the takers to use religious justification for their control of it—i.e., that God promised the land to them, or helped them get it. After a few generations of occupation, though, it doesn't seem to matter who first took it, and how they did it, as the possessors likely had nothing to do with it. So, their ownership changes from a moral claim based solely on power, to a moral claim based on a common interest in preserving expectations.

Regardless of the circularity of the argument, it functions effectively as long as the use of the property supports the subsistence of those who live and/or work on it. Generally speaking, laborers would rather gather subsistence from land peacefully than argue with a landed aristocracy over who held the primary right to control.

Problems, both ancient and contemporary, associated with the use of property within control economy have much to do with the loss of a sense of obligation by the "owner" to allow property to support the subsistence of its inhabitants. The response of the owner(s) might typically be "why should we care, it's ours and we can do what we want with it." But that argument may, from a nuanced perspective, be misleading.

When title to property was appropriated by force, it may have been so engaged for use as a generator of surplus, thus implying inhabitation, and a rent structure which allowed subsistence. This can change over a few centuries, but if changes in the perceived use and obligations of property fail to provide for essential needs of a public, the government (or its successors) will encounter opposition. If there is a moral right to the land, it would probably repose in its inhabitants. Morality of ownership in a control economy, however, derives almost entirely from the military seizure of the land—though often reinforced by the persuasive use of religious scripture.

This system offers a given ruler discretionary authority to control production—i.e., they can give the land to whomever they choose, on whatever conditions they choose, provided they can enforce obligation. This changes property from its more intuitively moral content, as someone's right to keep the product of his or her labor, to something with no moral content at all. In the final analysis there may be little point in calling it "property," because it is about the use of force to mark territory and lacks moral credibility in its claim of right.

5. The emergence of a sense of "property" supported by the forceful effect of military structures transfers all sense of economic order away from shared productivity and toward the concentrated accumulation of wealth. But it is not just a change of how things are done, but also, a change of the nature of intercourse between mind and society. It is useful to appreciate this, even as we enjoy the fruits of highly productive and motivated modern economies. Older states of mind—if dealt with complacently—will undo gains we thought we have made.

In order to express this idea, we might return briefly to the difference noted in the preceding chapter between adaptive and fixed complexity. In wild economy, the relation of mind and society is one of mind embedded in language, where productivity, normative expectancies and social roles are blended. The sharing of the productive output of a society within an adaptive system is a natural accoutrement of the emergence of society as a shared experience. It is part of the reality that language evolved to address.

However, this natural tendency of social intelligence to form into more holistically situated communities is, at a basic level, threatening to the logic of a ruler whose life and welfare depend on social formations that are much larger than such communities. Wild economic communities form autonomously—and go their separate ways—in large part because their participants think and act autonomously and thus associate with others they love, trust and depend on. Social groups that have learned how to fend for themselves generally prefer doing so to being forced into larger fixed social structure with unfamiliar and hostile neighbors.

The task of the ruler, therefore, is to replace adaptive structures of this kind with fixed structures governed by a principle of loyalty to the ruler. To recall, role stratification emerges in institutions (objects of fixed complexity), as individuals improve upon the use of skills acquired in the navigation of fields of information. So, part of one's success as king consists in knowing how to find people who can organize the delivery of products or services which the king defines as necessary. We are apt to see orders of social status emerging out of hierarchies constructed on the measured interest of an existing ruler.

Take the following as an essential division of labor in a control economy.

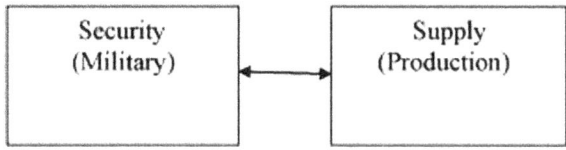

In its implementation, it is revealed in hierarchical structures held accountable to the continuity of the ruler.

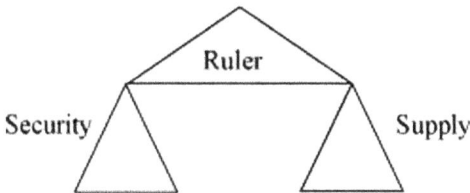

All in all, this represents a stable organization—favorable from the ruler's perspective, because it achieves dependency-based loyalty both horizontally and vertically. The military is dependent on supply but not in control of it, and supply is dependent on (or subject to) military force. Each hierarchic structure places individuals within those structures into states of dependency on rewards and punishments presumably distributed by superiors in the hierarchy. Importantly, the only adaptive or autonomous system is the one consisting of the ruler and his or her intimates, though the ruler's "autonomy" may in an abstract sense be disputed. He or she is, to a significant extent, captive to the same structures—though a comfortable captive.

Meanwhile, the conversion of economic order to a system of interdependent fixed hierarchies, moves consciousness into a state of inescapable dependency. It is a pervasive mindset of dominance and submission—of being dominated by the more powerful and of dominating less powerful individuals. This mindset is not very productive because benefits are received as entitlements granted from sovereignty—and these subordinate issues of productivity to issues of control.

Within such systems it is common for individuals in positions of authority to exact rents from other individuals who are dependent on their authority. We call it bribery today, and criminalize it, but in control economies it is the way things get done. In fact, one way of measuring whether an economy is transitioning effectively into what we refer to as "modern" may be the extent to which these behaviors have been modified.

The distributional structure of control economy is, accordingly, very top-heavy in its distribution of wealth, as the ruler—along with those on whom the ruler depends for the oversight of supply and security—are fastened to the acquisition and maintenance of points of control, and provide for themselves off the productive surplus of a much larger population of laborers. This is its most important law, i.e., to transfer all available surpluses to a ruling class and covering the security costs of doing so by paying much of that surplus to armies.

In this way, taxation falls primarily on persons occupying the lowest social strata. The authority and power of government, through numerous creative subsidies to its controllers, thus enriches a few at the expense of the inhabitants of militarily occupied territory.

Corruption of this kind and at this scale is an organizational effect of a governmental order dominated by the principle of loyalty, rather than the principle of efficiency (which includes justice and productivity). It is equally operative in economies with either modern or ancient technologies—for cars and horse carts alike—and can therefore occur within economies utilizing technologically sophisticated products and services made in well-organized industries. Corruption—whether modern or ancient—is something that nonetheless tends to stay hidden from view. No one confesses to or engages openly in it, because it is morally loathsome, and thus embarrassing to put on display. But it makes things happen.

As such, it tends to limit the productivity of a given economic order by failing to establish sufficient certainty in law to allow effective planning outside the hierarchies of loyalty that protect the ruler(s). Since loyalty-based hierarchies are highly variable, not openly revealed, and impact businesses with a productive interface with government, they frequently present risks that discourage innovation. In fact, to the extent innovation emerges autonomously, it is in the best interest of control structures to inhibit its development unless it can be tied to the safety of the ruler.

It might occur to some that a government of this nature should be actively resisted by the people, who typically outnumber the ruler(s) by huge margins. But that would reflect some degree of ignorance as to the shift of perspective that fixed hierarchy engenders. Since territory derived from central authorities ("property") is a very strong motivator, the strategic posture is to fortify what one has and to be cautious about taking from others—without the ruler's permission.

As hard as one works to protect and exploit what ruling authorities have bestowed, the prospect of losing it is regarded unthinkable. In well developed economies of control, one is apt to find a substantial class of persons who represent a social default position—of untouchables and slaves—there to reinforce the artificial sense of elevation of the masses and to serve as reminder of the penalty for subversion of the social order.

This, it appears, stands out as quite an unfortunate corruption of human consciousness, in that the value of a human being might be attached to (made dependent on) the maintenance of a position within a social hierarchy, and that loss of position might be perceived as the primitive equivalent of banishment from a tribe. In a universe ordered within a fixed hierarchy, the fearful disposition of a king or queen can—in a manner of speaking—become a state of mind that rules over an entire population, except perhaps those who have fallen to the bottom.

6. One way of apologizing for this unfortunate state of affairs is to shrug it off as benign, given that land never really belonged to anyone in the first place. Thus, the ruler's claim of title is only a territorial announcement—as a lion marks territory with his urine, and what happens thereafter is subordination similar to what prevails universally among species in competition. Rents taken as a tax on income may thus be regarded as part of the order of nature.

Once law dislodges from accountability to collective Other, a source of moral authentication of a given rule of law is essentially transferred to the ruler. If the ruler says the product of someone's labor is the ruler's, then it is. The laborers objection at this point is that such is the way slaves get treated—and to which the ruler's response is relatively indifferent, because as suggested above, control economies are slave economies. Slavery, making its first appearance in the control economies of the Bronze Age, continued throughout the Iron and Middle ages as a formally enforced property right. How does slavery fit into the mind of a society of dependents?

There are a number of considerations which complicate discussion about the legal recognition of slavery. First, it is not entirely clear what kind of ownership slavery is. In the case of property, a ruler's gift of property to one of his or her friends is apt to have strings attached, such as proof of loyalty and an obligation to make the land productive so that surplus can be paid toward the support of the ruler's army. Within the logic of control economy, the recipients' alienation of the property would typically return to the ruler, and not be offered for trade to another person without involving the ruler. Control of personal servants would, under the same logic come as a benefit tied to service owed to the ruler, and come subject to moral requirements that the ruler places on the beneficiaries of slave labor.

Second, the term "slave" probably does not mean the same thing as subsistence-based compensation, though there is often a coincidence between the two. Since the ruling class of a control economy functions off a margin between laborers' subsistence and their productive output, compensation strategies would tend to target subsistence as the cost of labor.

But the life of an agricultural worker may or may not have the sensation one tends to associate with the experience of slavery, even though compensation is at or below subsistence. People typically do not feel as though they are owned by another if they have a meaningful range of discretionary choices over matters of importance to them and are subsisting from the result of their own labor. There have been, on the other hand, quite a number of luxuriously supplied slaves, who feel they are subject to the ownership of others.

Third, the existence of a "slave" class has—as noted above—a motivating impact among other groups, who value the status and dignity associated with non-slave status. There may not be much to the status of non-slave, but there may be something reprehensible in the thought of being a slave, quite apart from being in a service relationship to another.

There is no shame in serving another but there are forms of service which effectively displace choices essential to the development of personhood. Choices related to sexual preference, and the formation and cohesion of a family unit are among the borders of choice which slave labor has traversed throughout history. Other intrusive duties might include being forced to harm another or to take great personal risk. There is, perhaps, enough moral intuition intrinsic to human consciousness that certain types of dependencies are apt to injure one's ethical identity.

Fourth, involuntary conscription to dangerous tasks may or may not signal enslavement. A person conscripted to labor at a quarry, may well be considered a slave, as the work is arduous and dangerous. But that same person conscripted to military service, subject to greater labor and risk, is not regarded "slave" and instead receives a relatively high social rank. Perhaps this is attributable to the role of soldier as protector of the "state" which is itself something which the ruler has marketed as worthy of protection, and likely sanctified. But soldiers are also called upon to bring desolation to numerous innocents, and at times to impose unjust punishments upon their own people. Are rulers that effective, and the general public so impressionable, that one can with a few words change a slave into a soldier, or the reverse?

In civilizations such as Greece and Rome, much concerning the ownership rights—and corresponding obligations of treatment—were written into positive law. Slaves could be bought and sold, and left to heirs, but the rights concerning slaves were limited by standards that may be surprising to some who have a view of history in progress—i.e., slavery was another bad thing that was overcome, and we don't allow that sort of thing now.

But there were treatises written by the philosophers of these ancient economies which sound much like commentators on the current state of social welfare programs. Comments included remarks about the passive character of the slavish personality, their propensity toward laziness and sensual indulgences, and their dependency on resources provided by others. Such statements lead toward the justification of slavery, due to the fact that a certain class of people is, for whatever reason, resistant to personal initiative, and need to be directed and cared for. That these individuals might be obligated by threat of violence to obey someone else who has acquired a right of control, seemed like a just exchange, given their overall character deficiencies. [20]

At the time of Greece, and then Rome, slaves made up about twenty five percent of the labor force, and discharged a diverse assortment of tasks—including the management of businesses. Some of the conditions are brutal—as in obligatory sexual labor, and in heavy public works projects—and some not—as in the performance of skilled labor and management. The simplest explanation of slavery lies in the fact that there are many necessary tasks which persons prefer not to do themselves. Getting others to perform those tasks with acts of violence made at least as much sense as forcing sovereignty and taxes on citizens with acts of violence. In a state where government itself communicates obligation through violence, the coordination of human affairs at other levels is apt to mirror coercion as an organizing principle.

This is not the case—as indicated before—because it has to be, but because an organizing principle is replicative, i.e., it affects adaptive choices through which participants in a system make sense of it. Slavery makes sense in micro-economic relations because it makes sense macro-economically. Where the governing principle of state consists in the service and protection of the ruler, then in accord with that logic, his or her principal agents exist in a state of service, who in turn exist as masters to others who exist to serve them. At some point existence, stripped of titles and privileges that the king confers on subordinate participants, leaves nothing left to define the person except "slave"—i.e., a person who exists for no other purpose than to serve. [21]

That is essentially what it means to have acquired a state of consciousness. There is within a stable and sustainable economic strategy a basis in which value is conferred on what it means to be a human being, and from which social relationships necessary for production acquire ethical content. The existence of slavery was thus close to the heart of control economy. One's existence is to serve, and the rest is naught but raiment bestowed by a ruler. This, of course, was quite a shift from life in a wild economy.

A number of rulers have established among their subjects, a personage entitled "freeman," a provocative word deriving from Sanskrit "pria" meaning "to love (take delight in)." A "freeman" however, was not what is viewed in modern times as an essential predicate of existence—rights of autonomy and self-expression—but literally meant someone who was loved by the king. This signaled, perhaps, an individual who was granted admission into a select group who participated in the sanity of the king—an environment in which love is shared in games of language.

Notwithstanding palliatives such as these, the logos of control economy imagines a fairly rigid and inflexible hierarchy motivated by a system of loyalties (reinforced with bribes and blackmail) that are only partially disclosed to public view. Such hierarchy is, at least theoretically, susceptible to reform into non-corruptible entities through a hierarchy of accountability in which a relationship of dependency between a manager and subordinate translates into structures of assignment and inspection that flow from the top (ruler) to the bottom (field laborer). This structure, in bureaucratic terms referred to as "chain of command," has difficulty maintaining focus on productivity, because productivity is always secondary to the safety of the ruler.

Indeed, work hierarchies governed by the principle of control tend to function as, or degrade to, audit hierarchies marked by the progressive generalization of task assignment—with larger more generalized tasks acting as a grouping for a set of smaller more specialized tasks. It works for organizations designed for one or two functions, but not for multi or omni-functional systems tasked to adapt.

As discussed in chapters two and three above, human work systems do not function naturally as abstractive hierarchies (progressive generalization of roles), but as logical hierarchies (methodologically integrated), and the ruling principle of human work systems is formulated through consensus building processes. The weakness of control-based work systems, and their dominative hierarchies becomes apparent as they attempt to get larger, and as they encounter environmental disruptions.

7. Growth within a control economy is a matter of neutralizing potential rivalry rather than the maximization and equitable distribution of productive output. Because such rivalry exists geographically—i.e., in other agriculturally supplied kingdoms, the logic of control requires the appropriation of the resources of potential rivals and the expansion of rule through conquest. The name ascribed to this phenomenon is "empire." While empire represents an innovation in the economics of city states, it does not materially change the order and rationale of control economy. It ultimately collapses under its own weight—but not without putting up a fight.

Empire is apt to become part of the game of survival in a world driven by military imperatives. Part of its logic is the avoidance of conquest through conquest. While there may appear to be some available defensive strategies, the danger of a defensive logic is that it is stationary and reactive, while an aggressive recourse is creative and active. Military organization cannot evolve effectively without an effective flow of feedback information of periodic military engagement. War tests the technology of armaments and strategies, and the viability of leadership. Since a defensive pose waits to be overthrown, overthrow is assured with the sufficient passage of time. Within a military logic, expansion toward empire is often the only economic strategy that makes sense.

Just as control economy justifies rule through the appropriation of religious deities, empire supports aggression with a cultural mission to civilize its foes. Along with the aggressive course of empire, therefore, one will encounter media effective in the transmission of culture—(1) the diversification of Deity, (2) the formalization of a spoken langue in a phonetic alphabet and (3) the issuance of currency and the support of its value. Though we tend to equate the third development with "economy" the others are part of the economic order.

The diversification of Deity allows a conqueror to offer its own culture as a palatable substitute for that which is displaced by conquest. It operates as a statement of tolerance toward the content of religious worship, and in effect disarms spiritually poised opposition likely to remain in the hearts of a conquered people. The pagan gods of the Roman Empire were presented in a way that accommodated and benefitted from local religious practices of a conquered people, to the point of cynicism.

A principal milestone in the transmission of culture is the adoption of the conqueror's language. But the spoken language is itself extremely malleable. Take, for example, the conquest of the Philippines by the Spanish. In less than two hundred years, a hybrid language later named Tagalag developed which combined native dialects with Spanish, but the temporary occupation of Spain prevented a more complete transition to Spanish. The language continues now and is close to the heart of most Philippinos. English, however, carries more official weight, is spoken fluently by a majority of population, and is used in most written commercial communication.

One of the first phonetic alphabets devised served the ancient Greek language and helped disseminate Greek through the conquests of Alexander the Great. Cities, streets, and numerous landmarks were marked with Greek letters. One needed to be able to speak, write and think in Greek to participate effectively in Alexandrian commerce. The Romans copied the Greeks, and thus spread Roman ideas around the Mediterranean, though the stronger reasons for learning Latin were commercial—to trade in goods marketed internationally, and to benefit from laws of property and contract devised under Roman thought.

This was related, of course, to the issuance of currency, as currency signifies the formation of a marketplace, and a conscious decision to allow markets to emerge and wealth to accumulate. A decision of this nature is not easy from the perspective of a dictator, who by nature tends to approach matters of social organization very conservatively. If a dictator holds control, and produces a surplus which supplies an army, why would he or she experiment with productivity if the result tends to produce rivals? The issuance of currency cedes control to others in that it provides access to resources through which others can organize.

If the nature of control economy were experimental and innovative, currency would have appeared near the inception of the Bronze Age, but did not appear, however, until about 600 B.C.E., as part of the formation of empires and phonetic alphabets used as a means of translating and teaching language among conquered states. [22]

The formation of commercial networks enabled by the issuance of currency is more of an instrumentality of Empire thinking, than it was a commercial innovation derived from the genius of empire builders—or part of the "advance" of civilization. It would not likely occur except where protections were in place regulating against dangerous accumulations of currency in potential rivals.

It is not much different than the decision of what to do with a person after they have been converted to slave. They carry with them subsistence costs, and generally speaking, it is cheaper to cover those costs and benefit from their labor than to deal with the security costs attendant to abuse and starvation. So, decisions about the formation of commercial structures are essentially defensive, while dictators continue at what got them to where they are and refocus on the expropriation of the retained earnings accumulated by others.

The beneficiaries of empire imagine a world organized as a Ponzi operation, where new acquisitions fund the cost of past acquisitions. The problem, as in all control-based systems, consists in the maintenance of control organizationally, in an environment where security costs exceed subsistence costs. This seems to have been what happened in Rome, about 2000 years ago. Rome's fall has attracted a number of different explanatory hypotheses. All theories seem to argue that the armies of Rome were not adequate to preserve the social order Rome had created, but have offered different reasons for it. The most modern explanations are economic.

One argues that a viable Roman economy never really existed, and that its source of wealth was based on the plunder of wealth gathered within its control. Rome reached a point where it had to levy taxes to support its military. This intruded on subsistence capacities of agriculture, thereby resulting in the cessation of agricultural production on a grand scale. The essential weakness of Rome was that it came under predictable economic pressures while functioning under primitive motives related to coerced labor. This left a void in what contemporary economies refer to as a middle class of purchasers. [23]

Another theory argues similarly that since political survival in Rome was based on the maintenance of a loyal army, the ruling Emperor was forced to raise taxes beyond the productive capacity of farms and businesses. Since there was no income to tax, Rome began to requisition property, still to cover military expenses. The ruler also passed laws preventing occupational transition, effectively conscripting individuals to continue in occupations which were not paying. This produced a fair amount of economic chaos, and frantic efforts to establish smaller self-sufficient economic units around landed estates which had been exempt from taxation due to long standing agreements within the aristocratic class. [24]

The problem of maintaining control over an empire—in Rome and in other contexts—falls within a "theory of complexity" which distinguishes between the costs of conquest and the costs of preserving conquest. Human behavior within a marketplace is quite complicated, and difficult to predict because such behavior is adaptive—meaning that the rules of the game change depending on the circumstances and on human perception of the circumstances. Rome's theory of control by use of positive law (commands) and military coercion wasn't enough to preserve order, and attempts to restore order by spending more on security was making problems worse. [25]

This observation essentially engages the questions we first summarized in the first chapter. Does a control-based strategy have inherent problems which cannot be resolved through increased control measures? Is big government doomed to failure?

There are reasons to say "yes" to this question. First, as a general rule, the adaptive responses of a marketplace increase as the types of economic activity increase. Thus, when one contemplates a shift from simple agrarian productive systems, to international trade and then to industrial systems, complexity multiplies faster than the control capability of a given government institution. Government then delegates productive functions to organizations it doesn't control directly, but endeavors to maintain control of by offering exclusive access to certain markets. Arrangements of this nature are likely to involve complex political negotiations, the effect of which may, or may not, satisfy the subsistence needs of the populace. These needs are likely to magnify if and when the public learns that neighboring states are distributing more to their subjects. The purpose of such combinations is to assure that government benefits in productive surpluses that emerge, and to prevent organizations emerging within the market from acquiring sufficient influence to depose the ruling authority.

The development of government sponsored "monopoly" of this nature are part of the highly variable reward systems—essentially corrupt—woven into the fabric of control systems. This particular strategy was, in effect, the strategy pursued by German nationalists prior to the Second World War, and is currently being pursued by China—where government acts as industrial sponsor to monopolies that share their wealth with the points of military control over the society. This species of corruption consists in the assertion of legal protections to business entities which feed gains to government leaders. Monopoly consists in the elimination of competition due to advantages derived from government.[26]

The corruption (and inefficiency) of control economies organizing around delegated monopolies are vulnerable to foreign or domestic overthrow. Their successors then attempt to eliminate corruption by endeavoring to manage production directly. This was, in effect, the social experiment of Communism put into effect by Russia in the early 20th Century. A fascinating aspect of this experiment is that despite its inception as a perceived antidote to the immoral practices of a preceding autocracy, its own version of control could not claim moral superiority. There were massive enslavements of industrial and agricultural labor at subsistence, with the majority of the surplus going back toward the support of military organization and bureaucracy.

In the process, Russia managed to industrialize, but did so through coercion, and thus without the enthusiasm and creative participation of its subjects. The logical outlet appeared to be in an ideologically fueled military expansion, occurring in midcentury following the demise of the ideologically motivated conquests of Germany. When a German empire failed, Russia then installed a Soviet Empire to assume control over Eastern Europe.

The German and Russian experiences, both beginning with ideologically compelling narratives (and the claim of "knowledge" of good and evil), nonetheless manifested oppressive influence over their subjects. In the case of German totalitarianism, there was a cultural ideal, and an authoritarian sense of order offered as solution to severe economic disruption in the systems of finance and industry. In Russia it was a theory of history and social injustice and blame cast upon monarchic authorities unable to address the disruptions associated with the industrial revolution.

From a number of different perspectives, it seemed that something new was happening, but from the perspective of organization that was not the case. In fact, it seemed like the same formula which had been in effect in the ascendency of Sumer. Versions of the human representing an objectified and stagnant ideal—Deity removed from a lively and responsive place within consciousness, to a place subject to the control of rulers. These ideals were, as always, used to unify and motivate public support of the new regime, while the true ruling principle was manifest in the hyper-militarization of government investments, followed by a government policy of Empire.

What was different at this point were much more advanced mechanical technologies available for productive output, allowing a much larger subsistence surplus. But since these technologies also affected the lethality of military technologies, they contributed to a sense of military urgency the world had not yet seen—and as a consequence, military aggressions unimaginable even from the perspective of the conquests of the Roman Empire.

Another difference between the emergences of these empires was an effective opposition lodged by systems of law and economy that arguably represent an improvement over the ancient model. These new systems claim to have emerged victorious in this competition. However, these new systems were and are in nascent form, and are only partially understood. The effect, it seemed, was the containment of conquest oriented governmental structures, and a sense of victory for a different version of economy.

# Chapter 5

# Behavioral Economy

1. A number of writers have argued that the domination of economy by military interests is an historical constant which has not and will not change. While there is an attractive sense of irony to this argument, irony may not be the best measure of the truth of it.

In the last chapter, we were preoccupied with how and why the notion of "control" is wrested from intuitively based self-organizing properties of language and arrived at the more cynical view that "control" leads to a military economy. The basis for this conclusion is that control creates hazards which recycle into an increased need for control. Within this logic, military priorities might prevent the sharing of productive surplus with the residents of a militarily occupied territory.

One way of challenging the logic of control economy is to allow for the existence of a benevolent ruler. But as we indicated previously, despite a ruler's best intentions, the aggressiveness of foreign states, and the expectations created by generosity makes the return of productive surplus to residents hazardous. The more likely strategy of a benevolent ruler—within the logic of control—is strengthening of the ruler's military, the redistribution of surplus as unexpected "gifts," and the hoarding of treasure as a reserve against future challenges. Benevolence as a ruling principle is secondary to safety—which is what proponents of the military theory of economy seem to be saying.

What if one could demonstrate that benevolence made the ruler even safer? Suppose that one could show that happy and motivated subjects produce more and that production can produce bigger armies. The problem in that argument is that benevolence leads to expectations which at some point make the populace more difficult to control, thereby making the ruler less safe than before.

It may be difficult to productively motivate people while they are working within the constraints of a given ruler's needs. The social psychosis of masses held within the drone of propaganda is one of a number of indicia that human behavior is complicated, and that motivation may have much to do with the establishment of an individual sense of sovereignty which is—in principle—antithetical to control economy.

But that isn't a consideration in the control-oriented ruler, as behavioral considerations are a means to control, and not the end. The ruler is not, in other words, looking to use control to make people happy and productive, but looking to use happiness and productivity as a way of securing control. The human species evolved a language, however, which allows it to pierce such burlesque. What remains is a state without credibility getting people to do what is necessary through threats of violence.

The name for economy which seeks to liberate natural motivational processes in order to secure and distribute larger surpluses is "behavioral economy" because of its interest in production as a behavioral phenomenon. It is also often referred to as "market" economy because of its interest in the adaptive behavior of persons pursuing interests in an economic marketplace. A defining characteristic of behavioral economy as here presented is that it occurred because of a shift of awareness of similar magnitude and importance to that represented in the shift from wild to control economy.

A description of behavioral economy thus begins with a critique of control economy, something already implicit in its description. It is not clear that the shift from wild to control economies was, in fact, a shift of human consciousness.

A credible—though not necessarily true—description of the great agricultural reforms if the Bronze Age is that these reflect less of a shift of consciousness than a shift away from consciousness. If within a definition of consciousness, one includes a socially formed ethical center, then a slave economy would reflect the opposite of consciousness. The use of deity as an externality whose design is to control or disrupt the natural development of ethical awareness can be regarded as a dissolution of consciousness, converting the human being as consciousness to something more like a beast subject to domestication.

Notwithstanding these refinements, there does appear to have been a change in the way humanity regards itself. The identification of ruling elite with godliness, or ethical purity, and the debasement of the rest as "labor" subject to manipulation, was quite a change of perspective, and was legally and economically stable. What qualifies it as a shift of awareness is the fact that its motivating force overwhelmed competing versions of awareness, and rulers along with the ruled had no choice on what to do. The question at this point is whether a new change of equal importance has occurred that has removed at least part of the world from the negative aspects of control economy.

Fair evidence of the fact that something new has happened consists in a nearly universal acknowledgement of the motivational inefficiency of control economy. There does not, however, appear to be much consensus in the diagnosis of the cause of this inefficiency.

One might begin with the motivational structure of master and slave. The slave labors at the behest of the master, and the master compensates the slave at subsistence. This motivational structure is inefficient because the master is obligated to support the slave at subsistence in any event, and so there is little to no motivation for the slave to produce more. The master starves unless he or she can devise punishments short of death to motivate the slave. This is the classic picture of a slave under the lash of the master.

But some might argue that this picture reflects an unrealistic extreme, and that a technology of motivation might be developed within a controlled economy through a process of experimentation. What will happen, for example, if the master shares a portion of generated surplus with the slave? Theoretically one might, over time, ascertain an optimal range of compensations for the generation of surplus—i.e., a point at which the portion shared stops producing more for master than the amount shared.

This scenario represents a beginning of what it is to think like an economist, as an economist would be careful to point out here that a problem arises where the slave accumulates savings as a result of shared surplus. So, a long-term cost of shared surplus might be the loss of the slave's availability as slave due to the slave's ability to purchase freedom. The master's countermeasure would likely consist in the passage of laws which either forced the slaves to consume all of their gains, or something having the same effect in eliminating rights of property attaching to slave savings. [27]

Another solution might seek to harness the slave's motivation to live as a free individual by offering freedom as an incentive to especially productive output. Things here get rather complicated, however, as issues of trust—or the reinforcement of trust through legally imposed obligation—become an important part of the motivational structure of an emerging economy. How does one know that the master will keep the promise? What kind of legal supports are necessary to establish confidence in a master's promise to a slave? When the slave obtains a legal right to enforce promises against a ruling class, does that, of itself, compromise a necessary feature of an economic order, where "human" is defined in terms of a relationship of service to a given ruler?

In the process of answering questions like these, some of the weaknesses of the slave economies of control present themselves as inherent, or intrinsic. If sharing surpluses generated by higher productivity tends to dislodge slaves from a state of dependency, their availability as slave is undermined—but sharing future output is essential to the maintenance of higher productivity, and the offer of shared futures are ineffective motivationally without legal protections that alter the status and commercial identity of labor.

This problem, it seems, offers the best explanation of why, for millennia, the control economies of agricultural cultivation sought to repress expectancies of gain beyond subsistence, and instead sought to increase fortunes (while simultaneously reducing the risks associated with neighboring surpluses) by plundering other treasuries through conquest, and with severe punishments administered to its subjects for the communication of resistance.

It is easier, perhaps, to identify a problem of this nature by discussing the ethical relationship between work product and property. There is more than one kind of property—one which we associate with personal labor, and another which has strategic significance to a ruler. The first ethically reposes in laborer, while the second is subject to claim by force of the controlling ruler. It was the basis of a famous distinction in common law between what is known as "personal property" and "real property" the latter of which is controlled by the sovereign and delegated to agriculture regions of production.

Where, however, does the notion of a "business" or "firm" fit into these schemata? One might argue that since a business is the product of labor, it ethically attaches as "property" to the builder(s) of the business, but on the other hand, because it fits more centrally in to systems of production affecting the entire state, it belongs to the ruler. The resources of the geographic region subject to organized labor belong to the ruler—

whether the ruler is a single individual or a collective—though the labor may attribute to someone's organizing genius.

As a general principle, the assignment of ownership based on the importance of roles is fraught with political disagreement, and as such, is not stable. In a control economy, the disagreement is resolved by having the ruler treat the resources of the state as his or her own, while delegating to a class of organizers special responsibilities and compensations.

This way of separating a ruling class from a class of common laborers is simple to formulate and enforce in agrarian productive systems, but ambiguity over the importance of roles between owner and organizer remains. This ambiguity worsens considerably when administrative constraints are considered. The ruler may want to own the business developed by one of his or her subjects, but may be incapable (for a number of reasons) of doing so.

The more serious concern, however, is in the threat that the organization of resources poses to the ruler because the ruler cedes control over currency and personnel to an individual. If the ruler takes the business, he or she effectively discourages creativity and resourcefulness in the formation of organization. But if one allows an individual to keep the business, they are at risk of being subject to the demands and influence of the individual in a number of different ways. This situation is, as indicated above, comparable to the situation of a slave buying his or her way out of slavery, and then avoiding the obligation of slave.

Macro-economically, this is apt to translate in the mind of the ruler as a risk of assassination and is thus unacceptable. Therefore, as control economy develops a need to promote the formation of businesses, so develops a need to establish a relationship of dependency between the business and the ruler. This, as acknowledged in the last chapter, is normally accomplished through the ruler's offering its coercive authority and wealth in the establishment of monopoly.

Monopoly is slightly more efficient than direct ownership by the government, only because the monopolist functions under threat of the removal of government protection of exclusive access to a market. The monopolist is thus motivated to reduce cost of business in order to generate surplus, and to maintain quality sufficient to assure the continued purchase of the product by the public. He or she must also assist the ruler in concealing surplus from the public, along with the payment to the ruler for the protective services of monopoly.

As discussed in the preceding chapter, when this sort of behavior is examined through the lens of modern market economies it is often called "corruption" because of a concealed relationship between a so called "private" sector of business and the ruling elite. But as the last chapter revealed, modern corruption may be more about the concealment of control-based structure of many modern economies, and not a change of a way of doing business.

While the inefficiencies of monopoly are widely known and appreciated throughout the world, they are naught but another device by which ruling elite appropriate surplus from labor. People pay more and receive less for monopolized products and services. There are certain kinds of monopolies, of course, that are useful and valuable, but sorting through and regulating such monopolies is unlikely and impermanent within the design of a control economy. The productive regulation of monopoly is only likely in a behavioral economy, a matter we will address in various ways below.

2. We like to think we are different now, but what is the substance of that difference? One way of explaining it is that we came to the realization that "civilization" under conquest economies lacked an important ingredient, which came gradually along with religious edifications emerging within human consciousness.

Another way of explaining the difference is that we never really changed, and that the deficiencies of control economy finally yielded to certain realities about the nature of the human being. The latter hypothesis would be that preferred by the movement in Europe we associate with The Enlightenment, and the emergence of science, beginning about five hundred years ago. The Enlightenment view is that if we understand things better, we can devise systems that validate and uplift humanity, and in the process, support more creative and productive risks.

Popular opposition to a debased view of humanity, however, had been around for a while, since the dawn of what is now referred to as the Axial Age. Some writers are impressed with the temporal proximity of spiritual movements in different parts of the world—between 600 B.C. and 100 A.D, which seemed to have in common an ethical value emphasizing kind and thoughtful behavior toward others.

One of the greatest of these is based on the narrative of the life of Siddhartha, a self-displaced prince of a kingdom somewhere near what is presently called Bangladesh. As the narrative goes, he became disillusioned with comforts of royalty upon the discovery of suffering in the world and set out on a quest to determine why suffering exists and whether there was a way to end it. Along the way he sampled the mysticism of a group of ascetics, who promoted the idea that the elimination of suffering and the achievement of enlightenment occurred only through the renunciation of all worldly comforts. But Siddhartha later discovered that this renunciation was unnecessary and achieved enlightenment through meditations which aroused compassion and assistance toward the suffering of others. The achievement of enlightenment had other benefits, apparently, as he transcended material consciousness and became Buddha, performing miracles and other supernatural acts, and could teach others to do the same—thus forming the basis of a religious movement.

Important in the development of Buddhism as a religious movement was a revised theology that consciously resisted the promotion of exterior deities—i.e., specifically renouncing God as an exterior or objective presence, and moving spiritual presence inward. One could live, therefore, without an externally derived positive law, and exist in a state of contentment by emphasizing a sense of goodness emerging from within. God's existence became almost irrelevant, but existence as an ethical phenomenon became relevant. Among a number of strategies adopted by Buddhists in the pursuit of their religious beliefs was the formation of remote monastic orders with no wealth to attract plundering conquerors, and they were able to preserve and promote their movement for centuries.

Another "countercultural" movement had been an important part of the Judaic tradition in the area currently known as the Middle East, which had come under the influence of civilizations located in what are now called India and Greece. By the time Jesus appeared, Judaism had already appropriated an internally generative monotheism (as opposed to external deity), and ethically benevolent moral precepts into its theology. However, according to the narrative of Jesus, Jewish rulers in Palestine had made a practical decision to collaborate with Roman dynasties and serve the Roman Empire—an understandable choice given the alternative. [28]

While a number of political movements arose with intentions to disrupt this collaboration, the message of Jesus emphasized the incompleteness of the vision of the human evident in Roman conquest and localized Judaic complicity. Human nature is not as slave, but as an existential expression of God, analogous to relationship of "father" to "son" and is revealed in loving-kindness, and in healing. This message effectively repositions deity more intimately with human identity—from an external to an internal influence, and with it brings the human forward as an expression of an ethical God, formed by God within an ethical universe.

This resembled the message of the Buddhists, developed some three hundred years previously, except a number of things interfered with the preservation of the message. It was, after all was said and done, expressed within the domain of an aggressively situated Roman Empire, and offered as a spiritual antidote to the withered view of the human as slave (existing only to serve the king) and thus by many as a refutation of the importance of coercively based dominion. The narrative includes the transcendence of a violent act—crucifixion—along with the emergence of a religious movement which flowered among subjects of Roman order, and later became the official religion of the Roman Empire. Rome fell, but the religious movement remained intact, moving its center slightly east to Constantinople.

But since the religious movement did not—as with the Buddhist movement—separate from a secular world, it was subjected to modifications designed, in essence, to replace the internally situated deity of personal salvation and healing with an external deity subject to human definition. Within a few centuries the basic narrative was revised, and Jesus was identified as the one and only offspring of an externally positioned anthropomorphic god. His role was to establish a procedure through which individuals might ascend to heaven if they suffered patiently with the various injustices imposed upon them by a secular ruler. Around this view was established a hierarchically organized Christian church. It was, in effect, a repetition of the old formula of control, except that religious organization was organized internationally, as a service agency to a gathering of monarchies.

This corruption, which had been going on for quite some time, ultimately came under examination. There were a number of transformative, and related, events occurring roughly within the same time-frame—i.e., the diversification and reformation of religious orientations associated with Christianity, the beginning of the scientific revolution, the exploration of and trade with other regions of the world, and the opportunity to form new republics in newly populated territories.

It is useful here to identify a value which was sufficiently impactive to break a rehearsed legal and economic narrative—in this case at least two powerful counter-narratives juxtaposing the human-as-beast (selfish and manipulative) with the human-as-spiritual (generous and honest).

One can thus make an historical argument to the effect that when an ethical view of humanity received sufficient stimulation, history would and did provide opportunities for systemic change.

The kind of change we are considering here had to accommodate a much more crowded environment, which meant there was no going back to wild economy, but had to celebrate the kind of value that once brought primitive and uncrowded societies to life. For this reason, one can hardly deny the historical importance of legal innovations arriving along with the tide of enlightenment philosophy, religious reformation, and science.

They were not presented as political arguments, but statements about human nature, and revealing flaws in the sense of obligation prevailing within control economies that had dominated the human landscape for thousands of years. The task of establishing these views within a productive legal and economic matrix that accommodated evolved production technologies and currencies was not attempted until the emergence of what some call the industrial revolution.

The attempt did not at first resemble a systematic implementation or plan, but instead proceeded as a set of thought experiments formed around seemingly naïve questions such as "what if we do nothing?" The answer to that question seemed self-evident—several thousands of years of war, an agricultural landscape freckled with castles and other military structures, and quite a lot of coercively organized human labor.

But since we have not left the laboratory of hypothetical thought, more questions might follow, such as "what if we limit or restrict military intervention of market participants, and thus eliminate death or enslavement as a consequence of competitive failure?" The process of answering that question produced a theoretical treatise on the equilibria likely to occur within a competitive marketplace—Adam Smith authored "The Wealth of Nations."

An analysis of this sort could continue indefinitely, the points of which all seeking to anticipate the behavioral consequences of the introduction of different kinds of restrictions (and incentives), all brought as legally enforced obligations—as Law. This sort of intellectual activity marks what theorists refer to as "modern" economics. Since it is a mentally transformative economic event reflecting an interest in many nuances of human behavior within a marketplace, it is here referred to as "behavioral economics."

At the core of behavioral economics is recognition that we might be better off doing nothing at all—i.e., not controlling, or in making nuanced adjustments affecting the incentives of market participants. The self-organizing properties of human nature are likely to be more motivated and efficient if the ruler stays out of the way, for the most part, and assists commerce by way of legal interventions—such as the incarceration of predatory monopolists.

    3. How do we conceive a state of law in which doing nothing, despite the formation of fiercely competitive institutions, is a plausible option? As indicated above, the first rule of behavior is the separation of military power from productive firms and institutions (market participants), such that the state is sole possessor of such influence. This does not, however, represent a change from control-based economies. Allowing for one and only one security force is an essential rule of control—i.e., to protect the ruler from invasion. It is also, an important consideration in behavioral economies. The state must be able to protect against the appropriation of its military force, or it will be dissolved by other control motivated institutions—and thus lapse backward into control economy.

    The real point of difference is the establishment of a legal boundary between productive institutions and government, which removes the ruler as a direct beneficiary of the competitive behavior established by the rules within which market competition occurs. This is quite a change, because it alters the basis and terms under which authoritative figures assemble military agency. The safety of the ruler, at least theoretically, can be eliminated as a ruling principle of economic order, and be replaced with something enlightenment philosophers referred to as the "common good."

    While it was not entirely clear what that meant, one thing that was clear is that it was the sort of thing that would be part of a consensus building process. Almost by definition, this process invokes a game of language, such that within a behavioral economy, the concept of "state" replaces ruler, and the "state" then must exercise military power in conformity with conscience generated by the "I" in conversation with a public Other.

    The behavioral economy thus begins with an effort to restore a lost process by which conscience forms through dialogue. The more basic problem in the design of a process is the accommodation of dissenting viewpoints—which was not a problem in wild economy given the liberty available to branch away from uncomfortable disagreements.

The conception of such an objective is somewhat complicated. There are three major features to the formation of something of this sort: (1) participative rule setting (the vote), (2) coherent judicial practices (the rule of law) and (3) the protection of personal liberties essential to the formation of identity (civil rights). [29]

It is a generally accepted wisdom that majoritarian consensus used as the sole basis for the establishment of law is not a good thing. Aside from logistical difficulties in management of majority rule as a basis of policy—there being a need for efficient, focused and adaptive decision making—the encouragement of majority rule frequently produces the opposite of conscience-based policies. Without more in the way of commitment to the continuity of dialogue, a temporary majority is likely to attempt to dominate a minority in unethical ways, thereby encouraging the kinds of political countermeasures which lead directly back to control economy. The vote is more of a stimulative principle which, in effect, forces dialogue on matters of obligation by establishing accountability of leaders to popular interests to share—rather than hoard—productive surplus.

A further commitment to law, in accordance with the "rule of law," refers to coherency and consistency in the passage and application of laws, within a lexicon that applies equally to all people, or rather, allows coherent universal participation.

This would, as a matter of principle, also avoid the formation of laws designed to appropriate "property" or "opportunity" (not easily distinguishable) from a select individual or minority assemblage of individuals. The "rule of law" thus includes a requirement that formal obligations expressed through sovereign political processes be supported by a convincing rationale—other than its tendency to benefit a single individual or class of persons. That is to say, law cannot be used merely for the purpose of the favorable transfer of surplus to a politically influential person or group, and thus in concept negates an organizing principle of control economies.

This constraint partners effectively with the placement of value on personal autonomy of those subject to government, and the protection of individual liberties. These protections are imposed as obligation of government, and thus represent a significant reversal of many centuries of control-based rule emphasizing the absoluteness of sovereignty. While many personal liberties are regarded as valuable by absolute rulers, it is not the value of the liberties identified, but the fact that they qualify the authority of sovereign rule.

In control economies, a civil right would not represent a coherent idea because the nature of control-based sovereignty is to establish ethical dependency in both the minds and actions of its subjects. But since this principle is renounced in behaviorally situated sovereignty—and replaced by a conversation that requires mutual adaptation between sovereign and subject—an individual has a formally recognized moral standing to assert his or her claim against sovereignty.

More interesting perhaps, are the types of individual liberties moved to a protected status. Constitutional protections extended to speech, association, religion and privacy serve to assist the subjects of constitutional government in the formation and preservation of autonomous personhood. This contention is correct, as far as it goes, but it may be useful to examine the structural change in political communication in order to understand how the protection of personhood reflects and enhances a shift of consciousness—i.e., a transition from control to behavioral economy.

Control strategies tend to replace a presentive orientation to communication with religion acting to validate a given ruler, but behavioral structures eliminate sponsorship of religion and use adaptive social value as an institutional surrogate for a presentive level of communication.

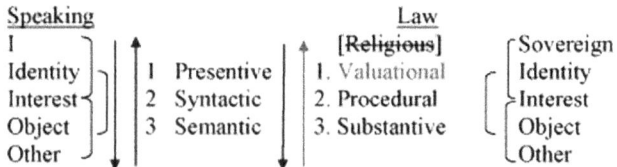

Given the exigency of competition, one is to be impressed at the resulting structures of government born in the eighteenth century which, despite a number of challenges, have been able to establish and preserve the peaceful exchange of information between large masses of people. But these structures are limited by the absence of awareness for why they are successful, something that makes the adaptation of these structures to disruptive occurrences in the environment lethargic.

Human behavior blends instinctively with a system that sets up the type of information exchange in which moral identities form. Along with this is an instinctive reaction to the constraining influences of totalitarian rulers. The legal removal of measures by which such rulers dominated their subjects was a matter of retrospection, that is, in remembering the means by which totalitarian societies of the past sought to intimidate and control their subjects.

The human being, as social animal, therefore did not need to be very self-aware to establish constitutional restrictions on government, because human experience had already revealed an impressive inventory of the devices by which ruling elites intimidate laborers—a list which, though impressive, is more of an historical record than a logically cohesive summary of the science of intimidation. The safer assumption is that human imagination has and will continue to find new ways to do so. So, while deep cultural self-awareness may not be needed to write the laws necessary to transition into a behavioral economy, it may have to become more self-aware to preserve such an economy against creative human efforts to undermine it.

It is therefore unremarkable that legally protected rights gather around those conditions necessary for the formation of identity. These would include a right to privacy, to the formation and practice of religious beliefs, to assemble and participate in associations, and a right to fair processes preceding the expropriation of liberty and property, all of which are essential to the formation and preservation of selfhood. Human interest in individualized selfhood is what motivates and structures a presentive level in political discourse.

The utility of adaptively integrated political processes is that they appear to accomplish what language standing alone cannot. They allow for the maintenance of governmental structures necessary to sustain much larger economies than those contemplated in a wild economy. This amounts to an innovation reflecting an awareness of the behavioral deficiencies of human beings placed in a crowded and competitive social environment and the various forms of madness engendered by such environments. As we explained previously, wild economies cannot sustain ethical organization beyond a certain population, and the burning question for thousands of years had been whether the species could form complex societies without engaging control-based government—i.e., rulers engaged in ruthless practices designed to identify and destroy rivals.

4. Was it, therefore, a shift of consciousness that produced this innovation, or a lucky combination of events? Does it matter? Well, if it was a shift of consciousness, then it is likely to be more stable in the future than if it was a matter of luck, as the preservation of such changes in the face of challenging circumstances depends more on the ethical. We will henceforth refer to economic behavior of this nature as "creative risk" because it occurs within an environment engineered to encourage

productive initiative. It is thus distinguished from "destructive risk" which is oriented less toward the formation of productive enterprises and more toward the elimination of rivalry and the expropriation of the accumulated savings of others.

An error in the evaluation of the motivational efficiency of unhindered commercial activity consists in the imagination of an ethical, as opposed to a practical difference between privately and publicly formed institutions. Organization is a matter of technology, the success or failure of which depends on a proper understanding of it. In a behavioral economy, institutional failure is treated as a correctible deficiency, diagnosed and treated as a matter of science—an economic problem.

A social priority is apt to be neglected if the organization of resources are insufficient to the scale of the project involved, the most important resource being the discretional sophistication of the governmental agent on whom responsibility for the success of a given project rests. This suggests a number of different scenarios.

1. A program run by individuals with insufficient imagination to understand and accommodate the complexity of the task involved. (incompetence)

2. A program run by sophisticated individuals who do not have effective implementational resources and authority to bring about desired results. (undercapitalization)

3. A program run by sophisticated individuals with ample authority, but who are subject to interference by political and commercial forces opposed to their mission. (corruption)

These problems do not inhere in organization, but are, rather, matters which challenge a technology of organization—and which may include knowing when to do nothing. The more compelling question—at least in the conception of behavioral economy—is not whether we can assure the efficiency of government programs, but how government should situate itself within an economic system that includes market-based pressures in most of its organizational choices.

The tendency of market participants to seek ways of avoiding competition is fairly regarded as an organizational constant. In other words, organization is present not only in the formation of firms to compete within a market, but also in efforts among firms to organize the market. As a consequence, the modern economist considers the impact of government interventions on the human tendency to cooperatively organize both within and among market participants. As a general rule, the role of government is to make it easier to organize to become more competitive, and harder to organize to avoid competition.

Many businesses—particularly those in weakly governed economies—find that the best way to increase profits is to find ways to secure government acquiescence to or endorsement of anti-competitive practices. A discussion of this nature leads us to the first aspect of innovation mentioned above—i.e., a government set up under motivations which avoid a sense of dependency on a given ruler. The development of an ethically coherent rule against such dependency is prescriptive, a legal matter. The implementation of a system that adheres to the rule is descriptive, an economic matter. Our examination of the ethical coherency of the rule is referred to in this chapter as "behavioral economy." Without an expectation of coherency, it is impossible to develop a meaningful sense of whether an economic order is moving toward or away from it. [30]

Our use of the phrase "behavioral economy" is designed as an acknowledgment that organization is a behavior that occurs within and between institutions, and that the task of government is to understand organization well enough so that it can be selective in the type of organization it allows. Organization is not dependent or ancillary to market processes, but part of the substance of them. As such, it is inevitable—and expected—that at some point market participants will attempt to recruit government officials to their commercial objectives.

The corruption of political processes tends to be good only for the few able to gain positions of advantage through competitive access to government. But the effect is demoralizing to those who either do not have access, or those who for moral reasons refuse to participate in corruptive exchanges. There isn't much economic literature about the behavioral impact of corrupt government on productivity, though it is as obvious as an elephant in a small room. If one allows the elephant in as a calf, one may not be able to get it out as an adult.

What is more difficult is determining the clarity, frequency and weight of interactive communication between the rule setters and the rule breakers before a stable social system emerges. Here the line between law and economy is apt to blur the most; as how we want people to behave (law) and how they actually behave (economy) become confused. The confusion is evident in the reward of a variety of anti-social behaviors brought on in part by the anonymity of those engaged in competitive activity.

There is a person who has acquired fame in the rehabilitation of dogs and who is able to vividly demonstrate how bad dogs escalate from relatively tranquil, to frightfully aggressive and territorial states of mind. He is frequently able to heal this tendency in the course of a single session by maintaining watch over the animal, and periodically interrupting the escalation of rage with corrective gestures, and thus leads the animal toward self-correction. These treatments are reinforced with socialization process—living for a period of time with others it had perceived as threats.

For competitive markets, however, there is little in the way of reformatory socialization available, as competitions within market environments unfold less like cooperative societies and more like pit fighting. This effect can be consciously changed through intelligent choices—but choices made as to behavioral ends and means are the appropriate province of government, where public trust and confidence in the formation of obligation reposes.

A problem arises with the formation of associations designed to conduct business. Since government is designed to preserve its continuity despite the independent organization of resources, a "corporation" can assemble resources without much government interference, and act with focused efficiency similar to that of a given individual and are afforded the status of "person" within the universe of commercial transactions. The decision maker for a corporate entity thus acts on the behalf of a collective interest defined in terms of production—not ethical principle—because the financial resources of investors have but one common objective in the generation of profits. These decision makers are, in effect, disabled from the aspects of self-expression which include socialization, and the real participation in the development of an ethical value. Their speech is limited to commercial interest, but can and frequently is, packaged in ethically provocative rhetoric.

This poses a problem in modern economies where the costs of communication through various available media are high, and corporate entities are able to utilize their resources to influence ethical discourse—and do so without any real ethical accountability. They can be engaged behaviorally through interventions—as in the case of hyper-aggressive canines, but cannot be engaged as real participants in the formation of socially restorative value. This is because they do not speak as human beings were genetically designed to speak.

Perhaps this is not really a problem, because the genius of constitutional government was to allow politics to function as a meta-market, while smaller commercial markets are all part of one mega-market. Within this paradigm, market-based competition is the only ruling social principle, where a marketplace functions under its own self-correcting nexus of obligation.

However, as this proposed paradigm is examined more carefully, it seems that there is a moral difference between competition within a commercial market and competition within a political market. Competition is not good unless it acquires value through the intervention of a credible authority. The source of intervention is thus burdened with an obligation which is inapplicable to participants in market games—the intervener is accountable to a moral principle in the formation of rules (good rules), where gamesters are accountable only to the rules of the game.

The suggestion that market processes are in some sense validated by political processes subject to the same standard of value as market processes amounts to the same fallacy identified in the evaluation of natural selection and logic. Natural selection does not identify the "good" in the operation of selection, but only the consequence of selective processes which may be either good or not. Competition does not "select." Rather, it is a challenge that motivates behavioral innovations. It is up to the designer of the competition to examine the behaviors it encourages, and accordingly, select rules that encourage desirable behaviors.

Behavioral economy did not emerge out of the formation of processes, but the introduction of value into processes, as well as forceful interventions oriented to that value. Therefore, a core principle of behavioral economy is the recognition that adaptive processes established for the purpose of game design rest upon a different level of importance as the game itself. As such, an economic system that fails to interface with an ethical hierarchy expressed through a system of laws is, in a manner of speaking, surrendering itself to fate. Economic order will assert itself, but it may not be the kind of order we want.

5. It may nonetheless be useful at times to refer to the politics of law-making as a game or even a marketplace, provided that one treats it

as a different sort of market, subject to a different level of ethical scrutiny. The same may be said of a number of markets, some of which deserve more vigilance than others. The marketplace of human labor is, within a behavioral economy, included among those deserving special attention.

An economy of autonomous organizations each of which have gathered their own resources together places the modern human within an entirely different landscape, so much so that the definition of what an economy is can be quite challenging. Within this environment, there is a tendency toward commercial oversimplification—i.e., the reduction of economic variables to objects, items purchasable by currency. This works well in most instances, but an exception to such reduction is the market for human labor. This exception is mandatory, because the principal objective of behavioral economy is to subordinate economy to human interest, and not the other way around.

A human being is an ethical terminal within a society of others bonded by language. Identity forms around a number of things, but one can hardly identify something more important than one's work. Moreover, one works as a contributor to economy, where nearly all put themselves to labor, and derive identity from it.

A behavioral economy, it seems, is a gathering of productively oriented individuals operating within ethically prescribed limits imposed by a collective operating within political processes which are prescribed, by design, to activate conscience. A market functioning without this degrades into a control economy. In a behavioral economy, the collective defines the terms and conditions of the economy—setting the ruling principle(s) of that economy—and not the other way around. Its purpose, therefore, is to serve a collective seeking—but not necessarily finding—a consensus-based sense of obligation.

Within such an economic order, government would treat a market of labor differently than a commodities market, and pass and administer laws that protect individuals from exploitative conduct. The fact that labor acts like a market is not an argument for leaving it alone, but quite the opposite. Market participants can own commodities, and are encouraged to think that they can, but they are discouraged from thinking they can own people. Thus, to think of behavioral economy as a way of sanctifying market competition is quite an oversimplification, inasmuch as every market carries with it different ethical considerations influencing decisions about intervention.

In other words, behavioral economy encourages vigilance in the establishment of obligation, to the point of being in control of the fairness of various competitions that emerge within it. The difference is that control over fairness is not so much designed to protect the ruler as it is to protect the participants in and beneficiaries of competitive behavior. There are no paradoxes—ethically or epistemologically—where a behaviorally situated legal system enacts controls to ensure fairness, especially in the regulation of labor practices.

Within a behavioral economy, the principal source of employment comes from the development of private enterprises—i.e., that persons with sufficient imagination and desire to organize businesses will put others to work. This classical assumption includes a self-correcting market in which businesses compete for labor, and thus refrain from treating employees as slaves for fear that they will lose them to competitors.

This rule of order, however, is widely acknowledged as untrustworthy, so much so that exploitative behavior prompted major political movements in the twentieth century to legally prohibit private employment, and having government act as a single employer. This, as it turned out, was not more than another version of control-based economy, and thus succumbed to the same coercive practices that control economies had been using all along—ideological propaganda, restrictive of individual rights of expression and privacy, and limiting wages to subsistence in order to pay for the costs of security.

Such developments reveal that the source of oppression may have more to do with practical difficulties associated with a natural human resistance to control, than with the malevolent intentions of system organizers. The problem of injustice appears to have been less about the evil of a given ruler than about the organizational pressures within which rulers act. The bad behavior typical of a control economy is an organizational phenomenon which can, at least theoretically, be corrected.

Behavioral economy alters both the character and magnitude of pressure on those placed in charge of government. It is more focused on limited objectives which alter the destructive equilibria toward which competitions tend. Ideologies are subject to dialogue and modification. Competitions proceed in accordance with rules that are socially vetted. Governmental influence over economic outcomes occurs through selective interventions within a marketplace. The assignment of work roles to individuals occurs, for the most part, within privately owned businesses because administrative burdens would likely overwhelm government attempts to do so.

The concept of ownership applied to a business is an elusive one, even to the lawyers who set them up under corporate codes, and among those who buy and sell businesses. The owners of businesses do not own the people who work in those businesses, but have somehow learned to use money and language to create systems of work, and some are better at it than others. For this reason, there is a bias toward the accumulation of resources in larger more centralized institutions that exercise significant control over the lives of their employees. The bias is based on the belief that an economy will be more productive if one allows organizational resources to accumulate with successful organizers.

Whether accomplished organizers in a modern economy will organize more production with accumulations in their capital accounts is, in a behavioral economy, treated as a working hypothesis subject to verification. They may or may not invest in creative risk, and if not, the behavioral interventions of government may best serve the public by helping to move the capital to individuals with the capability and interest in doing so. In control economies, the tendency is to over-identify the productive entity with its owner—as a king is related to his realm. In behavioral economy, production is a coalescence of roles, which over a period of time, goes through changes. To think of control over a business as "ownership" is a vestigial assertion of control economy. In a behavioral economy, the application of the concept of "property" to a business is derived from a government process capable of ethically bestowing a right to control and benefit from it.

The vestiges of control economy are likewise present in the emergence of an anthropomorphic metaphor to government—i.e., that government is like a person who builds wealth by saving money and refraining from borrowing it. Behaviorally situated governments, however, do not borrow against the obligations of Other, but against the inflation of their currency. If a government borrows in order to put people to work, the appropriate index of whether borrowing is appropriate is the effect of borrowing on the inflation of the government's currency—not the application of rote prohibitions against borrowing.

Similarly, the decision to tax individuals in order to cover government obligations is often viewed as a personal government taking money from people—reducing wealth. Taxation could be about creating supply at better prices than privately owned business could create. Taxation could be part of the redistribution of income from hoarders to spenders, and decisions of that nature are the appropriate subject of legislative deliberation over the optimal use of a nation's productive surplus.[31]

Government is not a person, but an aspect of a public dialogue—ideally establishing conditions necessary for the generation of abundant employment and protecting those that enter into a labor market from exploitative treatment.

There is nothing quite as important to the morale of a behavioral economy as a generally held belief among its members that they live in a world which will, with honest effort, supply their needs and will protect them against the appropriation of the product of their labor. As such, the "things" we refer to as "economy" and "market" are linked to a system of laws that preserve this underlying assumption. They are the creative product of law. Therefore, in a strong sense of the word, the economy resulting from a system of laws is the "shared" property of the people who enacted those laws. When a given individual or group of individuals form a business, therefore, they enter a field formed and nurtured by collectively derived obligations.

As in control economy, the rule evident macroscopically is the basis for its appearance evident microscopically. The basis of property as descriptive of an ethical relationship between a person and the product of his or her labor derives from that of an economy emerging from a public dialogue which issues and enforces laws.

There is an opposing view, which is that the market is more like a receptacle of creative activity and functions most effectively when receiving the product of this activity without interference. This view partners with another that businesses are apt to form more prolifically when they are unrestricted in their employment practices.

The proponents of this view are the same as those who argue that the concentration of wealth in fewer persons will result in the creation of more employment. Again, we encounter the remnants of control-based assumptions, here the assumption that allowing businesses to control more of their environment will stimulate creative risk.

That is a problematic assumption that should be tested by scientific observation. The better assumption is that there are environments in which creativity will flourish and others where it will not, and that one needs to understand behavior in order to engineer or organize a market. Such markets are not value neutral, but to the contrary, reflect the intervention of value though the laws that govern them. Consequently, almost all behavioral economies have legislated against discriminatory employment practices. The same principle would proscribe retaliatory conduct by employers against employees who refrain from immoral conduct, or who exercise protected rights.

It is difficult to say which of the two economic priorities identified above—i.e., (1) government stimulation of creative risk or (2) government promotion of fair employment relationships—represents the more central economic principle in behavioral economy. It may be that the stimulation of productive enterprise is the only viable source of employment, but as indicated previously, a view of economy as a shared creation of public dialogue includes the proscription of demoralizing and exploitative employment practices.

This is due to a much larger shift that has taken place, from one where the principle of order serves the safety of the king—and the hoarding of surplus for military purposes—to one where there is no king, and thus a larger emphasis on both the generation of surplus and the equitable distribution of it. Job security, wage guarantees, and the elimination of employer abuse are a high priority in an economic system dedicated to the elimination of enslaving work relationships.

While there is some theoretical basis for the belief that abundant employment opportunity will provide enough in the way of bargaining power for employees to eliminate unfair practices through their own selections, there are motivating factors within competitive markets that interfere with essential fairness, and that market selection itself cannot eliminate.

This should be self-evident in the fact that well-funded and organized firms are in a better position to bargain as employers than solitary individuals are as employees. And while the formation of employee collectives is useful at times, it is generally regarded as a poor substitute for obligatory principles governing both employers and employees. That being said, employees are generally quite fair with their employers because it is part of the nature of morally autonomous individuals to be fair. But on the other hand, the same is not the case with employers toward employees, because they are usually organized as corporate entities under competitive pressure, and this tends to blunt the sensitivity of their senior executives.

6. One might say that the persona of the corporate executive (terminology applicable to all institutionally bound consciousness) is a new phenomenon, but that would be wrong. It is actually a newer version of an old phenomenon of mind in the process of consolidating control and the elimination of rivals. The most common propensity of this mind is not promotion of creative risk through competition, but the elimination of competition through destructive risk—assimilation (conquest) and appropriation (plunder). It may appear to be competitive at a given point

in time, but is always in the process of eliminating competition, and has no real choice in the matter. The tendency is disruptive enough that modern corporations often take special counter-measures to invigorate their executives with motivational speakers celebrating creativity, collaboration, initiative and leadership.

This observation might be construed as a slight to the various corporate cultures prominent in modern economies, but it is better viewed as a way of initiating a conversation about how organizational structure influences investment. Modern economies have not, after all, eliminated the sense of risk associated with doing business. They have merely reduced it. Moreover, most continue to use delegative organizational strategies—command and inspect audit hierarchies—the design of which best serves destructive risk—conquest and plunder. So, when we attempt to discuss the viability of "marketplace" that is supposed to engage in creative risk, and to thereby create jobs, we can't do so intelligently without discussing the motivational structure of the institutions that will presumably make those investments.

Unlike laws prohibiting exploitative employment practices, investment choices are decisions about what to do with the wealth in excess of subsistence income that an economy generates—its productive surplus. An economy can, acting under collective mandate, either tax and distribute the income, or invest it. If neither occurs, then the economy is taking that currency out of circulation. This is not usually a good thing, and so modern economies almost always have well established financial markets where individuals can lodge surplus into institutions that are good at choosing how to invest it.

One of the aspects of a shift from control to behavioral economies is a general belief that financial markets are better at making these choices than governments, and that the proper role of government is limited to making make sure that those funds are safe against theft. Otherwise, investment choices are ruled by the evaluation of risk, and the behavior of institutions tasked to evaluate risk.

The largest challenge to behavioral economies is organizational—i.e., when financial institutions consolidate, and their behavior moves from that of participation in a market to that of a sovereign seeking control. This tendency makes the government's role of securing the market against theft many times more complicated, because as financial institutions (or group thereof) move toward sovereignty, their strategic orientation moves from creative to destructive risk. This will require some explanation.

"Finance" as a concept generally refers to decisional processes related to the investment of resources (capital) in the pursuit of production. There are two basic types of investments—i.e., (1) direct investment in and control of a productive enterprise, with a right to share its profits, and (2) the extension of credit to a productive enterprise with an expectation of repayment with a specified interest rate. The extension of credit through lending is generally based on more conservative evaluations of the resources available to cover the loan—which are typically offered as "security" (risk assurance).

In a control-oriented economy, almost all investment is direct investment with ownership by the controlling authority—and a general reluctance to allow private individuals to acquire control of productive institutions unless those individuals are subject to control. With a relaxed need to control, a behavioral economy opens to private individuals who buy and sell (trade) securities in markets designed for these exchanges. They make direct investments in what are called "equity" markets, and trade lending arrangements in "bond" markets. The essential predicate of behavioral economy is that government is less motivated and able to evaluate risk—both creative and destructive—than privately situated individuals.

These markets trade with currency issued by government, or by a governmentally regulated central bank, nearly all of which appears in the form of "credit" held in the custody of institutions which bank credit (banks). In order for markets to operate effectively, a central banking authority must pay close attention to the value of its currency, and issues currency based on perceived needs to preserve the value of currency—which can be a very complicated process based on the estimated value of resources circulating throughout an economy and the willingness of the public to make purchases. In contemporary behavioral economy, a central bank loans currency to centrally situated banks because they are in the business of evaluating resources available for the repayment of loans. These banks are happy to incur such obligation because they are allowed by government to relend many times the value of their obligation to government to other banks, and at a higher interest rate they are obligated to pay.

In addition to having access to credit flows initiated by government, they gather surplus from a productive economy (also referred to as "savings") which are also the basis for the issuance of credit to borrowers at many times the value of the deposits. These are savings which—in contrast to control economies—do not flow back to the ruler, but become part of a market. Thusly, most of the money in circulation is in the form of credit to institutions presumably well situated in a private marketplace to allocate resources to projects in which the rewards associated with risk are the greatest. Decisions on the best use of currency are therefore transferred out of the ruler's hands and into a competitive marketplace.

The marketplace also provides opportunities for the application of surplus toward the purchase of rights to profit in privately situated business. There are firms that gather resources from individual savings for that purpose, evaluate risk, and trade in exchange forums at prices which reflect anticipated productivity. Productivity in a market is determined by the selections of purchasers—i.e., the value of a business is proven by interest in purchasers for its product, which is in turn reflected in the market value of its stock which draws investment from productive surplus.

This is a theoretically powerful way to use the filtrative characteristics of the market to direct resources effectively, and places government in a good position to examine the market to determine if resources are being allocated toward creative risk (to increase productivity) and to intervene selectively where markets are noticeably ineffective in addressing or investing in collective needs. The situation changes however where a financial system, operating under competitive stress, organizes its resources in order to eliminate competitive stress. When that happens, a financial market moves from market-based efficiencies, to a position of rivalry with government over the productive surplus of a given economy. At this point, a financial system views government as its principal competitor, and moves from market-based competition to political competition.

The political argument is usually framed as follows.

> 1. The government is an inefficient base from which to make selections over creative risk, because it is administratively encumbered, and because it is poorly situated to coordinate with international markets. [32]

> 2. Government should therefore tax less (take less productive surplus) and allow that surplus to accumulate in a financial industry where principles of supply and demand will determine which selections are appropriate. [33]

There are a number of things wrong with this argument. First, the assumption that government is inefficient is not a behavioral "type" assumption. Behavioral orientations are more receptive to the possibility that the failure of a given organizational process is correctible.

But secondly, and more significantly in the context of this discussion, in a consolidated capital marketplace, principles of supply and demand become distorted. The controllers of that market assume positions similar to "ruler." The difference is that this ruler is not subject to democratic processes, and so the rules which evolve favor individuals who have no real legal accountability to value other than the protection of the financial controller.

The regulation of monopoly and the restriction of anti-competitive practices within productive industries have been around for quite some time, and there are practical economic models for the evaluation of their markets, and their conduct within those markets. But the situation is different in a "financial" market, which is not already producing something, but is instead regarded as an intelligence gathering network for the evaluation of risk, and the attachment of prices in accordance with risk.

All "currency" therefore "flows" in accordance with the credit reposed in this system, and thus all productive processes of the market are dependent on it. This tends to situate "law" precariously where competitive processes reining the financial system are replaced by cooperative processes. A well-organized financial system has the power to set agendas for government that conflict with values and expectancies of its constituents, at times in ways which threaten the entire economy. [34]

Imagine a king who assembles a financial system so that he can circulate currency, but in the process, cedes control of that currency to a single individual. That king has a problem if the individual to whom control is given decides to oppose the king. This problem is different than the problem the king has with someone to whom he has given control of a productive process. For any other process, the king can use his money to pay soldiers and other agents to replace or reform it, but if the process organizer has control of his money, that option is either not available, or so complicated that it is practically impossible.

This imbalance is visible—as in conventional monopolies—in the pricing of products and services. There will likely be a higher price placed on low risk products in the form of higher interest rates, but also in the understatement of risk on products which are insured through markets in the form of derivatives—run by individuals who work in a cooperative relationship with the vendors of those products. These kinds of things cannot happen without market consolidation.

The situation worsens where those who hold the earned surplus of an economy in the form of deposits, are granted liberty to provide investment services in the bonds and equities markets which place those deposits at risk. The regulatory task on the part of government to assure that conflicts of interest are not corrupting those investments becomes many times more complicated than the simple regulation of productive industries.

What is more interesting, perhaps, is the lack of separation between regulatory agencies and financial system profiteers. The organizational union of these entities makes the corruption of ethical principles designed to insure fair competition more likely, along with the subsequent deterioration of markets which depend on the application of rules based on those principles—i.e., a disconnect between law and economy, or worse, the subordination of law to economy. The most fundamental rule of organization—applicable to logic and institutions alike—is that organization forms within value and will degrade into more primitive forms of order absent more sophisticated and effectively implemented assertions of value.

The resultant economy functioning under credit controlled by a consolidated and underregulated financial sector tends away from the encouragement of creative risk and moves quickly toward destructive risk—replicating the business model of a casino. Casinos are organizations which involved pooled resources where one person's gain is designed to take in the form of a loss to another. Most casinos are designed so that the casino operator takes the difference between the accumulated losses and the gains—profitably but not productively.

In modern financial systems, losers are drawn in through the inflation of price bubbles which for a period of time offer gains to those willing to place bets, but the price inflations these represent are not tied to productive surpluses of any kind of business. They are markets conferring value on other markets—a perfect instance of self-referential paradoxes which have mocked human thought for centuries. Markets do not confer value on anything, but serve to motivate valuable behaviors.

There is, in fact, enough wrong with the celebration of and dependency on markets that at least from an organizational perspective, the term "market economy" is, at best, indicative of a transitional phase between control and behavioral economic systems. This transition is marked by episodes in which fear paralyzes the flow of credit (and currency) and market participants move into states of mind reminiscent of control economy.

When the public develops a belief that the flow of supply isn't secure, it stops taking creative risks and reverts to the appropriation of the assets and savings that others have already gathered. Economic depression ensues. There is room here for a credible hypothesis to the effect that what we refer to as "depression" in modern economies, is really the onset of the type of fear that used to dominate control economies, where people form relationships of dependency on institutions that deal in the currency of political influence.

Once we understand that we are gazing upon a major transition in the way supply is understood and organized, the agenda becomes relatively simple. The productive output of freely assembled organizations in a behaviorally situated economy is significantly more than what was available in militarily organized control economies. But there is a reason why economies such as these failed to survive in the past. Accumulated surplus attracts invasions, and invaders have in the past organized legally into control-based organizations. The objective, then, is to protect newly developed wealth against invasion, or rather, theft. The way to stop it is to understand organization.

# Chapter 6

# Requisite Economy

1. Much of what has been identified in the preceding analysis as "behavioral" is regarded in common opinion as a form of liberation. Yet the lessening of control over economic matters occurred because of restrictions imposed by law on the behavior of persons with governing authority.

While those who aspire to command others as kings and emperors may experience a sense of loss over these restrictions, they are spared the threat of humiliating executions imposed by others bent on conquest, and find themselves engaged in a salutary exchange with others who speak to them with sincere affection and disaffection. The ethic of behavioral economy imagines a human organism formed and uplifted by the shared experience of value.

In the last chapter, we identified behavioral economy with a "market" of privately oriented business organizations subject to reduced governmental influence. Governmental influence theoretically serves the market by setting boundaries within which competitive behavior can proceed and continue without self-destructing. The correct balance in this formulation can be elusive. Even if one is successful in restricting the invasiveness of government, without a strong government, markets are apt to consolidate into exploitative organizations—hoarding productive surplus and holding compensation at subsistence.

For the sake of clarity, and of continuity in the analysis of behavioral economies (also referred to as "modern"), it may be useful at this point to summarize the points which support our contention that behavioral economy represents a shift of collective human awareness.

These are as follows:

1. Behavioral economy acknowledges and opposes the theory of human existence evident in control economy, and promotes a theory which emphasizes existence as shared experience—both autonomous and socially accountable.

2. This shift rejects the placement of sovereignty in a given individual controlling a fixed hierarchy and replaces it with a system of law adaptive to public value. Decisions affecting productivity are transferred to markets subject to such law, thereby allowing cooperative behavior to flourish.

3. Unlike language, however, the adaptive process of law does not take care of itself and depends to a significant extent on a commitment by its participants to principles that activate public accountability in government, and the sharing of economic productivity.

4. Participative government behaves to some extent like a market, but is different in its functional purpose. That difference is essential to the development of rules for markets, which if not bound by rules tend to organize in ways that compete with government.

The dangers of a legal void are more pronounced in labor and financial "markets" because those markets tend to organize in a way that place controllers in a position of opposition to the social welfare of those who are supposed to benefit from an economy's productive output.

We are beyond the point of identifying a different type of economic system—an economy resulting from an ethical dialogue between government and its subjects—and now faced with implementational issues. How does one develop institutions that combine the conscious and strategic release of control with effective interventions that prevent the misappropriation of human labor and its productive surplus? This takes us from what, in principle, modern economy consists of, and toward the fusion of value with structure—Requisite economy. Since not all behavioral economies exhibit sustainable and durable processes, Requisite economy is properly viewed as a subclass of behavioral economy.

A likely consequence of developing a theory of government that allows conscience to rule is that someone might actually attempt to establish such a government. Government action is risky for a number of reasons. It affects large numbers of people who respond in ways that are often combative and unpredictable, and may fail to anticipate changes in the environment—changes such as resource depletion and the toxicity of products.

Most of those who participate in the design of a government—along with the economy that supplies it—would at least pay lip service to the need to form adaptive government organizations, for reasons similar to the need to design a car with a steering wheel and brakes. It may be that the shortest path between two points is a straight line, but cars need to do more than drive in straight lines.

Even in elegantly designed governments, there are likely to be differences among its citizens over how adaptive it should be—i.e., over how tolerant it should be in the numerous variants of human identity (of human deities), what the government did and did not promise at its inception, how long is too long for competitive exchanges to play out without intervention, and whether government has any business existing at all.

To make things worse, within a behavioral economic milieu, attitudes emerge that are noncooperative, such as a sense of entitlement to wealth that is not based on a credible theory of value. In tribal societies, those tendencies are identified and marginalized long before they are manifest in grandiose states of expectancy. In dominatively hierarchical societies, rulers suppress public expectations that compromise theirs. But what if someone develops grandiose expectations in a life unwatched by the tribe, or by the king? Can these be satisfied with something less than a crown?

In responding to questions like these, one is apt to become more aware of how important government is in maintaining some measure of social order. While we may not be beasts, we tend to behave that way if not obligated in some sense to Other. The question of implementation, therefore, not only contemplates an organization that discharges necessary functions of government, but that supplies what men and women need and want as social beings, i.e., a meaningful connection to and participation in that which obligates them.

2. The implementation or "institutionalization" of a theory of economy comes with the realization that markets are conceived and

sustained by law and are the property of the law-maker. If law abides in the socially evolved language of a people, then the productive output of their cooperative behavior is their common property (wild economy). But if for some reason—such as threat of invasion—they are crowded into structures where language standing alone fails to establish law, then one is likely to see a degradation of shared ownership due to the extraction of law from language, and its establishment through the formation of dominative hierarchy (control economy).

It is unlikely that a control economy will on its own adopt the kinds of cooperative enterprises necessary for the emergence of what is referred to in modern vernacular as "industry" and "industrialization." The kind of restriction on control necessary to the establishment of a legal order capable of comprehending and accommodating industrialization (behavioral economy) is likely to occur abruptly as a decisive formation or reformation, i.e., as a model which rules the behavior of government. It is useful to record this in a written compact of some sort.

This compact—referred to as "constitution"—amounts to a set of requirements deemed essential to an organizational shift from a government of control designed to protect the ruler and his or her intimates, to a government of shared control in a participatory democracy. Because the objective of this compact is to bring organization into being by identifying its defining characteristics, it falls within the rubric of "requisite organization." An often-used philosophical term for the identification of prerequisite duty necessary to the existence of social organization is "deontology," a term which identifies obligation, the presence or absence of which marks the presence or absence of a type of social order.

One might argue that Requisite order is present in a government of delegative hierarchy, which is valid as far as it goes. Delegative hierarchy is organized, and there are essential requirements of hierarchic accountability which terminate at a point of central control for that hierarchy.

Organization within a delegative hierarchy, however, extends priority to the organizational participants, while others who are subject to it are treated as a social environment external to the organization. Their welfare is secondary unless the organization includes them in a dialogue that impacts the government. This, it seems, is an important distinction made in varying degrees of clarity—i.e., that those who labor at subsistence are not comprehended or included within organization, but are instead only subject to the economic reality which is the effect of such organization. The task of placing a public within the comprehension of government—so that the public becomes part of its organization—is another thing entirely. As a form of organization, it is a topic of "requisite" analysis. [35]

The modification of social obligation (law), identifying a shift from a unidirectional or positive formulation representing from the will of a ruling individual, to a bidirectional or publicly adaptive rule forming process requires institutional reinforcement. It otherwise degrades into control structures that would, if possible, avoid the complex discomforts brought on by vocal constituencies.

Complicating design choices toward this objective is a need to simplify decisional processes as much as practical, so that government can respond to environmental changes. This consideration might therefore favor the formation of a relationship of obligation between an executive and an electorate. Since public consensus is awkward to engage—particularly in large industrial societies—public participation in rule making mandates for an executive is apt to function through a representative legislature. One might depict this diagrammatically as follows.

Executive ⟵⎯⎯⎯⎯⎯⎯⎯⎯⎯⟶ Legislature

Arguably, an interaction of this sort would activate a legal process similar to what is observed in spoken language depicted in the last chapter. Accountability to Other being the basis of a tripartite structure in language—presentive/syntactic/semantic—we might expect to replicate a similar accountability between an executive and a legislative Other. This produces a model of law resembling language—valuational/procedural/substantive. The modern use of the term "constitution" is a way of encouraging communication important to the establishment of social obligation.

This arrangement is not appreciably different than what democracies achieved in ancient Greek and Roman civilization, and which were made more stable where the legislature assumed authoritative and/or financial power over the deployment of military force. But for any given legislature, there are destabilizing influences tending to weaken its capacity to force cooperation with an executive agency. Some of these are circumstantial—due perhaps to exigencies brought about by productive crises (e.g., drought or resource depletion), or by external invasions.

Others are internal—due to diverse and antagonistic constituencies that are against the formation of legislative consensus.

Human beings tend to form consensus about what is right and wrong tribally—each gathering around a perceived range of acceptability, or deity. In the case of strife, their preference is to separate socially rather than to live within disagreeable proximity. But in a crowded social universe, that is not possible. The resultant pluralism emerging from social division tends to neutralize the socializing effect of public dialogue upon the executive, because the human organism cannot ethically process the noise associated with numerous and divergent moral structures.

The executive—humanly prone to ethically embrace a coherent social system—tends instead to function as a broker of divergent and incoherent social systems. Dialogue in this situation is not apt to lead to a benevolent disposition in either the executive or the legislature because the dialogue is not sized in a way that excites ethical participation. The establishment and maintenance of processes established within navigable magnitudes is the subject material of Requisite organization. In that sense, Requisite is a syntax of social organization that enables dialogue on collective obligations to proceed meaningfully.

Democracy, in other words, does not stand on its own, even if it is processed through a legislature. Without structures added to the political dialogue, either the executive or some legislative faction will contend for and achieve a dominant position. This is, in effect, the conundrum which afflicts any attempt to place a centrally positioned ruler/executive in a personal dialogue with very large collections of persons under the domain of "nation."

An effective response to this concern is to institute procedures that promote rulemaking as an honest ethical dialogue. This is accomplished in behavioral economy through the following measures.

> 1. Accountability of the executive not only to the legislature, but directly with the electorate in what may be referred to as the general welfare or public good.
>
> 2. Shared authority in rule-making—i.e., executive power to introduce legislation and limited power by the executive to countermand rule-making activity by the legislature.
>
> 3. Formation of an independent authority that hears, interprets and enforces ethical standards—both substantive and procedural—identified in the compact of government.

The third proviso engages government in the maintenance of an independent branch of government, so that disputes over the authority of government will not commingle with or become subject to corruption of the interests of a given constituency. The independence of a judicial branch within a tri-partite government is irrelevant to a control-oriented government structure, as there is no real compact with an electorate, and thus no reason to convert individuals from status of "subject" to a "citizen" with rights of participation in rule making. But where the comprehension of government sanctifies an electorate as Other in an ethical dialogue, a judiciary likewise moves to a point of independence in order to activate a conscience—the "I" of government in a state of dialogue with its participants—which brings ruling authority into a state of accountability with Other. The result is a Requisite structure. [36]

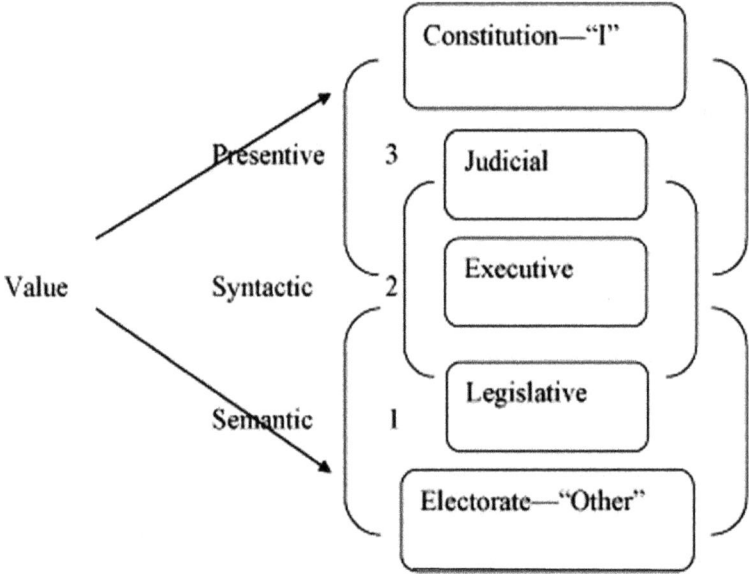

It is difficult to overstate the importance of this as a map of "government" now positioned between two sources of input—one which identifies "public" and "public good" as an electorate of citizens and another which identifies ruling principle as a "conscience" which embraces and includes a social universe bound by an information processing center.

An independent judiciary with authority to intervene in the event of controversy transforms this from an ethically neutral political system to an ethically active one. Such a system stands a much better chance of manifesting open and adaptive social structures, a favorable improvement over the closed and defensive systems typical of control economies.

The system literally comes alive as necessary elements fuse into a system which resonates with primitive structures embedded in social consciousness—moving thought from the government to our government. As a system open to intervention both from conscience and the collectively expressed will of an electorate, it carries with it the potential of durable perpetuity.

3. There are important uncertainties, however, that a map of this sort fails to communicate, and it is not yet clear whether this is a good thing or not. Does conscience stand alone as governing principle? Does the electorate tend to adopt or oppose the emergent principle? Is there a tension between them? This uncertainty, it seems, derives from a lack of clarity over the meaning of "value" and its relationship to the predicate "public."

That uncertainty in the comprehension of value might be a good thing consists in public acquiescence to uncertainties that can only be addressed through a political process. The "value" of the political process thus becomes the basis of popular respect for the policies adopted in the laws issued by government.

This orientation is different than that evident in control-based economy, which seeks public surrender to a ruler's position through manipulations combining the use of coercion and propaganda. In a control economy, "property" is conferred on individuals living within a social hierarchy accountable to the ruler, and the rightness of such control is not taken too seriously. Within a behaviorally oriented economy, the rightness to control that confers the status of "property" on a mechanism of production—like a business—is moved to a government which is expected to act in compliance with just processes.

We have discussed how in behavioral economy the notion of "property" undergoes transformation. Property, as something to which an individual holds a right of control, is ethically dependent on formulation of economy as something owned by its participants. Left alone, this formulation might indicate that the productive output of the economy is owned collectively, but that is not the case. Along with a shift from behavioral economy (as an ethical statement) to Requisite economy (its implementation), is the acknowledgment that individual rights of use and control stabilize social systems and are necessary to the assumption of any kind or risk—destructive or creative. While interests emerge through collective influence, they are experienced individually, and are at times asserted against the collective, if for no other reason than to establish right.

Within this setting, one is more likely to identify property as something he or she has "earned" through work. Earning normally suggests the acquisition of control through individual efforts that comply with rules established as a consequence of fair and open dialogue. It is occasionally difficult, therefore, to determine if someone has earned or stolen property because it is difficult both to determine not only whether they have complied with the rules of government, but whether the rules themselves are morally supportable.

Accordingly, the determination of whether someone is the rightful owner of a business—inclusive of business assets, processes, and reputation—derives from correct assumptions we make about compliance. The strength of perceived ownership is likewise increased within a context of right obligation manifest in a government exhibiting requisite structure—i.e., inclusive (effectively legislative), efficient (effectively executive), and just (effectively judicial). Together these influences gather in an economic order of "property" or rightful control. To the extent that these are weakened, such that government is perceived as non-inclusive, inefficient, or unjust, property weakens as an ethical concept, and becomes a matter of coercion. This subtly—though powerfully—impacts the morale of an economy bound by a respect for the value of property as something earned.

When economists, therefore, make a distinction between "private" property and "public" property, it is a distinction based on support of a private interest in control. There is a social interest supporting the encouragement of private individuals to apply themselves to productive labor, and thus for government to protect rights of control associated with labor. The public interest is in the productive effect of such encouragement, which is delivered to a market from which the public benefits through its purchases.

An important step in the development of this idea is the attachment of a right of an individual to control the labor of a few others—or perhaps many—toward some sort of productive output. Has he or she earned that right?

A common thread in the formation of behavioral economy is a government bound to its promise, with judicial mechanisms in place to interpret and effectuate that promise. This, as a consequence, favors a concept of government as a service agency which allows its citizenry to benefit from the productive effect of commercial organization, while protecting its citizenry from predation, enabling and often assuring access to necessary resources, correcting and/or limiting the harmful effect of market behavior, and providing benefits that markets acting on their own cannot provide.

Within this framework, there is no right to control others, but individuals may, through the accumulation of capital and the crafting of agreements, organize and control a business in which others submit to control voluntarily. It is, in fact, essential to a well-motivated behavioral economy that they do so. The withdrawal of government interference with private organizations, and the payment of a premium to organizers has proven to spur very productive behaviors—or rather, creative risk. [37]

In accord with these observations, it seems that a distinction between notions of "public" and "private" is useful only to a limited extent. Since all property is subject to a process of public endorsement, in a Requisite economy, property is best regarded along a continuum of rights that its owner is permitted to assert against government acting under the pressure of an electorate.

The practical implementation of a commercial reality based on property, therefore, includes the qualifications of control emerging from a government sponsored dialogue on the public interest in that property. The separation of objects and territories over which we seek control from that process tends to remove them from the universe of property altogether. One can keep what they earn, but that earning is subject to taxation and regulations on use. One can acquire a property interest in a business within a marketplace, but that interest is subject to restrictions derived from the assertion of public value.

Once government has bestowed a marketable interest on a given individuals use of a given item, one right against government in the property is not in its use, but in the value of its use. The owner can thus seek restitution for the governments interference with that use. The evaluation of rights extending to various items described as "property" is a nice source of business for the innumerable law firms that populate Requisite economies.

None of this, of course, means that private interest is irrelevant in the definition of rights associated with property. A businessman may claim, for example, that he needs a subsidy from government in order to make his business work. There he may be expressing a private value, but his argument for why the public would benefit from a government decision to extend the subsidy to him references a value to the public. This is apt to become a matter of controversy where the benefit he seeks is regarded as offensive to a public interest. Within the context of such controversies, or potential controversies, the government takes and issues licenses, permits, easements, tolls and taxes.

A different situation arises where competing public values are expressed as competing theories of government. In most cases it is not necessary for government to provide an endorsement of one theory of government or another. There are moments of dispute, however, where government is tasked with the problem of accepting or rejecting a theory of government due to a real threat to the viability of government—e.g., because a dissident theory seeks to neutralize its constitutionally extended authority.

One could argue that there is no public value advanced in situations where the whole notion of requisite government is negated. What this means is that at a certain level, it is nonsensical to argue for or against a policy if one does not accept that there is an ethical basis for government. In such situations it is best that the conversation not occur at all, but proceed as a negotiation over the use of force. And conversely, where there is a desire to promote ethical conversation, it is important to create situations that will make such discussion more likely, and that will produce results that are perceived is obligatory.

Without this ingredient, Requisite economy reverses backward into control economy, and property loses its ethical content. No binding conversations, no rules of entitlement. No rules of entitlement, no property. No property, no behavioral economy. Requisite structures are thus an obligation imposed upon government by operation of logic, as if to say: "If you want the liberative and productive advantages of behaviorally oriented economic system, you must work within constitutional processes." We place value on these processes, not as a casual matter, but because we have given much thought to what our political reality is, and take its existence seriously.

While it is important to establish a Requisite economy on resilient processes, it is unrealistic (anti-economic) to assume that rules will take care of themselves. Rules of themselves do nothing, as do orders and decrees. It is, rather, a matter of the value under which they are applied, and this depends on the ethical clarity brought to the formation of an economy.

4. This notion that constitutional processes are embodied within a revelatory expectancy applied to the human condition is consistent

with the Requisite logic outlined in the Chapter 2. To recall, the notation from which the concept of existence begins with expectancy in which the construction of an object "." is embraced by interest, and is changed to "+" in the event that its formation agrees with interest.

This is a "primary" interest which moves thought through stages in the navigation and mastery of a universe of objects "......+." Logic, and its resultant theory of rationality, is not a complex of structures, but of intentions, the phased integration of which result in structured wholes. Since interest is a manifestation of value, it is value which precedes the work from which integrated wholes—requisite structures—are implemented.

This review serves as a preamble, of sorts, to the discussion of a philosophical perspective titled "objectivism." Objectivism has not been received with much enthusiasm as an epistemology, but has been influential as the ethical foundation for at least one version of modern economy that vigorously resists government interventions designed to implement and optimize behavioral effects. Since the epistemology of objectivism resembles Requisite logic, it may be useful to portray it in order to distinguish it—and improve our understanding of behavioral economy.

> To form a concept, one mentally isolates a group of concretes (of distinct perceptual units), on the basis of observed similarities which distinguish them from all other known concretes (similarity is 'the relationship between two or more existents which possess the same characteristic(s), but in different measure or degree'); then, by a process of omitting the particular measurements of these concretes, one integrates them into a single new mental unit: the concept, which subsumes all concretes of this kind (a potentially unlimited number). The integration is completed and retained by the selection of a perceptual symbol (a word) to designate it. 'A concept is a mental integration of two or more units possessing the same distinguishing characteristic(s), with their particular measurements omitted.' Peikoff, Leonard. "The Analytic-Synthetic Dichotomy." in Rand 1990, pp. 97–98. The quotes within this passage are of Rand's material elsewhere in the same book.)

The integration of particulates into independent wholes rests close to the center of Requisite logic, but noticeably lacks emphasis on the way interest activates and controls that integration. This error—once an affliction of earlier versions of Requisite logic—is apt to be compounded in the derivation of an ethical philosophy, and ultimately, a theory of law and economy.

The error consists in the belief that rationality exists as a value neutral instrumentality that allows a given individual to shape his or her own destiny. An objective reality which includes a physical and social surround is formed to serve a solitary person. This person forms an ego or identity as the means of pursuing their happiness. Thus, within the objectivist universe, moral altruism—the identification of another's happiness with one's own—is naught but a form of egoism.

This view includes within it corollaries applicable to the formation of modern economies. They are as follows:

> 1. Any given individual determines his or her own good more effectively than either another individual or a collective of individuals.
>
> 2. Social relationships are negotiated arrangements through which individuals seeking their own good engage in trade with other seeking the same for themselves.
>
> 3. Since the good of one does not include the good of another, there is no such thing as a public good, but only the aggregation of private goods.
>
> 4. The productivity of an economy is a consequence of the creative effort talented and motivated individuals, not of collectives or of government systems.
>
> 5. The role of government is only to provide a forum or "market" through which individuals can freely pursue their own good without fear of coercion by the state, and by others.

The most common criticism of democratic processes by objectivist morality derives from the construction of a straw-man entitled "collectivism." The argument is that norms arising from a collective tend to devalue the creativity of highly capable individuals. Accordingly, highly capable individuals suffering from obligatory accountability to the collective are stifled and suppressed in their creative output. Modern market-based economies—the argument continues—are dependent on the creativity of highly capable individuals, and accordingly deteriorate where collective pressures predominate over individual liberties. A government sustained by democratic processes will kill the genius of market economy unless its naturally stifling tendencies are bridled. Thus, strong protections of individual productive liberty—including financial benefits accruing to successful individuals—is viewed as indispensable to the implementation of modern industrial economies. The inefficiency of emergent communist regimes of the 20th century is offered as proof of the validity of this critique.

This criticism, however, is flawed. As Requisite logic has demonstrated, nothing exists in consciousness without interest, and objectivism incorrectly regards interest as a solitary phenomenon felt by a solitary identity. As we contemplate human existence—and the formation of ego—within a language suffused universe, the supposed line of division between individual and public good blurs considerably.

Certainly, within the phased process of constructing a compound whole out of particulates, there are processes which proceed automatically, but they are activated by the interest termed primary, and function as secondary to that interest. The formation of interest sufficient to carry an individual through a developmental cycle is something that occurs within the universe of value acquired within a social universe. Recall the diagram reflecting value as a cooperative exchange between "I" and "Other" from chapter 3.

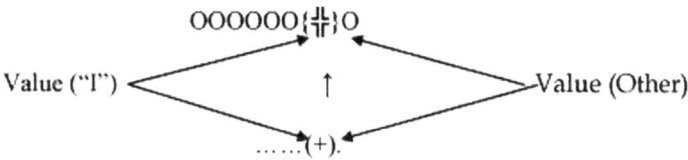

In a language suffused world, the mind is trained at an early age to process information so that it may be shared with others. This is most apparent in the conversion or primitive desires into socially productive values, and emergence of identity with content. The identity of objectivist philosophy has no existence or substance, but is, rather, only a terminus from which desires extend. They are wrong about this. Identity does have content, and we spend the better part of our lives engaged in social exchanges by which we discover it.

Therefore, the altruism that objectivists decry as illusory—as something which appears to exist but does not—is in fact close to existence. It is part of the formation of personal autonomy, not by surrendering to Other, but by including Other in the valuation of one's own existence. There is no autonomy in social isolation, but instead, autonomy exists in the affirmation of social existence and the regard of oneself along with others as a cherished participant in a social world.

Individuals living out the narrative of success offered in modern economic systems tend to understate the contributions of others toward their success. This consists in the collective protection of what they earn as property, and that its elevation as a right derives from their membership in a just society which fashions an economy that provides for a common good. At the moment they regard themselves as kings and lords with divine entitlements bestowed as rewards outside the processes of government, they have shifted away from the public value which enabled their success. They have as fervent objectivists moved ironically from an objective reality shared by many, and into subjective delusion. [38]

The horrors commonly associated with the communist regimes of the 20th century consisted less in the embrace of collectivist norms, than in the attempt to implement a socially inclusionary ideology through a dominatively controlled system. Communists misdiagnosed the problem of implementation—due in significant part to their ideological dependency on a Marxian historical script—and ignored the productive importance of enabling and stimulating creative risk.

With these observations, the objectivist claim against government disappears.

The genius of behavioral economy—now examined in its implementation—consists not in formation of a wall of exclusion between government and a marketplace, but in the development of contexts with the assistance of government in which creative risk flourishes. Markets are to a significant extent self-regulating, but they are prone to numerous imbalances requiring intelligent and nuanced interventions. The hope is that government is as adaptive to its environmental challenges in an industrial world as our spoken language was in the development of coordinated responses to more primitive surroundings.

5. Although the terms "market" and "regulation" are meaningful, they have up until now been used loosely. They were probably never used

in wild economy, and sparingly in control economy. But in behavioral economy, markets are the principal subject material, as the places in which someone buys some good or service that he or she wants.

As a practical matter, markets require a medium of exchange, or currency. They also require a system of commercial laws which identify ownership and control over goods and services, and the means of changing ownership through gift, devise or contract. Along with these laws are administrative mechanisms with the authority to clarify and enforce them. These comprise what may be regarded as essential public infrastructure for the establishment and maintenance of markets, and thus obligatory service of government.

Then there are goods and services which are good for the growth and viability of markets—thereby allowing one to get the things one wants—but are not practically available for purchase within a market. These might include transportation corridors such as roads, communications media such as postal services and telephone cables, human resource development agencies such as schools and libraries, places of rest and entertainment such as parks and beaches, and protective services such as police and firefighters. They comprise a public infrastructure serving many markets and in which government intervention is welcomed.

At this point one hardly mentions the word "regulation" because these are controlled—owned and operated—by government, and confer public benefits that return more to the public in value than they cost the public in taxes. There are at least three situations, however, in which government not only augments and supports the formation of markets, but interjects itself in some way into the dynamic operation of a market.

One of these is where for some reason an essential consumer need is served more efficiently through centralized market organization—i.e., monopoly, but the government chooses not to be the provider of that service. Public energy and water utilities fall into that category. Insurance services in many countries (including the United States) fall into that category in that those services are exempted from prohibitions against collaborative price fixing. As part of a bargain struck between government and industrial participants certain energy, water and insurance markets are subject to government oversight which, at least in theory, has power of audit and investigation, as well as the power to reject proposed consumer rates.

Another basis of regulation is where the nature of the good or service poses risks to the public. Government structures are therefore necessary to regulate the release of drugs, food products, professional services of various kinds, simple and complex financial instruments, buildings, factory waste and exhaust, etc. In recent years, governments have identified a public interest in the conservation of natural habitats and the historical artifacts of indigenous cultures and have empowered agencies to protect that interest.

Yet another basis of regulation is to preserve or promote the viability of a given market. This sort of regulatory intervention is more selective, and tends to identify markets and industries to which—again—the public welfare attaches. No one cares that much whether markets for pornographic literature or for cigarettes and alcohol deteriorate or self-destruct. But they care quite a lot about whether the petroleum and health industries are robust and responsive. Since most have saving for retirement lodged in firms which invest in equities, they are interested in the performance of the stock market. Here we are likely to see regulation not just in the form of monitoring and restrictive practices, but as well in the form of government subsidy—e.g., tax incentives, grants, loan guarantees and regulatory exemptions.

One of the ways that a government might influence market behavior, is to enter the market as one of its participants. This is perceived by some as the solution to the organization of market monopolies and price fixing trusts, where government activates competitive behavior by offering itself as a competitor. This is the final step before government might appropriate a market in its entirety. While this is theoretically achievable, it assumes that government possesses the competence to do this, and this assumption is often problematic.

Government enterprise is not subject to the same sort of accountability as private enterprise. A private business that markets an inferior or overpriced product will, in a competitive market, cease to exist. The dissolution of a government enterprise is a different matter, and often unnecessary, as porous accountability structures can be modified and adapted to market-based business models. This is visible in privatized medical services, postal services, transport services, water services and educational services—where government competes in markets alongside private enterprises.

The decision on whether to enter the market is simply a matter of public value—i.e., whether public needs require a governmentally funded provider. If private competition is needed, or if governmental intervention will injure the market, that itself is subject to the decisional priorities of government acting within a public dialogue. Such interventions do not destroy markets and governments that engage in such interventions do not destroy market economies. Rather, they tend to promote and stabilize the kinds of societies within which markets thrive.

A well implemented behavioral economy involves a government acting within resource constraints as an observer and manager of markets—an activity that seeks to elevate to the level of "science" an understanding of how markets form and are sustained, and the effect of government intervention on those markets. The "behavior" of markets is thus a highly regarded aspect of economic science.

The process by which suppliers bring a product to consumers is often referred to as the "organization" of a market. Market organization is mostly about how businesses form around a need that people are willing to pay for. The formation of a business is a managed process which includes the processing of the following risks by working with other businesses, and their management.

1. There is insufficient consumer interest in the product to induce customers to pay for it.

2. There are insufficient resources available to effectively move from start to sustainability through sales.

3. There are potential competitors in the market who will enter the market and offer a better product.

4. There are insufficient related infrastructures in place to support a business of this nature.

5. There is no one capable of forming and managing the processes necessary to the establishment of the business.

When these risks are low, there is little need for government intervention and a market will organize. What should the government do when there is a strong public interest in the product but other risks which discourage market organization? Should the government help organize the market by forming a business, or is it better for government to subsidize the formation of a business? Is it appropriate for government to reduce its risk by acting as purchaser of its own product, or by restricting the entry of competitors?

In evaluating questions such as these it becomes progressively more apparent that government participating in a behavioral economy benefits from a self-aware respect for limitations in its own capacity to manage. What seems to set government apart from privately organized business are consideration related to item number "5" above—the susceptibility of that business to management.

Given the improvement in our understanding of how to design jobs to fit the limitations of the human organism, there is some reason to regard the expansion of government interventions in market formation with optimism. To this end, a Requisite orientation to the expansion of bureaucracy—by its nature cautious and scientific—might bring government into comfortable limits through the invocation of practical rather than ideological constraints.

6. It appears, therefore, that the fear of government acting to overwhelm private business, could be more a product of our collective memory of the many abuses of dominative regimes than it is a defining feature of constitutional government. As we have indicated previously, a philosophical perspective which seeks to minimize or restrict regulatory interventions by government due to a view of the human organism that is isolated and alone (Objectivism, for example) is not coherent—epistemologically or morally, nor does it accept the numerous regulatory interventions necessary for an effectively functioning market economy.

That perspective serves a different purpose, i.e., as an ideologically conceived camouflage designed to resist the implementation of a modern behavioral economy. The resulting dysfunctionality evident in efforts to dismantle consensus raises a question over whether a behavioral economy—along with its benefits—is sustainable. This question includes two related questions.

1. Is there a way of processing ideological division such that a decision-making agency can at least theoretically identify and marginalize behaviors which will disrupt or disable the authority of government?

2. Is the practical implementation of such processing within the capability of individuals assembled as executive, judicial and legislative agents, or is the task of government in this context too great for human agencies to handle?

These questions derive from the values of Requisite organization—i.e., organization does not occur without the intervention of an interest that values collaboration, and that interest produces sustainable wholes only if human capability so allows. Any organization is, within the lexicon of "requisite," free to limit its universe of interest as an adaptive measure, and this is what happens frequently in control economy. Government simplifies its responsibilities and may in the process behave more coercively toward its subjects.

Something of this nature may be a motivation in contemporary efforts to shrink the size of government, and to delegate more authority (sovereignty) to state government. This motivation was a significant aspect of a conflict between the northern and southern states in the Nineteenth Century. Despite the southern attempt to make a philosophically sophisticated statement of its position, the attempt failed because it was promoting a legally and economically regressed theory.

It is one thing for a government to adopt a pragmatic approach to its own managerial limitations, and another thing entirely to disable the power of the government to make nuanced decisions about what it can and cannot do. One brings pragmatic concerns to a public forum, and is theoretically able to assess whether human resource limitations and institutional design allow for success. The other compromises the ability of government to act at all, and pursues the dissolution of authority as if it were an ethical mandate.

The resolution of the ideologically driven demand by the southern confederacy to dissolve the authority of the federal government was ultimately resolved by a civil war. It is doubtful that if the Confederation had succeeded in its attempt to separate from federal authority, it would have been successful in movement toward modernization. The notion of "property" and the regulated control over it—an essential ingredient in behavioral economy—would probably have lacked the ethical mandate necessary to carry it out. A state which confers the status of "property" against human beings fully capable of participating as citizens has, in effect, lost ethical credibility to bestow the status of property on anything. The soul of behavioral economy is the maintenance of the ethical credibility of government. Without it, the economy reverts to the order that preceded it.

The American civil war was fought over the question of whether control and behavioral economies can co-exist under a single government. It was neither the first nor the last of such wars to be fought, though it is likely that in future wars of this kind, the control-based faction will seek to conceal its true motivation.

We have noted that language reflects practical constraints manifest on a tribal scale that weaken when social cooperation is challenged by population increase. Something similar occurs within constitutional government—and a resultant behavioral economy—where ideological differences make coordination so difficult that the government cannot regulate commerce effectively. These differences are occasionally transcended through the coordinative efforts of gifted individuals, but there is little assurance that such individuals will survive the political vetting process of campaign and election.

Instead, the choice of leaders may result in control by lesser mortals driven by ideologically based antipathy toward one or more rival orientations. Even in these situations, the task of the executive working with a legislature is manageable if rivals share an interest in developing consensus through caucus and compromise, and thus avoid an unreliable hope that the political process will result in the selection of a "great" man or woman. The task of leadership in a complex political system is more complicated, and this is likely the case where ideological opposition places an interest in the development of consensus against an ideology that seeks to dissolve consensus.

Take the popular notion of a division between Liberal and Conservative—which seems to form with regularity in modern political systems. What if that changes from a difference in views about social policy to a difference in views about the very existence of government? Thus, a polarity which was once symmetric, and subject to compromise,

Liberal  Conservative

degrades into a different kind of polarity—consensual versus anti-consensual. This presents an asymmetric polarity, where compromise is extremely difficult because one side sets out to disrupt consensus generating processes.

Consensual  Anti-consensual

One might undertake a different strategy toward government and leadership in the second situation than in the first, perhaps aimed at identifying and marginalizing the disruptive influences through the reorganization of the political dialogue such that the anti-consensualists are isolated. The problem is the demands on the capacity of the executive within the latter scenario are more rigorous and require a strategic mind of superior strength to that required in the former.

At some point, ideologically voiced attack on the government process is apt to result in the disabling of government by making the management of consensus generating processes impossible. This imposes a paradoxical challenge upon government sustained by an essentially permissive or open orientation to the communication of ideologically based dissent. It is difficult for government seeking self-preservation—

as it did during the American Civil War—to ethically separate and limit political behavior aimed at process disruption. To the extent that proponents of this disruptive behavior have reduced it to a method or science, it is referred to as "fascism."

Fascism is, perhaps, the most famous and dangerous version of strategic disruption of constitutional government, but the installation of an oppressive surrogate is only one possible consequence of this strategy. It is also an effective way of removing government from its primary task of market regulation, and that is something likely to seem attractive to an interest (or collection thereof) which is opposed to the intervention of government in its marketplace. The assembly of a coalition of businesses within an anti-regulatory or radically individualist ideology (objectivism for example) is more about protecting a private interest than the advancement or development of a public value.

This does not become dangerous to constitutional government until strategies of disruption emerge. Examples of disruptive practices are as follows.

1. Disinformation—a process which seeks to undermine public confidence in facts essential for regulation.

2. Filibuster—a process through which a minority interest can stall or inhibit legislative action.

3. Scapegoating—the use of an individual or class of individuals as point of blame for social problems.

4. Position pledges—broad advance agreement not to exercise a government authority.

None of these activities are illegal, and are, in fact, constitutionally protected. Quite apart from matters of corruption, which can be made the subject of civil or criminal penalty, we examine here a systemic administrative weakness in law, where groups of individuals utilize legitimate processes for illegitimate purposes. One can imagine, however, the deficiencies in constitutional processes that involve both kinds of interventions. The safeguarding of constitutional government, given these considerations, requires much vigilance and determination, inasmuch as fascism is an organizational problem resulting from the failure to establish resilient consensus generating mechanisms, and a resultant environment that overwhelms the capability of its leaders. It isn't a necessary result, but likely in a system where the technology of organization is unsophisticated.

7. If we take the objectivist claim that economic prosperity is a result of the creative output of exceptional people, then we might embrace a theory of productivity in which government allows such people the room and resources to develop products and institutions. That could support a policy bias favoring less regulation and more concentration of wealth. We previously indicated skepticism toward this as an economic strategy because of a weak motivational link between wealth and creative risk. It is remarkable that this is not regarded among economic policy-makers as self-evident, i.e., that commercial success within a market attracts competition, and that resources would, in that event, shift toward the elimination of competition. If government is set up to reward such behavior, one would expect the rapid deterioration and decline of economic productivity, despite the popular mythological narrative that economic benefits flow to exceptionally productive people.

Assume for a moment that the assignment of resources to exceptional people is a good thing for an economy. Within the "exceptional persons" theory of production, behavior aimed at stifling government might be perceived as a good thing. Since politics is not a very good way of identifying such people, get government out of the way and let the market selection processes sort it out. After the sorting process, let them act as gatekeepers within an aristocracy of excellence. However, it bears repeating at this point that markets do not select anything, but only record the results of competition. The selection of excellent people rests in the hands of those who make the rules. The selection of persons excellent in the pursuit of creative risk is something that they do, provided that they know what they are doing.

There is a famous narrative of success in the business world involving the Procter and Gamble Company that benefitted from a change of orientation to intellectual property. Procter and Gamble's chief executive officer was an exhibitionist of exceptional organizational skill, adopting a policy of very strong control over its numerous intellectual property holdings. His attitude of control permeated the entire organization, and included a specially conceived hierarchy of laborers, their bosses, bosses of bosses, etc. He himself promoted a mythic image of competence, touting educational achievements, and the mastery of foreign languages. He thus hoisted himself to the top of the organization, and projected forward an emperor's vision of Procter and Gamble dominating its marketplace, while competitors paid huge premiums to license its technologies. He, in other words, satisfied at least one social image of the successful executive.

However, after about two years under this dominion, sales suffered, and the company lost about half its stock value. A sophisticated diagnosis of the company's difficulties revealed that its products could not be sustained through exclusive reliance on technologies proprietary to Procter and Gamble, and the emperor's vision of a self-contained city of technological treasure was deemed unworkable. He was fired and replaced by another individual with very little personal need to dominate others within his organization, as well as other companies. Instead he developed a cooperative strategy that coordinated with the technologies being developed in other companies.

Procter and Gamble thus became a nexus of interdependent relationships with competitors, and with potential competitors, and this apparently became the basis for the development of many excellent products that benefitted quite a number of businesses. Property identified as the acquisition of patents over various inventions and processes was valuable as a tradable asset, and could be sold opportunistically where it was integrated with the products of other companies in the development of new products. Procter and Gamble's profitability increased dramatically, and within five years it regained its stock value—and then some. [39]

There is a way of visualizing this comparison as a requisite phenomenon occurring within a Requisite logic. To recall, cognitive development within this logic is a phased progression revealing a strategic orientation based on the navigational capability of someone at work, within a given scale of magnitude. There is a repetition of phases within a larger context—symbolically expressed as a movement from interest "( )" engaging object "." and later interest "{ }" engaging object "O". Within the universe of human social or bureaucratic organization "." may be something like the work of a laborer within a production team, and work identifying "O" may be something like the formation of a comprehensive services unit for a business—a five-tiered organization integrating skills acquired which are necessary to control a sizeable mass of workers.

But the cycle of development which delivered this person to a position of mastery repeats within a larger context utilizing the same processing strategies. Thus, we imagine the replication of a developmental process.

|  | Intention |  |
|---|---|---|
| (+) | primary | [{⚊⚊}] |
| [(.)]+ | security | [{O}⚊⚊] |
| [(.)>+] | intimation | [{O}>⚊⚊] |
| [(>.+<)] | order | [{>O⚊⚊<}] |

As these logical images suggest, a preoccupation with "security" is apt to dominate one's thinking at one stage of development because they are not yet capable of integrating effectively with the next navigational strategies—which include intimation to other [{O}>⚊⚊] and then "order" [{>O⚊⚊<}]. The thought of bonding to other without having taken control over it doesn't fit into the mind of someone who strains at control over his or her surroundings.

It is no less apparent in the persona. Due to their perch on an occupational pyramid, there is much concern about the perception of others. That person may exhibit propensities toward narcissism, including a large but brittle self-image, while regarding others as minions. They are inclined to erect voluminous structures through aggregation, i.e., the stacking of simple structures. They identify influence with power and crave it. Since they are the standard bearer of an institutionalized value—the only one they know—an outsider's challenge on moral authority is taken as an affront. This version of "bigness" is thus in reality an expression of limitation.

Life might go on like this indefinitely, but that could become boring. That, and the excitement one associates with trying something new, is a signal of growth. It is fortunate, perhaps, that someone at Procter and Gamble had taken this step. In the story of Procter and Gamble's success, it would appear as though it benefitted from a leader's willingness to move from an assimilative pose to another that appreciated the opportunities available to one or more industries where trading relationships among rivals were pursued as business assets. Thus, a failing company within an industry blighted by destructive rivalries was remade within a vision transformed by a simple and natural integration—i.e., from a [{O}] to a [{O}>⚊⚊] and [{>O⚊⚊<}] brought on through the relaxation of control and extension toward intelligently conceived collaboration.

In the case of Procter and Gamble and its industrial rivals, there were financial advantages to cooperation that could be realized monetarily, as well as a legal infrastructure that was able to identify and protect intellectual property such that it could be traded within a common market. There was a legal and regulatory environment where certain kinds of organization were more likely to emerge than others. It was an environment attracting a different kind of excellence than Proctor and Gamble originally brought forward.

The legal innovations that made this possible were not available five hundred years ago. Exceptional organizers elevated to a state of potential rivalry with kings were either absorbed into the king's organization, ruined or killed. In a Requisite economy, bad things are not supposed to happen to good people. But it is often difficult to identify and promote good people, because "good" is not meaningful, economically, without a sophisticated understanding of organization.

In an ironic post-script to this story, Proctor and Gamble appears to have organized so well with other competitors in its markets that a few years later, it was subject to some hard fines in Europe for engaging in anti-competitive practices. It was probably quite an intellectual challenge for the regulators that imposed the fine to understand the situation, and to negotiate an appropriate sanction, but it serves to illustrate the kind of role government is tasked with. It's not a game for dumb bureaucrats.

This raises requisite considerations that occupy a limited part of the landscape contemplated in modern economics. One is encouraged to examine what relationship, if any, there might be between the type of market with which competitors are engaged, and the types of cooperative exchanges that contribute to the productivity of a given industry. While attempting to encourage such relationships, one also must consider how a given industry is sized, what practical obstacles exist to entry, what kinds of leadership is essential to the formation of its business units, and what kinds of additional leadership—often rare—which can forge market exchanges.

There are environments where exceptional people do well, and there are environments where exceptional people fail. Without an understanding of how roles for such people emerge and are satisfied, it is likely that whole industries will fail because a given theory of competition supports and rewards destructive behaviors. In other words, competitive selection, operating on its own, does not operate under a moral imperative to reward excellence. It is conceivable that markets will reward mediocrity.

A nice example of the failure of competitive pressures to evoke productive behaviors are news markets financed by commercial advertising. These markets are important to constitutional government because they house the media through which ideological disputes are publicly vetted. This tends to steer political communication, needed in the development of popular consensus, into a commercial marketplace that is ineffective in sorting through political controversy. The communications media are important forums of public dialogue, but the movement of public dialogue into an information marketplace may not be an effective way to activate the kind of speech which produces an ethically durable economic order.

The problem with the situation is that these markets do not, of their nature, offer to bring diverse ideologies to a common forum. Human social behavior tends toward validation and avoids uncomfortable social challenges, which include ideological disagreements. In accord with this tendency, each ideology becomes a separate market, and instead of bringing conflicting views together for the development of compromise, the mass communication market intensifies the sense of division between conflicting perspectives and reduces effective communication between them. This may serve the public need for entertainment—i.e., friendly political companionship, but tends to isolate rather than engage dialogue between differing perspectives.

# Chapter 7

# Regression and Progression

1. The productive behavior of individuals in the pursuit of their rational self-interest occupies a field of knowledge frequently referred to as "micro-economics." While this knowledge is not reliable in predicting the behavior of specific individuals acting in special or unique circumstances, it is useful in predicting aggregate behaviors of many individuals participating in a market.

We do not know, for example, if a given individual wishes to buy a work of art, and for what purpose, or what his or her tastes in art are. It may be for purposes of decoration, investment, a gift to a friend, or any number of things, but we do have some idea of what they will pay for it once they decide to shop for art, as there are issues of cost, supply and quality that tend to influence the decision about which piece of art to buy. Thus, one can set prices based on considerations of what individuals tend to do, and extrapolate what a given population of individuals will consume based on price, product information, disposable income, and fashion. All of these considerations are important to those in retailing works of art, and allow individuals to develop businesses within an art marketplace without much government intervention.

Government does, however, do quite a lot to enable art markets by passing and enforcing intellectual property laws, which are valuable to artists in marketing duplicates. Such obligations are an expression of government assistance in the compensation of creative labor, and thus an incentive to produce art. And it tends to move some emphasis from the marketers of art to the artists themselves.

We noticed in the last chapter's account of the success of Procter and Gamble that the promotion of "property" interest can have a significant effect on the way markets organize by elevating the bargaining power of innovators and forcing the marketers of innovation to develop cooperative relationships with new entrants. Where established participants embrace rather than suppress competitive innovation, markets that organize around innovation tend to reward organization focused on creative risk. Along with such developments, one is apt to notice a change in the kinds of behaviors which stand out as valuable.

Accordingly, micro-economic analysis takes interest in contextual variables likely to affect behaviors in competitive exchanges—thereby making micro-economics a study of game-based behavior. These variables include the capability of participants, and the rules that tend to promote or inhibit certain kinds of behavior.

As we previously observed, it is possible to design interactive exchanges or "games" that reward aggressive and simplistic behaviors to the detriment of more complex and moderately applied cooperative behaviors. Some might agree, for example, that the game of basketball benefitted from the establishment of a bonus for baskets made beyond a certain distance, as it tended to encourage the utilization of a broader range of skills in a more beautiful and inclusive competition.

In modern economies, there is still a tendency to regard economic competition as a primitive game of survival where the survivors are regarded "best" despite having behaved immorally. By that standard, one might devise a game in which sixty-four contestants are paired in oppositions where death results from the loss of a coin toss. Although, one contestant will survive the contest, it would be absurd to praise him or her for it.

Micro-economically, the function of law is to devise rules of competition that favor the better innovators, and that there is little for a government to do except to allow market purchasers to select the best products, and to assist in the flow of human and material resources to the organizers of those production systems. The accumulation of wealth in those organizers may be regarded as beneficial, as the accumulation is normally the consequence of a reliable selection process—purchase.

We thus benefit from a dual selection process, i.e., one where citizens of a nation-state law maker select laws and another where the same citizens purchase in markets enabled by those laws. These selections combined together constitute a simple rule of order for behavioral economy in which productive surplus is both maximized and shared.

This rule of order can—at least theoretically—function well, even where accumulated capital flowing to the winners is not reinvested by the winners but comes to rest as "savings" in accounts where others use them for investment. The managers of those accounts—"banks" for instance—invest the money as loans or equity purchases, hopefully to well-tested and skillful business organizers who employ citizens at competitive wages. In this way, productive surplus is shared with the citizenry of a well formed legal-economic system where capital, information and capability are moved to their most productive use. [40]

The problem with this expectation is that even though the laws of a sovereign nation may have made these surpluses available, the recipients may choose not to invest their accumulated savings back in to their own economy, but do so in the economies of other nations. Gratitude carries significant obligatory weight in families and tribes, but not in markets. The government's recovery of the reinvestment value of privately accumulated surplus presents a multifaceted ethical conundrum.

One aspect of this conundrum is that modern economic systems appear to benefit from shared innovation and investment between nations, and this benefit might thus come back to the nation which originated the surplus. The effective investment in human resources in other nations may, for instance, enable foreign populations to purchase more of the goods and services of laborers in the originating nation. But more generally, access to foreign technological innovation and raw materials is apt to be part of a bargain struck between nations, and thus enhance productivity overall.

Before the emergence of modern economic systems which protect rights associated with innovation as intellectual property, sharing between nations tended to cede competitive positions to adversaries, and increased the risk of loss in military competitions—a risk most would find unacceptable. Economic interdependency in a modern world, however, suggests a basis for a movement from military to economic competition.

The hazard of internationally situated commercial markets is that the behavior of the participants in such markets is more difficult to regulate, and are thus far more likely to organize into entities capable of overwhelming the political processes by which markets are contained. Most markets form on their own without assistance, but they are likely, absent regulation, to organize into monopolies, or their equivalent.

It is one thing for a government to enter into trade agreements for human and material resources with other governments, or with assemblies of governments, but quite another to surrender the liquidated value of productive surplus to persons over whom they have no control or influence. It may, in fact, be unethical for a government formed for the purpose of making wise and equitable distributions of productive surplus, to avoid its obligation to make intelligent interventions, and just distributions. This is, after all, what seems to separate behavioral economy from thousands of years of rule under militarily dominated subsistence economies.

A third problem with the formation of international markets relates to the morale of a behavioral economy, in that it is difficult for a citizenry to take its political processes seriously without the perception that the resultant economy is something it can influence directly. To the extent that the citizen is alienated from a shared political experience, they tend to place more emphasis on their gathered material resources as a surrogate for the security once offered by communities.

There is a strange complementarity to the use of personal property as a basis of security, and the formation of modern economies. Property carries more emotional weight for its users than the physical comforts it provides. It suggests fitness to develop a family, and is beyond that offered as proof of social status. These are frequently claimed not only as benefits of ownership, but as entitlements.

For this reason, there is a moral conversion of economy from something subject to common ownership to something that transcends governments, institutions and markets. The abstraction referred to as "economy" thus exceeds international boundaries, and may (or may not) serve the citizens of a nation. The game of risk is apt to change, where the task of obtaining one's supply is a matter of knowing where rivers of money flow, and bringing the largest tanks and canteens that one can find to them. The first priority is taking it, and the task of explaining or justifying the accumulation to others is just a matter of story-telling.

2. Within a world dominated by the credo of control economics, it is assumed that accumulated surplus will attract invasion, so much so that the establishment of military strongholds to protect such accumulations is necessary to a state's survival. Plunder is, for the most part, the principal reason for invasion, and the emergence of behavioral economy does not change the interest of organized individuals and entities in stealing what others have accumulated. The emergence does, however, change the strategy.

Strong-holding accumulated surplus in behavioral economies is accomplished through laws that obligate banking institutions. While banks store some of the economic surplus in physical currency and valuables, most of it accumulates in the form of credit obligations. A nation might militarily seize another nation's bank assets, only to find that the seizure was elusive, as the accumulated wealth of the banks disappeared along with the disruption of credit relationships occasioned by the seizure.

It was simpler for one nation to steal from the productivity of another in agriculturally focused economies. Then it was a matter of expropriating the land, and the gathered reserves pertaining to the use of the land. The strategy of plunder in modern economies is to purchase the business organizations in which surplus accumulates without disrupting their credit obligations, organize those institutions in a way to avoid competition between them, and politically arrange for the removal of regulatory obligations on how these institutions conduct business. As a practical matter, the theft is the result of agencies functioning without accountability to nationally formed political processes—a non-requisite organization. It is in that sense of the word, an invasion.

The neutralization of political processes that would oppose the invasion involves the same persuasive formulae that have been used in control economies. The first is to conceal or camouflage the theft by controlling the public dialogue. This occurs by controlling the media of public communication and announcing the threat of military attack. The second is to establish deities that promote a sense of popular worship of purchased luxuries, and a compulsive preoccupation with the accumulation of currency.

Our reference to conscious efforts to establish deities that promote an image of the human organism in a state of dependency on a financial system is only a way of acknowledging that much of what we think of as lack is not more than a state of mind. It may help to hold the problem of economy functioning outside consensus generating processes up in the light of a thought experiment. Let us imagine, as many have, a state of technologies evolved to the point where machines—robots—are able to satisfy nearly every productive function with which human labor is capable, and that they could be manufactured and controlled by one percent of the live human participants in that state's economy. Let us also assume that this one percent of manufacturers and controllers are co-participants in a representative democracy, and have no power to affect the military potency of government except to cast their vote.

Alas, in this situation, we have a "rate" of unemployment of ninety-nine percent, and many who have nothing to do except what they want to do, i.e., planning their days, organizing leisure activities and entertainment, engaging in conversation, and thinking of tasks to assign to their robotic assistants. People would work, that is, keep themselves busy, but they would not be doing so to acquire essential needs and most luxurious embellishments on those needs.

The question of obligation or law—now evident as a matter of distribution to non-working members of this society and its functioning economy—is not at all difficult. The economic reality does not require or even permit full employment to achieve satisfaction of need, as the labor of a single individual produces many times what is necessary to satisfy his or her needs, and so should be applied to satisfy the needs of a hundred others. Perhaps at this stage, the government's issue of "currency" would be in the form of a voucher, which is meant as a right of citizenship against other citizens who might—due to some mental disorder—take more than they need.

The only obligational concern with an economy of this nature is whether it is fair to indenture one percent of the "producers" to the task of supplying the rest. The most direct way of addressing this concern is for government to offer an incentive, which may yet be difficult if there is nothing left to be desired. And so, there is a need to modify the experiment to establish a list of goods which are not available to non-producers and which are considered desirable. At this point, we should probably admit to variance in taste and to relative scarcity of goods to satisfy the satisfaction of taste. We might therefore call this class of goods "luxuries" as extras or upgrades. Whether or not these luxuries have any intrinsic value, it would be necessary in such an economy for the producers to believe that they do, otherwise no one would want to be a producer.

Now the issue of currency becomes more complicated, as the need being satisfied emerges within a market of individual priorities that must be addressed individually. In order to supply the primary producers, there must be producers who identify variable markets for taste along with those engaged for the primary market, and they need incentive as well, presumably offered as a "share" of the market of luxuries. But since tastes in such a market are apt to be highly individual and variable, the role of government is apt to let that market take care of itself, and issue currency, not as a voucher for need fulfilling production, but to allow for the individual selection and exchange of luxury items.

Since the line of division between an item of need and an item of luxury is apt to be disputed—especially where luxury is extended as an "upgrade" on a item of necessity—the task of management then soon exceeds the capacity (and desirability) of selection on such issues by government. And it is therefore necessary that currency issue for all produced items—necessary and luxurious, at which point currency will tend to accumulate in the hands of a very limited class of producers, assuming still that the number of producers is quite small compared to the number of consumers. The producers within this scenario soon have accumulated more than they might wish to spend on their own needs and luxuries, and so are motivated to produce less—to the point in which production fails to cover the needs of society's members.

Aggravating a situation of this nature are several developments common in modern economies, and which are linked to the circulation of currency within a market.

There is a tendency to overvalue luxury. This is due to the failure of produced items to satisfy essential human longings which are non-pecuniary—i.e., aesthetically attractive goods and personal companions, the elimination of crowded spaces, and the deferential behavior from many who might otherwise challenge or criticize them. It seems that the more that human consciousness attempts to monetize these intangibles, the less satisfied it becomes. The result is a shift of consumption to luxury items, even while many lack essentials.

Producers are placed under competitive pressure to hoard resources. In an economy where currency circulates vis-à-vis production—and absent measures by government to insure the perpetuity of the producer—risk is a two-edged sword. On the one hand it encourages producers to find more efficient methods of production and better products, but on the other hand encourages capital accumulation for strategic advantage and defense against rivals. Fear thus manifests as excessive accumulation—one way in which government effectively subsidizes risk.

There is a tendency to undervalue the needs of those who are not participating in an economy's production. This tendency is reinforced by the other two. Having monetized social esteem, status needs hover like carrion feeders over producers' behavior. Such needs are experienced with intensity, in significant part because of the unforgiving nature of a competitive environment. Part of the experience is a tendency to dehumanize the non-producers, and regard them as a parasitic mass, even though the labor of non-producers is not needed. This as a perspective grows first in the minds of the producers, whose avarice directs anxious suspicion toward others who do not share their luxuries.

The point of the exercise is that even within economic systems of abundance, the experience of those functioning within the system can regress into feelings of scarcity with only a few subtle influences. Within such an environment, the recycling effects of insecurity and dissatisfaction are the basis for the establishment of religious attitudes by which a public is controlled. Overt religious observances and ritual are a superficial aspect of it. Rather, it is a matter of conditioning human value on something that another possesses—of dependency. Social manipulators have known this since the beginning of what we refer to as "civilization"—i.c., that the birthplace of object deities is internal. We allow others to steal from us because we have already allowed them to define us.

The transfer of labor to robots may seem remote to the economic systems to which we have become accustomed, but the automation of industry powered by cheap energy is where modern economies trend. Industrial output placed in the hands of a relatively small number of producers, however, can reduce labor needs in another way. In an international market of unequal nations, labor costs are apt to shift to poorer countries. A producer who delegates work to a cheaper labor market in an emerging economy is doing something similar—economically—to what the industrial automator does.

This is not necessarily a bad thing. It reduces the cost of production and makes products more affordable in the more developed country, and advances cycles of growth in less developed countries. The problem rests not with production, but with law, and the development of just distributional rules within the more productive economy. The economic question is behavioral. Does the accumulation of capital in a narrowing group of producers (production organizers) motivate more productive behavior? The simplest way to answer is "no."

When matters of fairness and motivation tend to point in the same direction—in this case against the accumulation of capital with a small group of producers—the issue shifts to consideration of the most efficient way to do so. One solution is to issue more currency for circulation, and to take measures to ensure that much of it finds its way to non-producers, and even more to those who are interested in becoming producers. The problem with this approach is that this results in even greater accumulations of capital in the main producers, who continue to sell their products and services, which after a number of cycles would tend to diminish the value of currency.

One might argue that this would never happen in a real world, but that would be incorrect. In contemporary economies, governments borrow money to cover social programs and military expenditures. If the source of repayment is the currency of the borrowing nation, then it is the issue of currency which finances these expenditures—offset perhaps by an expectation of increased productivity resulting from the investment of borrowed money. It doesn't fix the problem of redistribution, however—whether issued or borrowed against future issue—as currency tends to concentrate into the possession of those least motivated to invest it in creative risk.[41]

The more direct solution is to tax the accumulation of capital and redistribute it in a manner designed to assure that it flows first into the provision of essential goods and services. This strategy often uses the progressive taxation of income, and the direct government funding of health, housing, food and educational programs. It also takes measures to motivate banking institutions to finance entry into both primary and luxury markets. This is what we see in modern, behaviorally oriented, economies—i.e., the identification of essentials and the use of progressive taxation of income to deliver essentials as a guarantee.

This more direct approach becomes difficult, however, where productive and financial institutions internationalize, as it becomes difficult to determine to whom the accumulated currency belongs. Efforts by one government or another to invoke taxes against such accumulation are beyond the managerial capacity of international organizations—and these resources tend to flow into external investments in resource extraction (e.g. oil, and minerals), and in the development of industrial sites where labor costs are low. As governments compete for the flow of such currency, opportunities to tax and redistribute currency diminish considerably.[42]

As a general matter, one should avoid oversimplification of legal and economic issues. With that in mind, one might nonetheless accept as a working hypothesis that invasion in modern economies occurs through their financial institutions, and that fair evidence of invasion is the reduction on the taxation of capital accumulating among its organizers. If an economy is not engaged in taxation and redistribution, it is either superficially behavioral, or is in the process of reverting back to control economy.

Otherwise, the participants in an economy are taxed by its producers, though the tax is concealed from view. When a monopolist charges higher than competitive price on a product or service, the consumer is taxed. When the government borrows money, or issues currency to repay debt to monopolists, the consumer is taxed. These are taxes born disproportionately by lower income earners, which is the way control economies have always operated—i.e., transferring surplus from laborers to a militarily protected aristocracy of organizers, while persuading the public that they should be content with subsistence. Given that behavioral economy is a coherent ethical concept (Chapter 5), and that it can be implemented through "requisite" processes (Chapter 6), the most interesting issue remaining is whether it can withstand organized attack by the interests—situated internationally—that are displaced by requisite economies.

3. There is, in modern times, a debate over the appropriate role of government in the management of the flow of productive surplus, largely because the producers' receipt of currency encourages them to become consumers of the deferential behavior of non-producers. This social phenomenon, sometimes inappropriately referred to as "power," comes as an incidental effect of control over accumulated currency, which allows certain individuals to function as gateway to the consumption of luxury products and services.

In order to persuade others that this is a good thing, they construct a straw man that renounces distribution to non-producers, due to the fact that non-producers presumably have neither the will nor the intellectual resources adequate to organize productive enterprises. The straw in the position taken consists in its overgeneralization. Some non-producers are that way because they do not have the will or capacity to produce, but others fail because they are not afforded the resources necessary to enter the class of producers. Thus, in order that the marketplace will effectively attract capability and enthusiasm, the rewards of success must be both significant and reliable. But the argument begs an essential question lying squarely within the wheelhouse of Requisite organization.

Because these issues are not addressed by the proponents of the flow of unlimited capital rewards, it is better to view the motivational (economic) argument as a temporary distraction from the ethical (legal) argument they are making, which appears to be that fairness requires that the spoils of competition flow to and remain with the victor of competition. This argument refers to the ethics of a game, where the participants or contestants enter into a compact at the outset as to the rules of the game, and as the rules are adhered to, the rewards of the game are apportioned to the victor. Thus, to the victor is the claim "we won, and what we acquired is therefore ethically bestowed as "property"— an ethical entitlement to control.

The error in the argument is that a game designed to identify "winners" and "losers" occurs within a smaller set of limits than those of a government held to the task of enabling an "economy." A "game" is an instrumentality designed to draw skill and ambition from its participants on a given field of play. Modern economics is an activity of game design in which games are adapted to perceived social value. As with any game design process, the objective is to establish processes that identify and promote the skills which result in desirable performance. Many of our most popular games are continuously being redesigned so that more people will take interest in them.

A distinction between the productive effect of a game's rules and the distribution of the game's benefits, though nuanced, is an effective statement of the type of relationship between Law and Economy that comes under examination in constitutionally based (Requisite) governments. Ethically speaking we begin with equality as a baseline ethical principle, and thereafter justify separation from equality based on the productive benefits of unequal distribution.

This view was summarized elegantly by the late John Rawls, who in the formulation of the principle of constitutional government identified an order to the analysis of the ethical value of government.

1. The first rule of just distribution is equality—i.e., equal right to a fully adequate system of equal basic liberties compatible with the same for all. [43]
2. The abrogation of the first rule is justified if and only if it results in increased distribution to the least advantaged members. [44]

The first rule derives from the ethical postulate that every individual is their own "end" that that this end may not be combined or equated with that of another. The experience of similar pleasures of two persons, for example, does not equal twice the pleasure, because there is no mind experiencing such increase. There is one experience, and another similar experience, each representing an endpoint to that experience. This principle supports distributive equality because there is no ontological basis on which to justify favoring one person over another. Proof of the intuitive validity of this assumption is the behavior—as previously noted—of hunter-gatherer societies functioning within a wild economy.

The second rule is understandably more controversial because it admits that there are rationales by which unequal distribution might be favorable to a person receiving less—but only if all benefit. With this rule, the door swings open to the development of an economic order that utilizes unequal distribution as a motivator of productivity. A society in which games are designed by its government to stimulate productive behavior might qualify as a "just" society, provided that the rules of the game do not overreach its objective. A game that provides more reward than necessary to motivate productivity overreaches, because it lacks an activating rationale.

The game itself has no ethical value other than that which the designer brings to it, i.e., the skills and motives which the designer deems valuable. To say otherwise engages yet another version of the Russell paradox, the solution of which is to understand that objects do not confer value on objects, rules do not confer value on rules, markets do not confer value on markets, and games do not confer value on games. To say that there is a meta-game—such as a game of game design—where compliance with its rules validates the games it designs, invites unending logical regression, and the formation of entirely artificial and abstractive logical hierarchies.

One might say that such value does not repose in the designer's head, but must at some point repose in his or her heart, though we might engage games and other processes to help find what lies there. It's not always easy to do.

The foregoing paragraphs essentially summarize the ethical dilemma inhering in the formation of international markets. Game design is ethically required to undergo adaptations when and if the game's outcome involves consequences that violate the value or values for which the game serves as an instrumentality. Absent a game designer having the incentive and authority to make such adaptations, an essential implementative influence on competitive markets is lost, and along with it, the ethical substance and standing of their outcomes.

A market that has somehow managed to liberate itself from such influence is as much a threat to a nation organized under Requisite (constitutional) structure as a foreign sovereignty bent on conquest and is apt to regress into social systems led by individuals driven toward destructive risk. Within a theory of Requisite economy, there is no meaningful difference between a foreign nation and an internal faction somehow excused from participation in a nation's laws.

Values activated as antidotes to developments of this kind are simple: (1) An individual human being is something valuable, (2) one is no more or less valuable than another human being, and (3) unequal distribution is valuable only if it is done in a manner consistent with the equal value of individuals. This formulation adds to the two principles of justice discussed by Rawls, by stating what Rawls implied, but failed to express—i.e., that the human being is valuable, and such a being could not have equal value to another if not at first valuable.

But this acknowledgment leads thought toward a more complete and systemic understanding of the terms "equal" and "equality" as a social value. It is "requisite" inasmuch as it is constitutive of what "is" and reveals, correspondingly in its absence, the absence of organization. Requisite organization is therefore foundational to equality, and equality fails to exist in a theoretical or practical sense without it. Let us divide this into three parts.

First, Requisite did in its origin, commence with the expression of value toward the human organism as a special adaptation to a challenging physical environment, where value emerges as shared experience made possible through cooperative ventures enabled by language. It is one thing to be alive, and pursue desire, but quite another to be alive and to bestow value on life. One emphasizes the impulsive experience of an organism seeking to fill a void, the other emphasizes a socially derived orientation where existence—not merely what pleases existence—is deemed good.

Second, a Requisite order is moderate in what it requires from participants of organization—an attitude that derives from the assumption that individuals desire to live productively, and that work and social contribution are natural human traits. Though it is tempting to view assertions about a continuum of intellectual development, and resultant variability of individual capability, as socially divisive, it is quite the opposite. Respect for the equal dignity of social participants implies that they should not be required to do more than they are able, nor be confined to chores which frustrate their creative potential.

Third, given the need in egalitarian societies to link distributional rewards to productive contribution, an emphasis on the quality of organization (Requisite) is a more effective means of leading toward more credible and socially trustworthy compensations.

That is what a pragmatic and scientific response to the preservation of equality seeks to do—i.e., to treat departure from the establishment of equal outcomes as a matter of importance, especially in an international context where accumulated resources do not appear to directly recirculate to a society's game losers. It is unethical and demoralizing, in other words, to release concerns over outcome to a universe ruled by conquest and acquisition.

That would tend to place focus squarely on evolution of international markets, producers and financial institutions. It is foolish, actually, to adopt a theory of law or economy that supposes that markets are entirely self-regulating, or that if a valuable resource is left unguarded, it will not be taken.

While there is some moral credibility in treating the promised reward of an episodic competitive exchange as binding, a Requisite economy appreciates that a promise related to a given episode (referred to in bureaucratic contexts as "task") is limited in time. Rule adjustments are necessary so that one or more episodes will not destroy the moral continuity—and its derived productive continuity—of the competitive process. The conversion of Economy to a winner take all contest played out over a fifty to one-hundred-year time span is naught but an effort of non-cooperative environments to engulf a Requisite order.

There may, in fact, be a sense of entitlement that accompanies incompatible perceptions of how frequently rule based intervention should occur. Is there an episodic boundary to claimed moral right to the productive effect of competition? Is it appropriate to make an ethical claim to an episodic outcome when none has been promised by any authoritative institution? Are the business activities of highly evolved and internationally scaled productive institutions compatible with the limited ability of government to set the stakes? Are such institutions appropriate vessels for the formation of government policy?

All such questions are Requisite questions that engage authoritative agencies (government) in the task of managing economic outcomes. In a behavioral economy, it is not about whether to control or not to control, but how to manage our affairs in an environment—inclusive of many nations—where control over some processes must be released in order to establish productivity (and security) at another level.

4. In modern economies activated by participative government a feeling of moral entitlement deriving in significant part from having earned something attaches to property, which includes preclusion against government to interfere with the use of property. This works, so far as it goes, in one's personal use of money to purchase goods and services, but may not work for others, such as the movement of currency to the vaults of foreign economies.

The point is that it is difficult to have it both ways. If one claims property as an entitlement bestowed only by the power of the ruler, then their ownership (and right of control) is derived from and is apt to conform with the ruler's needs. If it is a moral entitlement, then the right is dependent in most part on the moral ascendency of the sovereignty of a participative government. There, unequal distributive choices should bear some relationship to the value of a recipient's productive input. This at least theoretically justifies the accumulation of huge fortunes, because one might argue that benefits of that nature are necessary to evoke the creativity, risk and labor associated with complex organizational invention. A Requisite economy cannot be sustained, however, where such fortunes are stolen.

Within the last half century there have been a number of changes in the world that present a challenge to the continuity of behavioral economy. These changes consist of the following:

1. The development of technologies of influence and persuasion—of behavioral manipulation—easily implemented through media subject to purchase.

2. A dependency in a competitive political campaign market on funding to develop influential messages with paid access to the media.

3. Large accumulations of wealth in internationally consolidated markets with an interest in influencing the rules by which financial markets operate.

4. A relationship of dependency between internationally situated businesses seeking unregulated competition and many of the political candidates seeking office.

It seems that the combined effect of these changes favor rule making which is accelerating the concentration of wealth in persons who are not very interested in pursuing creative risk. Since it is not necessary to influence government so much as disable it to continue in this regression, there is a significant probability that the gains of behavioral economy will be reversed over the next fifty years.

Those who designed the game in the form of constitutional government probably could not have visualized how strongly this confluence of changes might affect the ordering of markets and of productive affairs, but to give them credit, they designed an adaptive government. And so, there have been some attempts to restrain the effect of money on politics, and those attempts have resulted in some argument among capable policy advocates. One of the most important arguments arose in the opinions related to a case before the Supreme Court of the United States—labeled Citizens United v. Federal Elections Commission 558 U.S. 310 (2010).

Before that decision, the United States Congress had passed a set of laws preventing corporations and labor unions from making independent expenditures and electioneering communications in support of a given candidate and had formed the Federal Elections Commission to administer those laws. Citizens United was a non-profit corporation formed to oppose Hillary Clinton—then a candidate for the office of President—and sought to publish through the cable television media a derogatory movie about Ms. Clinton. The movie would have been a clear violation of congressionally enacted laws prohibiting corporate electioneering and expenditure. Citizens United brought suit to have those prohibitions nullified. The nine Supreme Court justices voted five to four for nullification.

The majority and dissenting opinions reveal different views about the nature of government, which in the end resolved as a difference in view over the relative values one should give to the preservation of political processes against corruption by financial interests and the constitutional guarantee of free speech. The majority, absent some demonstration of quid pro quo effect of corporate electioneering and campaign funding, was unimpressed with the corruptive effects that the elections laws sought to remedy, and felt that there was insufficient basis to override express constitutional protections for political communication established as the First Amendment in the Constitution's Bill of Rights.

That the prohibitions applied against a fictional creature—a corporation—did not remove the Citizen's United conflict from the scrutiny afforded political communication under the Constitution. It is common, in fact, for individuals to form groups that combine resources in order to amplify their political message. The corporate identity would not affect Citizen's entitlement to First Amendment protection—under classical analysis—but might affect the relative weight given to the speech interests of corporations. The majority opined that the affect would be negligible, in that the public political interest in the financial interests of corporations was as legitimate a basis of political expression as other social interests.

As is sometimes the case, the dissenting opinion represented a more nuanced and sustainable view of government. It is also far more consistent with Requisite values and structure of modern economic order—a nation that confers "right" on property through an ethically situated dialogue among its citizenry.

To start with, the dissenting opinion criticized the majority for failing to adhere to procedures designed to establish an effective exchange of information between branches of government, the breach of which were—in themselves—indicative of a disrespect by the Supreme Court of Congress. The Supreme Court ruling was, in effect, like cutting someone off in mid-sentence with a loudly expressed pronouncement—as one would do if they were not interested in what the other had to say. Though a formal matter, it was a matter of concern to the dissenters that the branch of government representing the collective will of the people was not being treated respectfully—because it did not adhere to procedural formalities by which respect is expressed.

Then the dissent faulted the majority for failing to acknowledge the importance of the problem which congress had addressed—i.e., that the accumulated capital in emergent corporate structures might pose a threat to the sovereignty of government by making election outcomes dependent on corporate based financing. It wasn't a new concern. As we have discussed earlier, rulers have for thousands of years been afraid of independent accumulations of influence (later manifest as accumulated currency) in organizations which are not subject to control, and similar concerns were expressed when the first constitutions in the modern era were being drawn. As originally conceived, the corporation introduced a potential for explosive economic growth, but should exist as a regulated entity, as it might tend to overreach its appropriate range of influence. This concern carried with it a mandate to the sovereign voice of the people to defend their government against appropriation by organized monetary interests, just as it would defend itself against rebellion or invasion. To many, the majority decision was like ordering that the castle gates be opened to a marauding army.

But in their defense, there was logic to the majority position. The political marketplace gathers all interests, economic and noneconomic. If groups can gather their resources to advance positions on foreign policy and the morality of numerous types of social relationships, why should they not be permitted to gather their resources to speak (or to amplify speech) on economic interest? To this question, the behavioral knowledge present in the social science of organization (Requisite) encourages us to distinguish the behavior of the human organism under corporate mandate from the behavior of individuals associating politically. The difference consists of essentially three observations.

The first pertains to the nature of what is regarded "free" and "freedom" in application to speech. Freedom viewed as nothing more than the absence of restriction fails to respect the organizational significance of language, which evolved so that the experience of socially cohesive values could be shared between autonomous individuals. This property of language thus distinguishes the organization of human beings in a society from the organization of a mound of ants—i.e., the mutual assertion of autonomy is foundational to the formation of an objective or shared reality. As such, free speech has more to do with the autonomous assertion of value than it does with the absence of restriction. The response of others to what we say can be quite restrictive, but our participation in dialogue as autonomous beings is where freedom rests.

A corporate entity tends to disable this aspect of language. The corporation is allowed to exist so that it will be productive, that is, to make a profit. The CEO of a corporation is legally obligated to advance the interests of the shareholders, and thus subordinate what he does and what he says to their interest in sharing in corporate productivity. What one hears from a corporate representative, therefore, is not "free" speech. It is the speech of an individual whose autonomy is completely subordinated to the commercial interest of an institution.

One might argue that the same is true of any individual who speaks on behalf of a larger group of people, but there are important differences. A group organized for political purposes is itself engaged in a consensus generating process, and presumably invites its members to speak autonomously within the organization. The rules of governance in a corporation, however, attribute influence over corporate action according to investment shares (monetary commitment) and so decisions on positions are apt to be based more on the financial influence of larger investors than on the ethical persuasiveness of the position of a given investor. Those finding themselves in a minority position in a political organization on a given matter of social policy can disaffiliate from that organization without losing an investment, but not so with a minority investor in a corporation established for a commercial purpose. Thus, a small minority of financially positioned investors may control the flow of resources to political causes with whom an overwhelming majority of the investor's corporate participants disagree.

Through the operation of a legal fiction designed to accumulate resources, select individuals can leverage far more influence than their status as citizens would otherwise allow in a constitutional government valuing equal political liberty.

A second observation involves an appreciation of the difference between a political and a commercial marketplace. As we have already noted in a number of different ways, markets do not in themselves confer value on markets, but a political market may confer value on commercial markets if the political market is itself actuated by valuable ruling principles. This, as a matter of observation, strongly suggests that more attention should extend to the rules of a political market than to those of a commercial market.

Most supporters of Requisite organization accept the principle of equal liberty (noted above as inoperative in corporate governance) as essential to the formation of a viable representative government—as well as its derived economy. That principle operates very differently, if at all, in a commercial market, as the rules that govern commercial markets are designed to identify and select the superior products and services—i.e., to commercially glorify inequality.

But in a political system, the measure of positive outcome is not in the identification of winners so much as it is in the enthusiastic input of that market's participants, the preservation of the same in the losers, and a fair actual and perceived relationship between distribution and productive contribution. A weakened sense of value due to the elevation of corporate identity over that of living individuals, and the use of that identity to advance significant political and social imbalances—manifest as unjustified inequalities—is apt to damage popular trust of institutions of all kinds, commercial and noncommercial.

In an environment of distrust, the worst behavioral traits of the human organism tend to surface. These are apt to include violent ethnic rivalries, predatory and fraudulent commercial activities, intransigent constituencies, and economic disintegration, ultimately. Our experience of the last one hundred years teaches that the beneficial advances of constitutional government fare poorly where property loses ethical credibility.

The third observation—again derived from Requisite organization—is that an organization must be able to defend itself against invasion and/or dissolution. This objective is fraught with difficulty, and not uniformly successful.

Germany was unable to sustain itself against dissolution following what history refers to as "The Great Depression." There the invasion could not be geographically isolated, as the invasion occurred from within, and a government that had lost credibility economically was disabled by a fairly small group of political manipulators. Along with the subversion of democratic processes was an almost immediate regression to totalitarian rule, maddened by genocidal paranoia, and bent on the conquest and plunder of other nations.

Such experiences in history ought to evoke a respect of the frailty of incompletely implemented and ignorantly conceived structures necessary for the establishment of modern behaviorally oriented economies. But in the decision of Citizen's United, the majority reasoned dismissively of the potential for corporate fictions to be used as a vehicle by a few individuals within and without the national boundaries of the United States to disable the popular sovereignty of its government. It is strange that a decision of this nature would pass within a political environment where close to eighty-five percent of the general population has expressed disgust with the efficacy of Congress, and large transfers of wealth had already accrued to a very small group of citizens.

As we examine law and economy through the lens of the social science of organization, we come to understand that it is more difficult to establish order than it is to destroy it, especially if certain ethical values weaken. It is probably fair to assume that when we place individuals within a highly competitive financial marketplace they will, if provided the opportunity, attempt to expropriate all the currency they are able. It is a fair presumed constant in the assessment of human behavior, and given that fact it is probably best to place the blame of dissolution on those who overestimate the resiliency of modern systems.

The last rationale of the majority opinion in Citizen's United appears to be that government—vis-à-vis the judicial branch—is poorly situated to oversee a government agency (the FEC) which will regularly make judgments that implicate constitutional rights. A similar justification supported the relaxation of oversight of the world financial markets between years 1998 and 2008, also presumed unnecessary due to the presumed resiliency of those markets. To say those markets self-destroyed would be disingenuous in an economic order which requires vigilant regulation. They were, in the final analysis, collapsed by the sloth of regulators. The wager by the majority in Citizen's United—exhibiting a similar attitude—may be even greater.

5. Perhaps it is unkind to put members of our judicial branch under criticism for complacency. Is it irrational for them to suppose that

government is more effective when it does less, and that markets—political and commercial—can thrive on their own? We ask again, is the relaxation of vigilance the safest alternative when the regulatory complexities become too great to be managed by ordinary mortals?

Except where a government is under attack, government has considerable choice over how complex its environment will be. And the choices made on a governmental level are better choices when they are supported by organizational competence. A decision to back away from regulation may or may not be correct, but it would appear that a decision of that nature should not be controlled by the perceived difficulty of regulation until those who are accomplished organizers have vetted the options. Regulation does not signify control, but rather the identification of the adverse effects of market behavior, and the implementation of ways to prevent them. That is, after all, the mandate of behavioral economy—i.e., the release of creative risk through the relaxation of control, while regulating against adverse consequences.

We have not spent much time examining the problem of resource extraction and have instead examined economy as an organizational phenomenon. This is partly because transportation technologies have reduced the importance of a nation's natural resources and magnified the importance of organizational intelligence. Also, while natural resources have been an important factor in the growth of nations like the United States, there are numerous countries that are resource rich and yet very poor.

In fact, the need for foreign resource extraction has made restrictions upon internationally organized businesses inconceivable. Given that every industrialized nation in the world is dependent on burning of fossil fuel to power engines that magnify the productivity of fewer people, and that oil must be extracted and carried at considerable distances, one might devise an economic theory that completely de-emphasized organization and emphasized petroleum products. As with all resource-based economists since Malthus, they see the end of the world approaching with the depletion of oil.

They have a point. There is a limited supply of oil and an accelerating demand for it, and if we were to run out today our economies would collapse. But it is not going to run out today, and not even in the next ten years—perhaps better to estimate twenty to thirty years. Moreover, it seems that there is an abundance of alternative energy available at a comparable cost in solar energy generation—currently available, and much more implicated as the field of plasma physics evolves over the next fifty years.

Transition to better energy sources is not likely to become simpler in the coming decades if action is delayed, as competition over dwindling supply will tend to stress the regulation of markets and strengthen the position of international businesses that finance and effectuate these resource extractions.

There are, for instance, well organized resource acquisition businesses focused on the extraction of fuel, though it is not in the best interest of the world and all of its economies to consume those resources. There aren't enough of them and they are leading to environment challenges likely beyond the capacity of modern economies to adapt. These businesses are organized internationally in a cooperative relationship with an international finance industry, and prosper in a world economic order which stays the same.

The risk is destructive, because it takes resources from others within economies that redistribute a very small part of the gain to the inhabitants of those economies. Given that government in developing countries is not typically robust and accountable, they are vulnerable to corruptive pressure. We have, in other words, fallen into a market structure that fails to address the urgency of a transition to renewable energy, and nations in a state of dependency on international business models functioning without effective government supervision.

6. A number of commentators write with excitement of an emerging global order that involves increasing economic interdependency among nations, and a persistent and non-coercive pressure on preindustrial nations to modernize. Yet there is a lack of clarity in this writing as to what modernization consists of, except to emphasize the benefits of cooperative economic behavior. Not the least of the benefits of this development is the possibility that international conflicts will be more easily resolved without resort to military force. Stargazing of this nature—for better or worse—invokes a theory of the history of the world.

This particular theory of history lays emphasis on the emergence of communications and transportation technologies, making the coordination of affairs in different parts of the world easier. It is important to acknowledge, however, that from any given platform identified as "present" there are numerous potential futures, all of which depend on the choices made now. We have, in the last few pages, identified a potential scenario accompanying the globalization of economy which suggests exploitative international combinations centered about an unregulated finance industry.

At least one theory of history imagines a superhuman consciousness as God or Messiah who will resolve our organizationally based predicaments through an external act of intervention—something like fire and brimstone. This version of history is not attractive to a scientific orientation, not simply because it is implausible, but because it is not ethically satisfying. The scientist would hope that if there is a God, that being would include humanity in the solution, and that human beings would act rightly out of understanding—not through a mysterious spectacle. And this leads us to a more interesting question—i.e., does the human need to change what it is find it necessary to address the organizational problems of the near future, or is it sufficient that the human understand itself better?

As a species, we should hope that it is the latter. If in fact the consciousness of the human organism does change from time to time, such changes appear to take place very slowly—over thousands of years. Since we are on an economic course which will reach crisis within one hundred years, waiting for a new shift of consciousness is not more than the kind of complacency which leads toward destructive competitions. We are, after all, only about five hundred years into what is arguably a shift of consciousness that produced democratic governments and modern energy rich industrial economies.

Another problem with waiting for a leader is the naïve supposition that there is no organized resistance to the kind of changes that are necessary. The resistance is there, and benefits from impressive resources. Its stewards are intelligent and cruel. They are encouraged by the dependency of a popular movement on single leaders, because when the leader is gone, the movement goes with it. They are also encouraged by the fact that political campaigns are expensive.

The strategy of organized opposition to the shift of consciousness we associate with liberal democracy is worthy of a lengthier analysis. It is useful to note, in passing, that it is not a political movement. The boot stomping marches and racism of the Third Reich were just one of its expressions. It is, rather, an organizational strategy bent on disabling democratic processes, so that its beneficiaries can appropriate the wealth flowing through markets. It is a totalitarian countermeasure to political freedom that may be occurring within a time span that occurs outside our present sense of history. It could, for example, be something like an ancient philosophy responding to a modern one.

The real antidote to focused attempts to undo human progress is organization, or rather, the kind of organization embedded in consensus-based language systems that are successful in activating conscience. Compared to these, totalitarian organizations based on relationships of control are crude simulations of real organization.

Along with breakthroughs in the social science of organization are opportunities to understand ourselves well enough that we might preserve our gains against organized resistance and avoid a regression into the kinds of political systems motivated by fear and effectuated by military organization. Part of this understanding is that it is not competition per se that has produced the luxuries of the modern world, but our adoption of obligatory processes (law) that transform competition from a destructive to a creative process (economy). More importantly, perhaps, we have come to an understanding that we could do so without changing what we are, but rather, by understanding what we are.

As it turned out, this understanding was less disappointing than the beliefs of those who had for many centuries established dominative organizations to protect rulers, and to defeat rivals. Near the center of species self-awareness is value—i.e., that the autonomous existence of a human being is a valuable and socially cooperative awareness. The emergence of modern structures was less a change in human consciousness than it was the assertion of the principal value activating human consciousness, and the implementation of controls that prevented fear from corrupting the natural gravitation of human beings toward cooperative societies. It wasn't something new about what the human was, but a more sophisticated and ethically empowered awareness of what always was.

Because social science movements, such as the Requisite movement, place such emphasis on the role of capability in social organization, it is tempting to overemphasize the organizer. This works to some degree in the understanding of a single institution but is much less useful in understanding transformative social movements, or in the development of laws suitable for the maintenance of productive economies. We may be better situated to handle the serious challenges to our way of life by imagining a world in which ordinary people embrace great values than one in which great people assert control over complex constituencies. This seems the preferred course for Requisite—or any other social science movement—in the achievement of coherency as an ethical philosophy.

Accordingly, one might want to consider whether "trust"—as the ethical moniker of the Requisite movement—is an adequately stated summary of the value of human organization. Though valuable, "trust" lays emphasis on the confidence that participants have that they will not be harmed by others in a given social organization. Again, value of this nature transfers emphasis to structure, and derivatively, those who control it. But this only seems to beg the question of what activates the formation of trust inducing structures. Trust, it seems, is better described as a beneficial aftereffect of cooperative behavior motivated by value placed on the autonomy and welfare of the participants in a social system.

Trust inducing structures are valuable because people are valuable. It may therefore be more productive to focus on the emergent value of the axial age, which placed emphasis on a human relationship to value, which is the value of modern democracy, i.e., "freedom." The "freedom" of requisite economic order is not so much about the absence of restriction, but the affirmation of the value of human existence. In many great religious texts, it is also referred to as "love"—a term having many different meanings.

These considerations lead us to some useful insights on how to approach the problem of global organization in an international market which—while energizing—threatens to undo the beneficial advances we have made to this point. This may be more operationally conceived as addressing worldwide stresses related to the generation of energy within a universe of liberated marketplaces. If we assert too much control, the productive output of those markets will strangle as national sovereignties seek—usually to no effect—to arrive at consensus on distributional issues. But if we assert too little, the consolidation of international finance practices will move increasingly toward wealth extraction (destructive risk) rather than wealth production (creative risk). It will be necessary to examine the transition behaviorally within a set of laws adequate to the needs of all.

It is likewise important not to underestimate the need for an accelerated and orderly development of pre-modern economies. Their populations and economic output will grow significantly over the next fifty years, and they will generate and consume energy. The transition, however, to sophisticated and sustainable energy and water production technologies requires a modern economy—meaning effective legal, health, educational, financial, transportation and utilities structures. Under the present trajectories of growth, putting our own house in order—though necessary—is not enough. Accordingly, we should pay as much attention to technologies of organization as we do to other technologies, and regard all of it as necessary to our own survival.

As we as a species become more aware of ourselves, we are apt to realize that "order" and "organization" are not about the imposition of hard but of soft controls—of the management of outcomes that benefit from the exercise of liberty. Requisite principles might therefore be viewed as welcome in addressing organizational problems on many economic levels, because it is in the end a better thing to find ways to cooperate than to deal with the other harsh consequences waiting only a few moments away. It isn't necessary to change very much, but to instead understand the changes that have already taken place. That should be transformation enough, at least for now.

# Postscript

I have omitted comment in the preceding pages on ways to go about bringing the rest of the world into modernity. This is due less to the lack of opinions I carry around with me than to the realization that we have not ourselves completed that transition. The best thing we might do for others is to be what we profess to be, and that will require some effort on our part. I suspect that I will spend some time—as I have recently—on listening to others instead of trying to tell them something. But time is not really on our side, at least as I and others interested in the future tend to see things.

There are some things that have come to my attention since I completed the first draft of this manuscript that should be noted, and that don't fit well into the narrative. One of these is the status of Requisite Organization as an intellectual movement has not in its mainstream applications matured much further than where Elliot Jaques left it. I attribute this in part to the fact that RO has not established itself well as it should have as an academic course of study. The interest of "management science" within the academic universe appears to have shifted from structure, along with its motivational support, to the marketing of leadership prescriptions. This is not to suggest criticism of Jaques or any others who share his views, but to restrictions in application that tend to remove RO from other more stimulating forums. It is clear to me now that RO would rest well in the academic disciplines of developmental psychology, and the application of psychological models to the understanding of market behavior. Organizational Development—as a field of study—is too narrowly situated to receive this research.

Since writing this book, I am grateful to have had the opportunity to read Luc Hoebeke's book "Making Work Systems Better" and it is apparent from reading it that the use of Jaques' research has and will lead other commentators along a similar path. Almost as an afterthought, Hoebeke devotes about twenty pages of text to the economic implications of RO, which are quite similar to my own observations. These are identified as nine controversies, the points of which are:

1. Disciplinary boundaries of economics are changing.
2. Economic competition only partially describes market economy.

3. A revised definition of "ownership" challenges old conventions.
4. Innovation is a socio-political phenomenon.
5. The market driven media distorts effective governance.
6. Planning (control) is in conflict with innovation (creative risk).
7. Scale affects viability of representative democracy.
8. Global economies effectively circumvent localized controls
9. Governance is a matter of establishing a balanced value system.

It is, perhaps, worthy of note, that he makes a point similar to my own in the understanding of RO research, that is, that shifts from one work level to another each involve not only a shift of form, but a shift of attitude and strategic orientation. This addition to RO is what allows one to talk coherently of the human organization as similar to an organism—adaptive and socially responsive.

I am very much encouraged to see that a shift of emphasis—from economy as competition to economy as organizational—tends to bring thought into a more nuanced and productive approach to economic development. He criticizes some of Jaques' conclusions, as do I, but I think Jaques' error can be pinpointed and rectified. The error consists in being overly preoccupied with the form of maturation, and not sufficiently preoccupied with the motivational substance of it. With that modification, it is relatively easy to see human organization not just as an organism, but as an organism functioning within an adaptive language system. With that, the use of RO research as a basis for understanding a wide variety of organizational phenomena becomes plain and obvious. It therefore belongs in the forefront of more than one academic discipline.

Conversations I've had with other RO practitioners since writing this book strongly suggest that the error is being repeated among quite a number of Jaques' followers. I can't say it is for lack of intelligence, insight or capability on their part. The difference, as I indicate in Chapter 2, has to be extracted from the logic made accessible by R.O. Gibson, and comes about through the realization that thought can't exist without selection, and in the human cybernetic universe, selections are a matter of wanting something. As I pointed out, Bertrand Russell made a similar mistake—historically recorded as Russell's paradox, as did I until I saw the problem. For those interested, I have attached an explanatory appendix of how information processing strata derive from R. O. Gibson's logic, and how to repair some of its deficiencies.

The error, unfortunately, casts us into a somewhat deterministic universe. We are within it subject to structures instead of the generators of structure. There is a tendency as well to devalue value, and to view states of motivation as less unimportant and more locally dependent experiences than they really are. We find ourselves located within an ethical universe of peace and quiet rather than enthusiastic collaboration. The prime ethical directive tends toward escape rather than opposition to the various tyrannies devised by the human species. It fails to see the problems of others as an important aspect of our own problems. Though ethically coherent, it is, as such, not ethically satisfying. Nor is it an effective survival strategy in dealing with the challenges likely to emerge within the next one hundred years.

I make this observation because it appears that the deficiencies of past social organization will not likely disappear soon enough on their own accord, and require focused resistance. One of the lessons of history, however, is that such resistance is futile if directed at the person (not the principle) and if nothing constructive is being offered as a replacement. It is necessary to know what to oppose, and "better" to oppose non-confrontively by advocating the modification of governance processes. It can be done in a way that harnesses the power of language. It's a good time to get started in that direction, inasmuch as political tensions related to the cold war have abated, and the pressures one would associate with resource depletion are—relatively speaking—still below red line.

As I see things, there are at least two areas where the introduction of RO as a social science technology would accelerate economic development significantly. The first is in the installation of autonomous judicial structures capable of identifying and sustaining rights within a rule of law. This would involve a shift from politically dependent claims of control over real estate, business, innovation and employment relations to stable and enforceable rights of ownership. These structures tend to separate modern from pre-modern economies, and make the extension of affordable credit within a financial system possible. My thoughts on this subject are essentially duplicative of those of the famous developmental economist Hernando De Soto. De Soto's dream of extending affordable credit to an indigent work force is far less dependent on the enactment of laws than on the development of a dependable judicial and social infrastructure—and thus almost entirely an organizational problem.

The second lies in the replacement of government investment in military security with investment in water and energy utilities infrastructures. It seems, perhaps naively, that international assemblies of nations can provide effective security against invasion or rebellion, and can condition the extension of security on national compliance with requisite governmental processes. They can also do this without interfering with the autonomy and governance of developing countries and taking on the logistical nightmare of "worldwide government." It doesn't seem out of the range of human capability to make those selections—realizing in the process that unitary control through coercion is, by definition, not governance. Since abundant water is feasible within an economy supporting abundant energy, the substitution of military complexes with energy complexes suggest an effective point of focus. Here again, we are talking of interventions (not all governmental) that challenge us to develop and replicate organizational designs.

On the other hand, depending on market-based world financial system offers little to be optimistic about. It has neither the capability, nor the motivation, to address security issues. It may, in fact, be the opposite—i.e., using locally assembled coercive unitary control structures as an instrumentality for the extraction of wealth from indigent populations. It may on a larger scale be viewed as part of the transfer of wealth to a financial system formed into a collection of gambling houses—all celebrating destructive over creative risk. Knowing the difference between trustworthy finance and exploitative consolidation is, in the end, the kind of thing that becomes clear within a Requisite economy. Elliot Jaques, and others working with him, started us in this direction. We might within this paradigm—with some luck—be able to ascertain the root of corruption, and thus oppose it more effectively.

# End Notes

[1] There is considerable debate over the mechanism operating in the emergence of market failure, along with the mechanism of the ultimate recovery of the market. Disagreement among theorists appears to have less to do with what happened (collapse of credit in a banking industry) than with why it happened (what economic policies and practices bear the blame). Two major explanatory schools—one named after John Maynard Keynes and another simply entitled "Monetarist"—emphasize different aspects of government intervention in economic affairs. The Keynesian school argues that underutilization of human resources activates a cycle of contracting demand for goods and services and reduced investment manifest in further restriction of available employment, thereby implying that an authoritative source (government) should break the cycle by putting people to work with newly issued currency. The monetarists—led by Milton Friedman—believe that the decline of employment generating investment can be resolved through monetary policy, i.e., using the banks (instead of government) as processers of expanded credit availability. Since currency and credit are, in essence, about printing money, the real or substantial difference between the schools is, again, about the efficacy of government as a stimulator of growth versus the efficacy of market driven lending institutions. Both schools appear to agree that the incentive structures of private lending institutions should be scrutinized, but disagree over the degree of scrutiny that would be effective on the part of government.

There is likewise a strong consensus among economists that the Second World War had a stimulative impact on economic growth, but there is disagreement about the favorable developments of the war which brought that about—along similar lines. Some argue that full employment activated by military conscription and the armaments industries was the prime mover of growth, while others emphasize that it was the emergence of businesses and the concentration of resources and technologies in newly developing industries which produced growth. All seem to agree that high government debt and highly progressive tax rates to cover that debt did not impede the momentum of the recovery, once currency began to circulate through purchase and investment.

[2] An illuminating treatise on the subject of Micro-Economics was authored by Samuel Bowles (Microeconomics, Behavior, Institutions, and Evolution, Princeton University Press, 2004). This is an important

book from the standpoint of advancing a theory of Law and Economic Order because it identifies quite a number of situations where market driven self-interest fails to produce efficient results, and how institutional formation and intervention can affect market equilibria. This analysis is a necessary link to a theory of economy which emphasizes the ethical and practical basis for government as a source of assistance in human cooperative activity. Our work here is not technically micro econometric, but certainly suggests modifications of policy which would make Bowles and other game oriented theorists much more important in the evolution of macroeconomic policy.

[3] The development of a child's acquisition of a concept of volume is a small part of Piaget's overall theory of cognitive development, but essentially illustrative of the theory of development he authored. One important aspect of his theory is adopted throughout this book—i.e., that the comprehension of wholes not only proceeds in phases, but that development proceeds in cycles that move comprehension to a new order or stage of comprehension which engages objects of comparable type and complexity across diverse contexts. So, development is more than a matter of acquiring control over a given object, but a process where control over a given object becomes a transferable skill manifest in similar types of objects encountered in diverse situations. He refers to this as an "empirical abstraction."

[4] The summary of findings over the next several pages derives from considerable direct communication with Jaques in a seminar given at the University of Southern California in January 1979, as well as an impressive list of publications authored or organized by Jaques. His work is aptly summarized in General Theory of Bureaucracy (London: Heinemann Educational, 1970), Levels of Abstraction in Logic and Human Action: A theory of discontinuity in the structure of mathematical logic, psychological behavior, and social organisation (London: Heinemann Educational, 1978—with R.O. Gibson and D.J. Isaac Editors), Requisite Organization: Total System for Effective Managerial Organization and Managerial Leadership for the 21st Century (London: Gower, 1997), and The Life and Behavior of Living Organisms: A General Theory (Greenwood, 2002). These publications can be obtained through Requisite Organization International (ROII) directly. A more diversified resource center for past and ongoing research in the field of study begun by Jaques lies in Global Organization International. Both resources centers can be contacted on line.

⁵ This critique references an article published by R. O. Gibson and D.J. Isaac, "Truth Tables as a formal device in the analysis of human action" Levels of Abstraction in Logic and Human Action, London: Heinemann, 1978.

⁶ That work was completed by this author in various phases, beginning in 1979 as a paper submitted to Jaques, and later in expanded manuscript form submitted to Jaques and his colleagues in 1980 and 1983. That work included the assertion that there were four and only four information processing modes, and was in fact the basis of a discussion with Jaques that the use of a five-phased cycle of information processing was an error unless a fifth stage is identified as a point of transition between one order of complexity and another—i.e., completion of one cycle doubling as commencement of another cycle. This work is now submitted and fully explained in a 2003 book entitled "On Freedom" within the chapter entitled "Intellectual Freedom." That book carries with it an appendix explaining the notational system used, and the debt owed to G. Spencer Brown in his groundbreaking work Laws of Form. Also, attached to this book is an appendix describing the transformation of a first order logic to an information processing logic emphasizing the link between interest and logical structure.

One of a number of reasons for the completion of the 2003 manuscript and its publication in 2016, is that while information processing vocabulary was accepted into the lexicon or "science" of stratified systems, its relation to first order logic did not accompany that usage, nor was there explanation of how those descriptors adopted an essentially cyclic theory of cognitive development consistent with the theory develop by P:iaget as well as a theory which relates structured output (as processing mode) to motivational state.

⁷ The designer of the information processing vocabulary was the author of this book, and the original deficiencies of the expression of the logical basis—as states of intention—are those of the author.

⁸ This distinction brings the Requisite movement considerably closer to what Piaget was attempting to describe in his use of the term "empirical abstraction" to explain the movement to a new "stage" of development—i.e., that mastery of a given object invoked the capacity to transfer that cognitive act to other objects of similar "type" or "form." But here we are seeing—as if through a microscope—that abstractions of this nature are nested within a newly formulated interest or expectancy. Mind, in other words, has to work through a cycle of familiarity with a given object, and then after having effectively integrated the experience

into an internalized pattern, is released into contemplation of that object as a "type" forming within a higher order expression of value. Parallel processing does not, as some interpreters of Jaques seem to indicate, consist in the collection of serial processes—or rather, an accumulation of series stuffed into a system. It is instead the emergence (a transitional state) of object standing apart from but giving meaning to an entire field of data—even though only some (or one) of its particulates may be perceptible.

⁹ This is not a trivial point of controversy, as it is quite difficult without this insight to appreciate a distinction between simple "hierarchy" as a developmental progression, and superficial hierarchy appearing within the abstractive lability of a spoken language. There was an attempt by Jaques and his wife Kathryn Cason to identify "four and only four" states of information processing by using four connectors of first order logic—(1) either/or (disjunctive), (2) both/and (conjunctive), (3) if/then (conditional) and (4) if/and only if (bi-conditional). Though Jaques made an effort to link four information processing states to these logical connectors, the effort fails because of a failure to appreciate that a conditional expression is, in first order logic, not the same thing as an implicative expression used in logical syllogisms. Nor are biconditional expression anything at all like what happens in what modern psychologists refer to as parallel processing, except on a very superficial level. Gibson, who was the discoverer of the "four and only four" logical processes recognized that movement between levels involved more than a change of connective function, but a change of purpose and perspective that the schema of Jaques and Cason fail to recognize. One cannot, for example view parallel processing as a concatenation of serial processes. There is much more to it than that, and engages one somewhat deeply in set and relations theory. To get an idea of the complex and engrossing nature of parallel processing, a good resource would be paper authored by Louis Kaufman, Constructivist Foundations: Vol 4, " Reflexivity and Eigenform, The Shape of Process," July, 2009.

¹⁰ An explanatory footnote may, at this point, serve to clarify the intended use of a "map" of conscious experience. This has already been the subject of considerable explanation in this author's monograph entitled On Freedom, in the chapter "Political Freedom" where the interdependency of individually formed identities in language provided the basis for a revised understanding of law as a species of language—having the same structure and dynamism. As may already be apparent to the reader, a key to the understanding of language consists in the revision

of "information processing" to identify two different sources of value—one reflecting the intervention of primary value and another reflecting the strategic use of three (not four) processing instrumentalities each representing a value derived from their efficacy in the navigation of a field of data gathered within the domain of primary value.

What this mapping provides is a proposed still photograph of consciousness poised to bring perceptual experience into shared social experience. The "I" part of the diagram identifies an influence which seems to come within as a governing expectancy which is independent of control, and is sometimes referred to in religious experience as "I am" in order to emphasize that it represents an imperative of existence manifest in efforts to construct existence out of a unordered void. It is equally manifest in the presence of other beings "Other"—an influence which touches and forms our own existence intimately. In language we do not control these influences, just as we do not control "conscience" but respond to them within a matrix brought into being through language.

[11] One of these is the system developed in antiquity among Greek philosophers—Plato and Aristotle—which identified Reason as the basis of ethical judgment. According to Plato, the human organism included a "rational" element, with its own interest in the discernment and formation of social harmony as a basis of existence. Another system emerged in a philosophical movement known as "the Enlightenment" which culminated in the assertion by Immanuel Kant that Reason was the basis of a moral imperative of consistent and universal application of moral rule as the basis of ethical formations such as law and virtue. There are a number of other proponents of reason as the basis of ethics, which is by many regarded as the basis of modern ethical consciousness. This analysis, however, suggests a more socially interactive and intuitive process which identifies Reason as a relative rather than absolute experience, and thus Reason as one of the effects of the value placed on shared experience.

[12] This note may help address a skeptical reader's discomfort with the use of the term "deity." In a scientific world, there is a tendency to think of deity as a superstitious effect of primitive society, and even to regard contemporary Judaic, Christian and Islamic deity as an expression of scientific ignorance—and there is some truth to that criticism inasmuch as the externalized deities of the modern world are used more as placeholders and palliatives than they should.

The importance of using the term in this book derives from the fact that we don't have much control over what we think "good" or "acceptable" mean. These emotions seem to vary to a degree between societies, and as we observe their effects in others, we behave as anthropologists taking note of their idiosyncrasies. But the experience of value within one's own culture or society is something different. There are virtues we extol, and a range of acceptable expressions of individuality, and a perceived need to be in agreement with others about what those are. We want to believe in a transcendent ethical principle, a good which is shared with Other, and so consciousness embraces that as deity, even if it refrains from using the term "god." We know intuitively when we fall outside those boundaries—when we have sinned, and our sense of self existence or selfhood (Identity) weakens or dissolves.

What does one call that influence, and where does it come from? As the preceding discussion on evolutionary genetics suggests, one might call it the "brain" but what is the "it" which the brain registers, and so the question fails to have a satisfying answer. The use of the term "deity" leaves that question unresolved, and hopefully, untainted. As such, it serves as a balancing figure in an equation (a linguistic equation that includes the communication of ethical value).

[13] The stratification of language into three tiers—as opposed to the two of "semantic" and "syntactic"—is set forth by this author in his completed manuscript "On Freedom" in Chapter 4 "Political Freedom." The term "presentive" is appropriated from some of the work of Nathaniel Lawrence (deceased) in a paper he submitted to the International Society of Time in 1977, and adopts his referent for it, i.e., not merely the use of language to present "self" but of the way "selfhood" is embedded in the structure of language.

As one becomes more comfortable in the understanding that semantic and syntactic features of language are distinct only as matters of emphasis—not as separate and isolated cerebral functions—it becomes apparent that value is a part of the shifting emphasis occurring within the mind of speakers and listeners, and that the organizing point of referral for value is "identity", or rather, the formation, preservation and participation in selfhood.

This view of mind as operating within organized complexes, landing upon and shifting from states of intention which include and integrate a compound (but limited) complex of experience, represents a shift from existing models from language as a data processing function of brain to a developing informational organization of mind. And, as we are eager to repeat, organization does not occur without value, and value is individually seated in "self." If one attempts to imagine language without self-reference, he encounters incoherency similar to that which troubled Wittgenstein.

There is some temptation to view self-reference as a component of semantic reference, that is, to view it as an aspect of meaning, and there would be some truth in that. Meaning as a register of linguistic output is riddled with express and implicit statements about the identity of the speaker. But in doing this, the point being made here is missed—i.e., that identity is fused to the process in which meaning (as productive output) is uttered, and would be incoherent without it. It is "present" in the formation as well as in the effect of a linguistic event. This marks an end to certain forms of nonsense—like talking computers. If they aren't experiencing "identity" they aren't engaging in language.

[14] See Gowdy, John M. (1998). Limited Wants, Unlimited Means: A Reader on Hunter-Gatherer Economics and the Environment. St Louis: Island Press. pp. 342; Dahlberg, Frances. (1975). Woman the Gatherer. London: Yale university press; Erdal, D. & Whiten, A. (1996) "Egalitarianism and Machiavellian Intelligence in Human Evolution" in Mellars, P. & Gibadfson, K. (eds) Modeling the Early Human Mind. Cambridge MacDonald Monograph Series

[15] See Lee, Richard B. & Daly, Richard, eds., ed. (1999). The Cambridge Encyclopedia of Hunters and Gatherers. Cambridge University Press; Lee, Richard B.; Guenther, Mathias (1995). "Errors Corrected or Compounded? A Reply to Wilmsen". Current Anthropology (36): 298–305; Lee, Richard B. (1992). "Art, Science, or Politics? The Crisis in Hunter-Gatherer Studies". American Anthropologist (94): 31–54.

[16] See, Sahlins, M. (1968). "Notes on the Original Affluent Society", Man the Hunter. R.B. Lee and I. DeVore (New York: Aldine Publishing Company) pp. 85-89.

[17] See, Jonas Langer; Melanie Killen (1998). Piaget, evolution, and development. Psychology Press. pp. 258; Leonard D. Katz Rigby (2000). Evolutionary Origins of Morality: Cross-disciplinary Perspectives. United kingdom: Imprint Academic. p. 158. It should be noted, however, that the emergence of more sedentary agricultural economies resulted in some class based division due to the accumulation of domesticated livestock, though not on the order of the slave economies emerging in the Bronze age.

[18] See, Marcus J Hamilton, Bruce T Milne, Robert S Walker, Oskar Burger, James H Brown The complex structure of hunter–gatherer social

networks: Proc Biol Sci. 2007 September 7; 274(1622): 2195–2203. Published online 2007

[19] See "The Development of Social Stratification in Bronze Age Europe, Antonio Gilman, Current Anthropology, Vol. 22, February 1981—an interesting article, accompanied by several interesting comments on the article, essentially setting forth the weaknesses in the view that social stratification at the inception of the Bronze Age occurred and continued due to beneficial social effects of management—referred to as "functionalism." This criticism is part of a larger debate between "conflict" based theories within a Marxian school of interpretation emphasizing an historical/material dialectic between haves and have nots, and a structuralist school emphasizing the relationship between social structures and the managerial utility of the establishment of a ruling class. Our analysis tends to fall on the side of conflict based theory—with a twist consistent with ongoing efforts in this field to reconcile the functionalist and conflict based schools.

There is "functionality" to the organization of states around military assemblies which acknowledges the importance of protection in relatively sedentary agricultural societies subject to invasion. Our analysis is focused on the logic of social formations functioning within escalating fear of invasion. (This was, in essence Gilman's response to the contention that aristocracies confer an economic benefit on servient masses.) The point of equilibrium within a social universe of this sort is exploitative because non-exploitative strategies are not apt to survive. Within a social universe that rewards sociopathy, there is rapid decline into a highly exploitative equilibrium that has a predictable and stable dynamism.

In Jaques' last book, The Life and Behavior of Living Organisms, Jaques falls squarely within the functionalist school of this debate, emphasizing that advances in civilization were attributable to the visionary perspectives of social organizers and managers. This book contributes to the functionalist view by pointing out that management applied to complex social structures is important to the progress of civilization, and occurs opportunistically only when conditions favoring such organization combine with the manifestation of visionary capability. This book seeks to place this insight within a sense of "history" which acknowledges organization as an important aspect of history, but that the shift from adaptive structures to fixed structures impeded the formation of modern economies. Most of the kinds of visionaries capable of envisioning and implementing a modern economic order—though of great capability—would likely have been killed in the universe of control economy.

Much of what Jaques thinks of as visionary capability is enabled by contextual variables affecting the nature of the contest. In modern economies, therefore, we are apt to encounter greater numbers of visionaries not merely due to greater numbers of people, but because game rules have shifted allowing visionary capabilities to be utilized. This is, perhaps, less important to the understanding of bureaucracies than in the understanding of economies, where ethical controversies and rules over who will prevail within them are elevated.

[20] See Aristotle, Politics 1:5 (Jowett, Trans)

"The same holds good of animals in relation to men; for tame animals have a better nature than wild, and all tame animals are better off when they are ruled by man; for then they are preserved. Again, the male is by nature superior, and the female inferior; and the one rules, and the other is ruled; this principle, of necessity, extends to all mankind.

"Where then there is such a difference as that between soul and body, or between men and animals (as in the case of those whose business is to use their body, and who can do nothing better), the lower sort are by nature slaves, and it is better for them as for all inferiors that they should be under the rule of a master.

"For he who can be, and therefore is, another's and he who participates in rational principle enough to apprehend, but not to have, such a principle, is a slave by nature. Whereas the lower animals cannot even apprehend a principle; they obey their instincts. And indeed, the use made of slaves and of tame animals is not very different; for both with their bodies minister to the needs of life.

"Nature would like to distinguish between the bodies of freemen and slaves, making the one strong for servile labor, the other upright, and although useless for such services, useful for political life in the arts both of war and peace. But the opposite often happens--that some have the souls and others have the bodies of freemen. And doubtless if men differed from one another in the mere forms of their bodies as much as the statues of the Gods do from men, all would acknowledge that the inferior class should be slaves of the superior.

"And if this is true of the body, how much more just that a similar distinction should exist in the soul? But the beauty of the body is seen, whereas the beauty of the soul is not seen. It is clear, then, that some men are by nature free, and others slaves, and that for these latter slavery is both expedient and right."

[21] As a sequel to the quoted text from the politics of Aristotle, it is interesting, perhaps, to examine the comments of Aristotle evolutionally—

i.e., descriptive of the way consciousness restructured under the effect of a control economy—where dominative hierarchy organizing social assemblies of fixed complexity reigned over the affairs of great masses of people. Here Aristotle engages in a form of reasoning that recurs frequently among the ancients. He examines the nature of consciousness—a hierarchically organized phenomenon—and reflects upon society as if it were a replication of consciousness. The beast within man thus produces servient roles within a social order that are similar in kind to the stratification of mind.

But one might have noticed that the platform from which Aristotle separates base from elevated aspects of mind consists of the view that rationality as a value neutral organizing presence governs man at the highest level. Since the ethical man is servant to reason, so too the ethical polity supports a condition of obedience of servant to master. There is some elegance to this formula, but there is a philosophical snare hidden within it. That snare is similar to that which afflicts, from time to time, the theoretical formulation of Requisite organization—as structurally rather than intentionally governed.

The problem is with the understatement of the role of value in the development of social organization, and how that value engages individual consciousness (man) as participant in an adaptive exchange between "I" and "Other." Reason is not the ruling principle, but one of the effects of a value placed on shared experience, a value which embraces individual along with collective existence, compassion toward suffering, forgiveness and kindness. If one treats Reason—in Aristotle's work frequently manifest as abstractive hierarchy—as identical to or the source of such value, the nature of law and economy strongly favor dominative hierarchy, and fails to achieve the creative potential of social organization under more liberated formulae.

If value is, it doesn't need reason to make it so, but reason as we think of it may be regarded as an effect or manifestation of our relationship with it. So, the "reason" of Plato and Aristotle may be better viewed as a version of mind, rather than the substance of mind, and in the context of control economy, an attempt by man to "know" good and evil, or rather, to subordinate good to human control processes. Reason is something we gain understanding of as we gain understanding of ourselves, and may ultimately be something quite different than we—in both ancient and recent times—imagined that it was.

[22] While the issuance of symbolic commercial objects appeared relatively early—2300 B.C.E.—these were used in restricted contexts to

identify measures of grain (and other produce), the appearance of coinage used as a universal basis of compensation and trade across a variety of commercial markets did not appear until much later—between 800 and 600 B.C.E. See Wikipedia articles "Coin" and "Currency."

[23] See Arnold J. Toynbee, A Study of History (abridged edition 1947)

[24] See Bruce Bartlett, "How Excessive Government Killed Ancient Rome," Cato Journal, No. 14 (Fall, 1994)

[25] See Tainter, Joseph (1988) "The Collapse of Complex Societies" (Princeton University Press) It may be worthwhile to note that Tainter's approach to the evaluation of Roman decline is the closest available to a one size fits all theory, mainly because Roman decline is used as example to a much more broadly located theory of civil collapse, and the relationship between such collapse to the adaptive power of government.

Implied in this analysis is a point somewhat similar to what we have been examining in the course of this book, i.e., are government structures conceived as adaptations to a fixed expectancy of control able in the long run to deal with a host of stressors they are apt to encounter, not the least of which are the loss of social morale and productivity, disease associated with impoverished concentration of mass populations, and heightened security costs associated with unresolved conflict. Such concerns corrode social and economic order, and lend credibility to ideologies which express disapproval of the expansion of government. The question left unresolved, of course, is whether certain strategies for the management of complexity are part of the available technologies offered within the social sciences, and where—whether in the conception of government or in the formation of administrative mechanisms— solutions to overburdened institutions are properly applied.

[26] See Ian Bremmer, The End of the Free Market, Penguin, 2010.

[27] Some liberty is taken here to identify how an economist thinks, which is something interesting in itself. Not that economists are ethically prone to undertake measures to assure the perpetuity or availability of slave labor, as the rightness or wrongness of the availability of slave labor is a legal, not an economic consideration. The professional function of an economist is to systemically evaluate the consequences of environmental changes, which include changes in obligation, and the availability and cost of labor as a major economic consideration. Were an economist, however, to conclude that a change of obligation would place stress on an economic system, a dialogue between economists and lawyers would

commence which included the evaluation of what other government interventions might be required to avoid the adverse consequences.

There are times when the introduction of obligational reform may so disrupt the systemic provisions for available human and natural resources that economic disruption would be severe. This, it appears, was a significant part of the debate over the abolition of slavery in many parts of the world in the latter half of the nineteenth century, and over the recognition of the rights and powers of labor unions in the first half of the twentieth century. These debates were similarly resolved in part by an economic evaluation, i.e., that economy would not be destroyed, and that great masses of people would not face starvation if controls designed to insure the availability of cheap labor were lifted. The controllers of labor might have to take a loss, but economy would continue under a more liberal set of constraints. It was important to know that, as an economist might know, before transformative shifts of obligation could be implemented.

[28] Judaism may well have been the first of the major world religious movements to function within the kind of ethical parameters associated with the Axial Age—though at least two reputable authors identify Confucianism as the first major religious movement emphasizing kind regard toward all human beings as essential to happiness. See Jaspers, Karl; Bullock, Michael (Tr.) (1953). The Origin and Goal of History (1st English ed.). London: Routledge and Keegan Paul; Karen Armstrong (2006). The Great Transformation: The Beginnings of our Religious Traditions. NY: Knopf.

A good reason to look closely at Judaism as a headwater to global transformation is the capture and enslavement of the people of Judaea by Babylonian conquerors, and the need during that time to make a more universalized statement about the value of human existence when faced with unthinkable cruelty. It was a stress of this nature in which God—as an externalized anthropomorphic tribal companion—was transformed into the ground of ethical existence common to an entire species. The god of Moses worked for a select group among many served by their own gods, but the God of Judaea under the Babylonian enslavement was part of an evolving monotheism—i.e., one and only one God which is identified with the source of all of what really is, all good. This was the God identified in the first poem of Genesis—"In the beginning"— written more than one thousand years after the story of Adam and Eve. While the theology of monotheism is elusive, it is transformative in the sense of being moved inward as a basis rather than effect of existence.

Writing concurrent with this transformation inserted the Golden Rule into the Torah (Leviticus 19:18) and identified the love of God along with the love of Other as ruling principle (Deuteronomy 6:5,22:1-4). This change occurred hundreds of years before the famous narratives of Siddhartha and Jesus were written—though these narratives may have helped to advance and clarify the kind of protest nascent in Confucian, Taoist, Platonic and Judaic traditions, by stating clearly that the nature of being consists in a value which negates man-as-beast.

[29] It might be useful, at this point, to set ruling principle of behavioral economy (shifting influence from a ruler's fear to participatory dialogue) apart from pragmatic constraints and expectations (the institution of constitutional government). One must commit to a different sort of economy, which includes a more ethically situated concept of law before one makes discriminating choices regarding institutional design.

Therefore, we are now in the process of defining the ethical precepts of a complex cooperative system in which a government gazes intelligently and cooperatively upon behaviors in a marketplace which is only partially self-correcting. In the identification of these three principles, we are looking at different facets of the same thing—autonomous beings (acting under protections to autonomy), engaged in a participative and persuasive dialogue (consensus oriented to agreement between I and Other), expressing itself in rules of conduct (ethical obligation).

Productive behavior within a system which strives to integrate itself ethically—as ruling principle—reveals not just one but many different kinds of markets, some of which have graver ethical implications than others. The signal characteristic of Behavioral economy is the evaluation of markets as behavioral phenomena within an intelligent and participative government, and the marginalization of the fear of given ruler(s) as a basis of selection.

[30] The word "rent" refers to extra charges on a product or service due to the unique situation of a given firm's relation to government. One charges a "rent" for the occupation of property which requires no productive input by the owner except to make it available. As we have indicated, economies based on ruler-based dependencies all emphasize special relations to government, and monopoly is—more or less—the rule rather than the exception. This book originally contemplated a chapter or more to the concept of surcharges to consumer where private firms successfully procure acceptance by government of "rents" but there

are already some very good resources available. See, for example, Joseph Stiglitz, The Price of Inequality, W.W. Norton, (2012).

A nice example of "rent" might be the override consumers pay for health insurance in the United States, whose pricing structures are specially exempted from laws prohibiting monopoly and price fixing. American consumers pay close to twice what consumers pay in single payer health systems, and yet there is much confusion over what to call the surcharge, except to use the term "rent" or "tax" for a cost structure which has no competitive market corrective factored into it, and depends almost entirely on special position acquired within a matrix of laws designed to preserve competition. It is, perhaps, one of a number of ironies of an economy divided into government and market that direct taxes by government to support a cheaper program are considered a burden (notwithstanding their relation to ethically based consensual processes), where collusive pricing to support a more expensive program is deemed acceptable. The difference is that in one situation, the tax is hidden (and thus easier to collect), more or less, while in the other it is not.

[31] These concepts are regarded as elementary among modern economists, but are often neglected within the arena of political discourse, inexplicably perhaps except as noted above in the poor comprehension of what a "government" is within the universe of behavioral economy—i.e., a stubborn tendency to oversimplify the relationship between government (law) and the effect of law on production. There are two important economic concepts which may help to loosen attachment to the view of government as "person."

One of these involves the simple realization that when government spends its tax revenues on labor, it produces taxable income in those who receive it. But what is received is not received only by the government employee or service contractor, but by others who receive funds through the private expenditures of the same people who receive government money. Government has placed its money in circulation, some of which is subject to taxation. Assume, for example, that all the money placed in circulation is taxable at 25 percent as it is received (an admittedly unreasonable assumption). The government theoretically recoups the expenditure from the tax revenues generated from four generations of payment—i.e., 25 percent from primary recipients and 3 groups of secondary recipients—unless there is offsetting currency inflation due to productivity lag which is less than equal to the expenditure (see below—"multiplier).

Another concept is referred to by Keynesian theorists as a "multiplier" applied to the stimulative effect of the circulation of currency on consumer behavior (aggregate demand). Theoretically, an increase in demand brought on by a change in an endogenous variable such as government spending, will likely result in a change of an exogenous variable such as investments in production (e.g. hiring more laborers) which increases production—thereby offsetting the inflationary effect of such spending. In an economy where there is significant underutilization of human resources, therefore, the effect of spending stimulates production over the course of several generations of spending (The percentage increase of which is called its "multiplier.") until markets achieve maximum or optimal use of available resources.

Crucial in the evaluation of a multiplier is a comparison of the consumptive behavior of those who pay for it—and the tendency of spending to reduce other business costs. This would tend to favor the transfer of resources away from individuals who are not spending currency toward those who are—implemented through progressive taxation—such that the de-consumptive impact of taxation is more than offset by consumptive behavior of its recipients. It would also favor the use of government-based spending on necessary infrastructures such as health care (born largely by businesses) and transportation and communications infrastructures. Expenditures resulting in weapons stockpiles or other materials intensive technologies would reduce the multiplier.

[32] This hypothesis—like most—is only partially true even under ideal circumstances, but the point here is not to prove its truth or falsity, but to bring thought into proper zone of scientific skepticism. Since it is a much-debated hypothesis, and is provably true or false, the orientation of a behavioral economy rests in proof—and not in a sense of irony contained in phrases such as "less is more." Sometimes it is and sometimes it isn't, and determinations of whether it is bringing thought into zones where it is possible to reach agreement or least form consensus.

[33] This argument was in fact part of the argument for the repeal of Glass-Steagall (see endnote 30 below) but is the subject of more detailed consideration in Chapter 7 below. International commerce, particularly in the financial and energy sectors present obligational issues of a different kind than we deal with in this chapter.

[34] There are a fair number of theorists who attribute the 2008 financial crisis to the repeal of the Glass-Steagall act of 1933, which established a regulatory wall between banks which served as savings and

loan depositories (commercial banks) and banks which found money for investment (investment banks)—a true statement only as far as it goes. The rationale of Glass-Steagall was that when banks combine power as both depository and investor, conflicts of interest arise tend to (1) consolidate banking institutions in order to achieve market power and (2) to develop investment markets (using depositor credit) which pay large premiums to the banks at high depositor risk and low bank and bank officer risk. Critics of this repeal (Gramm-Leach-Biley Act of 1999) correctly foresaw a "requisite-type" problem in the administration of standards of care, institutional motivations, and the establishment of accountability controls. Proponents of the repeal argued that competitive pressures within the financial marketplace and regulatory standards preventing undue leveraging of depositor assets were sufficient to reign the finance industry within conservative boundaries typical of fiduciary relationships, and cite the bi-partisan advocacy of the reform as "proof"—of sorts—of its reasonableness.

Other factors, however, suggest a more sinister narrative. The repeal occurred within an environment of heavily funded campaigns of pro-bank legislators, and the impeachment (and resultant neutering) of a populist presidential figure. Moreover, a few years after the enactment of Glass-Steagall in 2004, and chief executive and Congress benefitting heavily from campaign expenditures from in the financial sector lifted leveraging restriction—affecting the safety ratio of extended credit to secure assets, and defunded the part of the Securities and Exchange Commission which investigated and enforced safety rules governing the issuance (by banks and other entities) of securities.

In the meantime, the banking industry increased its level of consolidation to include very strong interdependencies between investment insurance products (derivatives) issued by finance companies acting in near partnership with investment banks, and the conversion of home equity into tradable securities (with derivative markets endorsing their value)—all of which created the superficial impression of conservative risk (AAA rated), but which underneath revealed very high risk. Even the rating agencies (paid to evaluate risk of loss on investment) were cordoned into compliance with the dominant financial institutions.

Much of the newly leveraged credit flowed into the inflation of the housing market, and threatened to collapse the economy on a global scale upon the discovery that home prices were unsustainable based on the comparatively low productivity of the middle class—the result of overleveraging and the dissolution of the substance of regulatory safeguards.

The point of the illustration is not to cast blame on one political party or another, but to lend substance to the notion that some markets have a more direct rivalry with government than others, and this is particularly true of the financial marketplace.

[35] Our recognition of the relationship between the organizing properties of language and its manifestation in the formation of objects liberates us—to a degree—from the use of logical hierarchy as the prime mover of social order with an individual situated in a position of control. Such organization may function effectively in a state of dialogue with an entire society of participants, but will succumb eventually to influences which overstress the capacity of the central figure.

The reduction of all organization to logical hierarchy tempts contemporary practitioners of Requisite organization. Accordingly, it has been useful in this work to notice that logical processes—phased processes involved in the formation of "object"—are based on but not identical to linguistic processes. Logical hierarchy (higher order prevailing over lower order) involves the introduction of obligation within a limited universe, and will adjust the size of that universe to fit the capability of its organizer. Linguistic hierarchy (inner engaged in a phased dialogue with outer) sets boundaries within a theoretically unlimited universe.

And that—by way of translation into the emerging vocabulary of Requisite—is a way of stating the nature of the problem. The spoken language can't handle the complexity of social relationships in an industrial society—and neither can dominative hierarchy. The implementational solution, therefore, would favor the establishment of a language-type process as "government" rather than attempting to do the same through logical hierarchy. This alters, somewhat, what we might look for in leadership, i.e., not only high organizational capability, but an intuitive grasp of the ethical power of language as a means of sharing experience. We may, in the process, need to expand our view of what "intelligence" and "capability" mean.

[36] This, as with all maps and pictures, represents an easier way of expressing a complex of related and interdependent processes than is most often available in the serially oriented structure of our spoken language. The fact that it is corralled into a picture, however, invites one to view this as another version of fixed object that one might regard as they would an apple or a bureaucracy. That would be a mistake.

Notice that here the institutional components embody a tri-partite entity, each representing a processing center within a single government of co-equal branches, and value which inputs as a sense of Other (an electorate) and I (the basis of existence—constitution). The citizen doesn't stand outside of this model, but is lifted into it as a state of engagement, in a game of language in which someone places themself. It is not a picture of an object, or person, but of our own experience as a political creature in the thrall of an effectively implemented behavioral economy. This shift takes some getting used to, i.e., "it's not the government, it's me." And that, it seems, is the basis of the resonance of it. The structures of government replicate the structure of our engagement in language, which may at a given moment produce many ethical deficiencies, it is nonetheless an ethical process. Laws generating from this process therefore have ethical content which is different than the laws issued under dominative sovereignty.

[37] At this point it is appropriate, perhaps to note that property as an earned right of control has social implications which are entirely dependent on the impact that such control has on others. There are certain kinds of property which are essential and necessary to the maintenance of security over one's own welfare and his or her family and community, and rights of control which involve others in lifelong commitments and states of dependency. The practice of discernment at the level of government over these can be nuanced, and require an understanding of social obligation which properly attaches to rights of control. These considerations often require government scrutiny and intervention of the kind manifest in organizationally aware—manifest in the establishment of values and institutions equal to and in agreement with expectancy of ordered individual liberty—Requisite orientation. Thus, the behavior of a corporate CEO in the exercise of control over interests affecting thousands must be addressed as the exercise of a different kind of property interest than that of the same CEO managing a private household. See Eliot Jaques, Social Power and the CEO: Leadership and Trust in a Sustainable Free Enterprise System (Greenwood, 2002).

[38] Having pointed out the self-refuting tendency of objectivist philosophy—subjectivist moral isolation failing to recognize that objects (especially socially formed organizations of famous entrepreneurs) are objective because of, not in spite of, shared social value—it might be best to leave well enough alone. Objectivism is partially correct in its orientation, but fails through the use of a mono-valent ethic (self apart from other) rather than the bivalent ethic discussed in Chapter 3 (self-discovery in cooperation with Other). Only the latter is effectively organizational in nature.

But Objectivist philosophy is, to a great extent, consistent with a more primitive view of Requisite which lacks the benefit of a theory of language, along with critics of structuralism—Wittgenstein for one. The more primitive view tends to celebrate largess of organization, and fails to make nuanced qualitative distinctions between smaller organizations which represent more adaptive and integrative constructs, and larger organizations which are not more than the repetitive application of simple processes—true of a number of monopolists, for example. Similarly, a writer who develops three great ideas in an article may easily have done something more complicated than a writer who develops a single good idea, and repeats him or herself over the space of twenty books.

This may, in fact, be the ultimate "tell" on both objectivism and primitive Requisite philosophy—a preoccupation with the magnitude of output at the expense of quality (form over substance, effect over cause, wealth accumulation over wealth enablement). True Requisite is less about the celebration of the complexity of persons than it is about the understanding the complexity of tasks, and moving human resources toward their completion.

[39] See Mark Blaxill and Ralph Eckhardt, The Invisible Edge, Penguin 2009. In Blaxill's account, the story is designed to illustrate the importance of using a collaborative strategy in the development of products in an industry where technological innovations are difficult to anticipate and control. It seems that the importance of the book consists in its way of revealing how dominative strategies can in some sense be disabled through the extension of legal protection to market entry devices—such as technological innovation—and that there are productive collaborations which involve types of organizational skill nonetheless which can flourish without conquest and assimilation.

[40] This suggests a number of useful Requisite interventions by government would not be onerous or impractical to implement. In the last chapter we identified an example of how market productivity may be enhanced through the insightful behavior of one of its participants, and in this chapter legal protections on intellectual property which facilitated entry into (and resultant diversification and competition) markets, which themselves favor productive behavior at a higher level—creative collaboration as opposed to audit strategies.

Interventions utilizing understanding of this sort might emerge from either the finance industry, government, or both in combination—as economists working for such institutions are not, after all, blind to social science research, and are accomplished in the development of models of all kinds for anticipated returns on investments. Thus, before making a determination of the likely return on investment, it is necessary to assess the number of players in the market, the related technologies necessary in the development of products, and of equal importance, the amenability of a marketplace to effective leadership along with the sophistication of available leadership within the market.

There are few arbitrary limits on what government auditors are entitled to consider in the evaluation of a bank's assets, and such evaluation is already a common practice in the determination of the leveraging to which a bank is entitled against those assets. An analysis which factors the organizational dynamic of a given market into an evaluation of institutionally calculated risk would be measurably enhanced by the simple utilization of social science in the evaluation (1) the complexity associated with the development of favorable returns and (2) kind of leadership incentives and capabilities which the market offers. The translation of organizational potential and value into financial models would not be very complicated.

Government itself might utilize Requisite in evaluating its direct investment in the development of industries on which the public has a vital interest, as in the health and energy industries. At least two major government subsidies (Solyndra and A123Systems) appeared to have failed in large part due to miscalculations related to the organization of the solar panel and energy storage industries, or rather, an incomplete analysis of the risk and complexity of the organization of those industries. One must have a sophisticated understanding of both what organization is, as well as its relationship with real people in order to assess the timing and magnitude of subsidy—all of which lie close to the heart of Requisite analysis.

The administration of the regulatory process is itself a task of organization which requires that the regulator anticipate behaviors based on his or her understanding of the strategic orientation of the players in a market, and the formation of an information processing and gathering organization which operates efficiently. One cannot understand strategic behavior in others without understanding how the mind acquires control over and manages a field of information—and without having a comfortable sense of the scale and complexity in which those strategic orientations take place. Even if government doesn't have the resources necessary—such as to pay an attractive salary adequate to draw capability from the private market (though it should be noted that effective regulation has very good ROI because the revenue yield from taxes and regulatory penalties greatly exceed the cost of hire)—it might have designed intermediate processes engaging quasi-public entities subject to public account.

[41] This assertion is a matter of controversy in modern economies. If the "credit" of government consists in the anticipated productivity of its economy, then debt repayment will come from tax revenues deriving from that productivity, and as such, government credit is tied to its economy—and that the issuance of currency will not result in the devaluation of it. As debt accumulates, a certain nervousness arises among those who are accumulating currency that the source of debt repayment will be the account-holders of that accumulation, and thus that debt accumulation is really naught but a form of deferred taxation against a wealthy class—assuming that it is politically difficult to tax persons living at close to subsistence and who vote. So, the escape strategy of a wealthy class is to internationalize finance and to disable the taxing power of government. This, it seems, serves as a better explanation for legislative intransigence in the assessment of progressive taxation, i.e., not because it will reduce economic productivity (See Congressional Research Service, Taxes and the Economy, An Analysis of the Top Tax Rates Since 1945, September 2012) but because it will transfer wealth more equitably to non-military social needs, and interfere with the use of internationally based deposit accounts. Such intransigence thus provides a nice example of Requisite failure in government—of law and economy.

[42] The problem is—like most things—a bit more complicated than one might capture in summary of this nature. Since the depositories of currency accumulators exceed their consumptive needs (and desires) by many times, the emphasis shifts from accumulation in the form of income (which is at least theoretically available for taxation) to accumulation of deposits representing diverse interests and investments which are either immune from taxation (retirement accounts, for example) or are subject to very low tax rates (investments classified as capital gains) or are regarded as business expenditures (as in accelerated asset depreciation) or are shielded as gains by offsetting fictional losses. All of these avoidance measures became much easier for banks to use when consolidating at an international level and when restrictions eliminating the wall between commercial and investment banks were lifted.

The common thread of machinations of this nature is that there are many ways to avoid taxation of assets while preserving control over accumulated currency—the primary purpose of which is to gain strategic advantage in the exploitation of opportunities created by economic strength (normally destructive risk) as opposed to the advancement of socially beneficial innovations. As a general rule, accumulation of the sort we see on an international scale are not used to create, but to take—and thus are weighted heavily on assets tied to very predictable and established use. In order to tax, of course, one should be able to comprehend the strategy of control over assets—much more difficult when tracking the movement of money between accounts of diverse banks in an international system.

[43] See John Rawls, (1975) A Theory of Justice (revised edition) Harvard University Press (1975), at p. 53 Rawls first cast this principle as follows: "Each person is to have an equal right to the most extensive total system of equal basic liberties compatible with a similar system of justice for all" which is somewhat different in substance than a principle of equal distribution because it accommodates choices preceding distribution, allowing, for example, that someone might choose to earn more by working harder. Rawls engaged in periodic modification of this principle to address H.L.A Hart's criticism that the use of the phrase "equal basic liberties" doesn't say much except to identify a principle of equality, and Rawls felt the criticism was valid, and thereafter modified the expression to" Each person has an equal right to a fully adequate scheme of equal basic liberties which is compatible with a similar scheme for all." (See John Rawls, Political Liberalism, Columbia University Press, (1993), at p. 291) Since we are here focused on issues of distribution, we have cast that principle in its "default" form as a principle of equal distribution, assuming that all have an equal desire or interest in the productivity and thus make equal effort to obtain the same. It seems to this author unnecessary to make nuanced attempts to set equal "liberty" apart from equal "distribution" as Rawls' second principle provides a basis on which to individuate distribution in accordance with variation among individuals in social contribution attributable either to effort, efficiency or ability. Rawls himself acknowledged difficulty in applying this as principle in connection with the problem unequal distribution of individual capabilities.

[44] John Rawls, A Theory of Justice (revised edition) p. 47

# Appendix

As stated in the main text of this work, the evolution of a theory of Requisite organization benefits from a significant body of work which both examines human behavior in stratified organizations and the arrangement of truth functional logic into a stratified matrix which bears resemblance to that behavior. The use of logic as an observational filter has been part of the evolution of terminology used to describe people at work, and so it is probably suspect to say that the resemblance appeared as an independent source of validation of Requisite descriptors. They have been coevolving.

That being said, the use of logic has been useful because logic itself has been around for quite a while and has been worked on with the purpose of simplifying thought and thinking to its essential form. It is as well accompanied by a calculus—from which judgments of true and false, complete and incomplete, valid and invalid, and ordered and disordered may be made. If there is something at the core of a strategic or problem-solving orientation, chances are it has been conceptualized within the language and notational devices of abstract logic.

As much as we might say that good has followed from the simplification of a descriptive terminology, the use of logic in the formulation of these terms is more than a simplification. It is also a theory of mind, or at least a significant aspect of a theory of mind that in this case challenges the simplistic view that hierarchy occurs through progressive generalization.

This is something that managers have known from, let us say, "the start," in that effective management is much more than the delegation and inspection of tasks, but of understanding the constraints and resistance of the field in which work occurs. Similarly, in real logic, or at least the logic taught in contemporary textbooks, logic has very little to do with progressive generalization and very much to do with the strategic use of information in making arguments. As such, logic is a purposeful activity, and is incoherent without identifying expectancy and motivation. The extensions of logic are understood through their intensions.

The examination of work is, at some level, an examination of logic, in this case a universalized description of a mind seeking something. The reason why logicians and other cognitive scientists have been getting stirred up over work is due to the fact that there are work behaviors that appear to traverse context—constants. This encourages the social scientist to move from anecdotal observations, to functional terms identified as universals within a symbolic language.

The following jobs have been classed, for example, into stratified work titles, while using Requisite observations as background. (Andrew Olivier (AO), Some Background to Requisite Organisation Models, 2010, www.workcomplexity.com.)

> Level I: manual worker, admin clerk, front line sales person, call center operator, police constable, artisan, technician, claims assessor, miner, chef, front line supervisor.

> Level II: doctor, dentist, bench scientist, front line manager, researcher, lecturer, faculty officer, area sales manager, head chef, systems analyst, accountant.

> Level III: manager, project leader, research program leader, human resources manager, academic department head, practice head, logistics manager, colonel, ship's captain, call center manager.

> Level IV: Financial manager, dean, general manager, principal advisor, senior consultant, one star general, deputy director.

> Level V: CEO of a freestanding company, MD of a division within a group, director general, vice-chancellor of university, two stars general.

Now, if we were to try to describe what persons at these levels were "doing" we would probably be utilizing an intuitive sense of graduated complexity required in each of those job roles. And the task of description, therefore, is to keep the logic consistent throughout the description. There would be some attempt at Level I, for example, to use descriptors that are friendly (consistent) with added skills one wishes to identify at higher levels, which is to say, to maintain the consistent appearance of progression throughout the descriptive process.

Thus, in the same article we are provided with an illuminating set of descriptors that emphasize "leadership" as the basis for the movement from one level to the next.

Level I: lead self.

Level II: lead team.

Level III: lead others who lead team.

Level IV: lead multiple functions/processes.

Level V: lead business.

Logic here unfolds using self as baseline and thereafter identifying a progression which gives some sense of expanding magnitude or comprehensiveness of role, as well as a potential for the identification of methodological shift from one level to another. An awareness of methodological shift is most noticeable above at level IV, where the author shifted from a spatially conceived sense of comprehension (self → team → leaders of teams) to a work role involved in "functions" and "processes." The analysis is coherent (and easy to follow) because an interest has identified a universe of discourse (leadership) which allows the logic within that discourse to be expressed.

Something changes however where as a matter of science we become preoccupied with the development of trans-contextual constants. How did we know, for example, how to build a hierarchy of leadership if we did not already have an intuitive sense of how development works—independently of context? Just as science is involved in a search for theoretical constructs which apply in diverse contexts—as in Newton's theory of motion—so too does social science search for a logical substance from which applications like the logic of leadership development above may be "explained." The search is for a more universal set of coherent descriptors that can be used or identified as the "basis" of more context bound descriptors. Therefore, why not go to the logic of propositional calculus and build a descriptive matrix that can be used everywhere?

The hierarchical structure in propositional logic—at least on three levels—is obvious to those who have taken a course in that logic, probably because the logic was conceived in terms designed to break it in to its essential components, and provide the basis of a calculus of demonstration or argument. Also, those who teach logic are likely themselves to formulate a developmental progression that moves from simple to complex judgments in order to make teaching more effective. This progression works well in academic textbooks on logic for the first three levels.

Hence we have a (1) proposition about the world— "p", (2) a way of combining propositions about the world—"p" and/or "q" and (3) and a way of drawing inference from one proposition that is known to another—"p" and "if p then q" therefore "q". At each successive level, we have a very clear sense that something has been added into the logic, and it also appears to be something that could explain stratification in organization. As in the example above, we have self-leadership "p", team leadership "p" and/or "q", and leading (or teaching) team leadership "p" and "if p then q" therefore "q". [Notice how we are inclined to add parenthetically "(or teaching)" based on what we learn about logical progression from a more abstract logical platform.]

From this point, academic textbooks on logic move away from the use of logic as a truth-functional calculus into what they call a theory of binary relations without much in the way of explaining that movement except to point out that logic at (3) indicated that propositions which implied other propositions were, in effect, working from an assumed relationship between one proposition and another –"if p then q". But if one desires liberation from the linearity of syllogistic inference, and comprehend systems of interdependent propositions, they must loosen attachment to the content of a proposition, and thereafter treat propositions as points or vertices within an ordered complex of propositions.

In other words, change the language of propositions to a language of sets whose members stand in varying "types" of relationships to each other. This too resonates with the logic of leadership on display above, as a relational logic appears to describe the actions of a leader who has loosened preoccupation with a linear process "leading leaders" to system wide functionality. [Again, notice how we are inclined to reframe the descriptor to remind others that "functionality" and "process" are interests which embrace an entire system.]

This is one problem in the attempt to use propositional logic as the descriptive basis for stratification in organization—i.e., the lack of continuity of descriptive language or notation in the movement between propositional logic to relational logic. But the problem expresses itself in other ways.

First, propositional logic was not devised to account for intellectual development conceived or mirrored in organizational hierarchy. It was meant in the first instance to describe what we mean in ordinary language in saying something is or is not true. In order to have a coherent theory of logic that accounts for such development one needs to include a principle of limitation at each logical level, such that something we refer to as "capability" might be expressed as limitation which allows some processes to occur and precludes others. Propositional logic has no such component—though it may well be implied by virtue of the fact that the gradation of complexity in logical processes is responsive to the incremental addition to logical operations.

Second, related to the first, propositional logic invokes what appear to be more than one incremental process at each level. There are, for example at level two in logic not one, but four connectives—the disjunctive "p or q", the conjunctive "p and q", the conditional "If p then q" and the bi-conditional "p if and only if q". At this point, it becomes very interesting to note what academic textbooks on a theory of relations identify as not one, but four different types of relations—symmetrical, anti-symmetrical, transitive and reflexive. The question then became—how do we treat intellectual development as incremental if each successive logical level appears to introduce a whole complex of new ideas.

The first proposed solution was brilliant, but incorrect—impressed, perhaps, by the fact that in both the logic of connectives as well as the logic of relations, the complex of ideas numbered "four." According to R.O. Gibson and D.J. Isaac (identified as Jaques collaborators in the text of this book—and primarily to Gibson by Jaques on issues of truth functional logic in private conversation. Their combined authorship on truth functional logic is referenced collectively as the "Gibson" logic) the introduction of four main ideas in each successive level of logic suggested an order, of sorts, where each level introduced an explicit and implicit duality. The implicit duality was there but was providing the basis of a movement to the next level, where it would become an explicit duality.

This amounted to a fascinating hypothesis about human intellectual development, i.e., that as we as human beings appear to land on solid ground—seeing a world as black and white—we are at the same time undermining that ground so that we might comprehend the world from a better vantage point. And so, Gibson inserted a process of development which at each level introduced two pairs of dualities, using truth values in the use of tables as a means of expressing the expansion of capacity—involving four new ideas at each level, as follows.

Level I: Propositions—False/True [Negation, Assignment] (Brackets identify the "implied" duality)

Propositional Statement "P"

Express duality
F
T

Implicit duality
Not F, Not T Negation
Not T=F, Not F=T (Assignment)]

The express duality of "false" and "true" is treated as a self-evident baseline. Implicit in the process of determining f/t, however is an awareness of exclusion between them, evident in the functional application of negation, and the rule of assignment (one or the other but not both).

Level II: Connective Association—Disjunctive (or)/Conjunctive (and); [Conditional (if-then →)/Bi-conditional (if and only if ⟵ ⟶)]

Propositional group ("P", "Q")

| P /Q | Express duality | | Implicit Duality | |
|---|---|---|---|---|
|  | P or Q | P & Q | P → Q | P ⟵ ⟶ Q |
| t /t | T | T | T | T |
| t /f | T | F | F | F |
| f /t | T | F | T | F |
| f /f | F | F | T | T |

The express duality is revealed through contrasting columns of truth value, where P or Q is true if only one value PQ is true, and P&Q is true only if all values are true. Implicit in the process of functioning with the confines of disjunctive and conjunctive expressions is the emergence of awareness of interdependence, such that a value for one includes value for another.

Level III: Functional association (Argument)—Prime formula/Composite formula; [Functional expression/Rule of Induction.]

Propositional function/argument ("P" includes "Q")

Express duality

| Prime formula (determined) | | Composite formula (undetermined) |
|---|---|---|
| P | P ← → Q | Q |
| T | T | T |
| T | T | T |
| F | T | F |
| F | T | F |

Implicit duality

Functional expression   Rule of Induction

This use of truth tables varies to a degree from Gibson's original expression of it, but this expression nonetheless helps his case for an explicit/implicit duality. A real problem in the use of terminology is variance by which logical ideas are expressed where, for example, "argument", "function" , "syllogism", "induction" to some authors mean the same thing and to others mean something entirely different. It is therefore better to stay focused on the unique characteristics of the form, and its utility, which is visibly different at this level.

What was implicit at Level II—intimative association between P/Q—is now set out as the basis of an argument for the truth value of a proposition which has yet to be determined.—P is known, and P includes Q, therefore Q is known. Implicit in the extension of inference to a range of composite values is an emerging awareness that P, Q are functionally bound in a relationship—thereby supporting a rule of induction, or validity. Q is revealed where P is known, and a premise including Q with P.

Level IV: Relational association (order within and between sets of propositions)—Symmetrical (no order)/Anti-symmetrical (order); [Transitive, Reflexive]

Propositional relationality (Statement of rationale by which "P" includes "Q", "R", and/or "S", etc. within a relational type represented here in the small case "r".)

Express duality:

Prime/Composite set X=Symmetrical relation (for all P and Q in X it holds that if PrQ then QrP)

Prime/Composite set X = Anti-symmetrical relation (for all distinct P and Q in X, if PrQ then not QrP)

Implicit duality:

Prime/Composite set X =Transitive relation (for all P,Q and r in X it holds that if PrQ and QrR then PrR)

Prime/Composite set X =Reflexive relation (for all P in X it holds that PrP)

Here again, in order to make Gibson's developmental theory more comprehensible, we emphasize the utility of the change in logic being used, and note particularly that the range of attachment expands from "P,Q" to "P,R"—or any other variable one chooses to place within the relational set. Here the utility derives from a movement from the simple statement about inclusion—p includes r (and likewise in reverse order) in a symmetrical relation—to a statement of the order of inclusion in an anti-symmetrical relation—PrQ but not QrP. In one instance p and q have no particular "location," but in the other P and Q are located within a continuum such that a change in location cannot occur because the position of each is established through a relationship of order that covers the entire system.

Emerging, therefore, is an implicit duality within the use of relations as a means of "locating" ideas is the inclusion of remote ideas as part of an ordered complex. Thus "transitive" describes a process, an expanding process of relational constructs—occurring within an ordered sequence, and a reflexive standard by which P has one and only one place within a prime/composite set or "complex."

Level V: Contextual association-- technical definition of "term"/ technical definition of "predicate"; [Universal Quantifier/Existential Quantifier]

Propositional Universe (Statement of principle by which terms or variables within a domain or universe are placed within it)

Express duality:

Technical definition of "term": a complete relational construct that qualifies as an object or variable within a set of constructs constituting a universe—an object fitting within a prescribed range of variance.

Technical definition of "predicate": operator which when attaching to "term" in the form of a proposition allowst the determination of its truth or falsity.

Implicit duality:

Universal quantifier: statement that a given predicate applies to all terms within a universe.

Existential quantifier: statement that a given predicate applies to at least one term within a universe.

Here we can see that what was implicitly taking place at Level IV, as the development of a rationale of inclusion for all members of a relational complex is at Level V expressed as a principle of inclusion that delimits a universe or context. Predicate is what introduces the duality of False and True, in application to a term within that universe. It seems that in this version of a hierarchy of logic, we have come full circle, except having developed language suitable for logic of a higher order calculus.

As "universe" or "context" allow one to establish a domain of (and to speak coherently and consistently about) all kinds of universes many of which are abstracted terms identifying "types" of lower order complexes. "Universe" thus avoids confusion apt to accompany vagueness over the acceptable range of variance, and allows logic to be contextually labile. It is, in a manner of speaking, a syntactic courtesy designed to place its users on the same page.

As useful and progenerative as this "logic" of explicit and implicit dualities was and is, its value as a basis of description for human development in complex institutions is, perhaps, more apparent now with the benefit of further thought and experience in the development of logic-based descriptors. We have made some rhetorical modification of the theory. This was done out of respect for what the originator of this progression might have done with the benefit of experience, but also so that we might more accurately identify the difficulty of using propositional logic as a basis for the description of stratified hierarchies in institutions. And there are several problems with it.

First, though we can solve the problem of identifying "capacity" at each stage by being clearer about the utility that added logical function— added logical function identifying expansion and comprehension of a larger group of propositions, we are nonetheless dealing with an awkward hypothesis to the effect that in doing something new, we consciously appropriate a new duality. Common sense strongly suggests that when someone attempts something new, he or she is singularly focused on doing one new thing, and that doing so does not involve the conscious introduction of a duality, but that the emergence of a new duality is naught but a description of the transformational effect that a new process has on a integrated collection of old processes. Duality is therefore better viewed not as the cause of logical improvement but of the effect of the introduction of a singular improvement that strikes a contrast with its predecessor.

Second, the dualistic nature of Gibson's implicit dualities are difficult to conceptualize, except to note that they represent different processes, but they do not carry over readily into and define dualities present at the next level. It is well understood that his intent was to accommodate four-part complexes of ideas outlined within each methodological level that first order logic engages. But it is unnecessary to accommodate them within the rubric of implicit duality to account for their joint appearance within the lexicon of propositional logic—most noticeably in academic literature at Levels II and IV (disjunctive, conjunctive, conditional, bi-conditional) and (symmetrical, anti-symmetrical, transitive, reflexive). We can accomplish the same thing within the following paradigm.

1. Unimproved state.
2. Improved state.
3. Act of transition or conversion
4. Rule of conversion or completeness

Third, the Gibson hierarchy strongly suggests that a fifth level of development marks a point of return to logical form evident in a first level, and that he suggests a quatripartite cycle—i.e., four and only four forms of logical operation with some provision for the treatment of a fifth level as a point of transition to a higher order of complexity. Indeed, when this author first endeavored to correct Jaques in the use of a five-tiered system in 1980, Jaques conceded that Gibson had already been promoting four-tiered progression. The problem with Gibson's presentation in his 1978 publication, is that he begins with terms False and True as undefined, and apparently uses Level V as an opportunity to define what a proposition is—i.e., a predicate attached to a term—with "truth" being existential verification of the applicability of a predicate to a term. This makes the identity of form between Levels I and V difficult to discern because of reluctance to define "false" and "true" in the first instance.

Fourth, the use of propositional logic is itself a cumbersome instrumentality for the description of logical levels, because not all cognitive acts are reducible to linguistic acts—or if they were, they might themselves be difficult to capture as statements about complex objects. Since we tend to organize relations spatially and temporally, there might be some advantage in developing a notational system which conveyed the emergence of organization pictorially, and in a way that both presented an increase in complexity from an established baseline of complexity and identified and confirmed the improved efficiency of higher order logical processes.

A notation of this sort has been available in the logic of information processing which identifies an information baseline as a bit "." and utilizes programming technologies to find a desired bit "+" within a field of data. Since time and capacity are part of the logic of information process, it is desirable to improve the navigation of a field by partitioning the field so that unnecessary effort and expense (capacity) is avoided. Thus the use of a symbol ( ) to indicate "interest" brought to bear on a field of data searches for the bit of interest "+" within a field ……+.

(.).,.,.+. to (……+.)

The act of grouping or partitioning options represents a more efficient way of navigating the field, and thus resonates with what occurs in human intelligence as it attempts to condense singular parts into complex wholes, so that knowing the value of one object allows one to know the position of the others. The empirical question is whether this process of consolidation engages one in a process that resembles the emergent logic processes identified by Gibson and Isaac in their 1978 publication. The answer is, essentially, "yes" and in fact allows us to suggest improvements in his analysis.

The use of "information processing" as a metaphor in understanding logical hierarchy is, however, precariously close to identifying the human being with a computational machine, inasmuch as we often describe computers as "information" processors. Yet computers compute and/or process data, not information. Data becomes information through the intervention of interest. A machine having interest is not an artificial intelligence, but to the contrary, is genuine in every sense of the word. Information is a sentient phenomenon.

As basic a distinction as this is—i.e., a primary difference between expectation and creation, intension and extension, there are only a few logicians to date that seem to appreciate its importance. Ludwig Wittgenstein in his Tractatus and G. Spencer Brown in Laws of Form have led the way, Wittgenstein did so by emphasizing that human propositions are, by design, subject to environmental resistance that disappoints their proponents, and Brown by formulating a logical calculus that uses a circle about a space (.) as a motivated intervention that once created alters its maker.

If there is hierarchy in the universe, it is not a hierarchy of structures, but of interests inasmuch as there is no way to say one structure is better or higher than another without first introducing a value that makes it so. What we learn from Gibson's significant contribution to Logic is that the limits of a given level of information processing express themselves as dichotomies, or rather, as incompatible alternatives. As one moves into a higher level, they are consciously superseded and redefined.

Level I—Declarative processing. The first step is to avoid an attempt to use undefined terms "false" and "true" as a starting point, and instead to move the basis of their definition from Level V to Level I. We begin with a universe of discourse—a field—already in place. A "term" or "object within that universe substitutes well as "." and "interest" now represented as ( ) substitutes effectively as a technical definition of "predicate." The use of this notational system, taken from G. Spencer Brown's work, is explained in the Appendix to On Freedom, Poetic Matrix Press, 2016..

Interest, however, has magnitude, or rather, it is situated such that it can only embrace a given particulate within the field. This, in essence, defines what a proposition is, i.e., an interest brought to bear on a space or location separated or distinguished from a value neutral manifold. The expression "+" does not attach to "." intrinsically, but only acquires that status because interest selects it from among a group of objects which in of themselves have no value, i.e., from "." to "(+)". Interest is thus an intervention of value that provides the basis of separating or distinguishing one space among others as valuable. This occurs as a random search, with no limit except those of probability on the repetition of error. To avoid the repetition of error one must be able to remember, but recollection is not allowed under the rules which limit capacity.

We thus have four logical ideas within an information processing vocabulary that correspond to four ideas extracted from first order logic.

| | |
|---|---|
| Object | Term |
| Interest | Predicate |
| Distinction | Negation |
| Selection | Rule of assignment (either, not both) |

So what happened to "false" and "true" as an explicit duality? It may help here to note that Gibson admitted to uncertainty in the development of descriptors at this level, and his doubts appear to be justified. For one operating at a baseline, the judgment "false" or "true" is something added to the process, and in a logic where capacity is strictly limited the insertion of an interest-based distinction, there is no room to adjudicate "false" or "true" but rather instead only to experience error and satisfaction—and these are not the same. Likewise, the logical function of "negation" is at its most primitive level one and the same as distinction, or rather, the conversion of a neutral state to a positive.

It is, perhaps, useful to acknowledge that nothing new happens at this level as far as the "processing" of information except to identify "+" as valuable. The processing instrumentalities allowing for the formation of object were already in place. The one thing that changed is the addition of a new interest to an old one.

Level II—Cumulative processing. Likewise, at level two, except that a new interest in remembering—which derives from a baseline interest—integrates such that one might avoid the repetition of effort. Only then can one state coherently that the assignment of "true" and "false" have meaning. Knowing they are false or true includes remembering error and satisfaction. So, there is one and only one additional interest that offers to transform a less efficient strategic orientation.

| | |
|---|---|
| (.)…..+. Unknown | P or Q Disjunctive |
| [ ] as interest in knowing | P & Q Conjunctive |
| […..(.)]+. Changing unknown to known | P→Q Conditional |
| Knowledge cancels ignorance | P←→Bi-conditional |
| | (Either not both) |

Is there effective correspondence between these ideas? A disjunctive expression is true if but one of its components is true. The same is the case for the class of unknowns—the search is productive if but one space satisfies interest. A conjunctive expression, however is true only if all its components are true—and that seems to describe one's interest in knowing, i.e., to be correct in its expectancy of each member.

It should be noted that first order logic is somewhat careful to treat a conditional expression differently from an implication. Conditional expressions signify that one follows after the other. Implications signify that one includes the other. When field is limited to two possibilities (and knows that it is so limited), knowing one allows the inference of the other. There is far less certainty in broader domains, such as in the expression P→QRST. After knowing P, one still doesn't know or expect anything except that one of QRST is true. It is also evident in the fact that propositional logic regards the following two expressions as equivalent.

| p/q | - p or q | p → q |
|-----|----------|-------|
| t/t | t | t |
| t/f | f | f |
| f/t | t | t |
| f/f | t | t |

Since distinction and negation are here treated as equivalents, [(.)]+ is the logical equivalent of - p or q, and p→q, but does the same apply to a bi-conditional? The bi-directionality of the expression suggests that it does, but it is also true as a formal and explicit matter, as a bi-conditional expresses a rule of exclusion similar to that encountered at Level I—i.e., for a given object subject to distinction, it either places in the class of unknown (disjunctive) or known (conjunctive) but not both. The way of writing this in the language of propositional logic is as follows.

[(-p or q) or (-p and q)] and -[(-p or q) & (-p&q)]

This is proven as equivalent by the following.

| p/q | -p or q | -p &q | (-p or q) or (-p and q) and -[(-p or q) & (-p&q)] | p←→q |
|-----|---------|-------|---------|----------|------|
| t/t | t | f | t | | t |
| t/f | f | f | f | | f |
| f/t | t | t | f | | f |
| f/f | t | f | t | | t |

The table above sets forth a form of "proof" of the equivalence of two expressions "either but not both" and "one if an only if the other", though it must be conceded that truth table proofs have never been particularly satisfying, perhaps because we as humans do not organize our affairs this way. We do, however, try to keep track of the "things" we

268

do, and avoid the repetition of error, and as the "things" we do get bigger, the likelihood of error increases. If we don't know where we failed, we are apt to repeat it.

Level III—Serial processing. A benefit of the use of a bit or particle to represent a baseline is that it could be very small or very large, because the symbol "." fails to specify how complex an object it represents. One might imagine that if it were something very large or complicated—like a scientific theory—the repetition of error is quite likely. Even the best theorists might be unsure of what they are building, what the evidence suggests, and of the language they are using to describe events. The expression "." could be something as simple as clearing one's throat, or as complex as building an industry.

That does not mean however that the size of "." is unimportant, though its measure is not important. What is important is that the size remain constant throughout a developmental process, otherwise the logic dissolves into formlessness. This constancy is not evident in things we do as a matter of routine, but it is on things we have to work at, which is to say, our own limits tend to define the magnitude of the tasks and responsibilities we undertake. And so, the assumption of baseline task constancy in a world of work is reasonable, particularly in competitive environments on matters of importance, where people stretch to their limits.

It is very often useful to be able to anticipate consequences instead of having to experience them. For big projects where lives and fortunes are at stake, it can be nice to know that with information of the nature "P" will produce information of the nature "Q", especially where "Q" spells disaster. Let us say, however, that we know that "P" will produce any one of "QRST", where "Q" means disaster, but "S" means fame and fortune. That would be "+", of course, but to get there it isn't enough to remember error, but to avoid certain errors altogether. This capacity represents the next step in logic, where we avoid the preclusion "knowing" and "not knowing" by implying.

| | |
|---|---|
| [.....(.)]+. Supposition | Prime formula (variable) |
| → Intimation (interest) | Composite formula (function) |
| [(.)] →+ Demonstration | Extended use (proof) |
| Intimation cancels supposition | Principle of induction (validity) |

It is not difficult to appreciate the similarity of these two arrangements of logical ideas, as well as to appreciate that their arrangement in fours represent four different aspects of thought occurring at this level as (1) unimproved state, (2) improved state, (3) a process of conversion and (4) a rule of exclusion. Likewise, it may be apparent that for the group on the left, a "rule" of exclusion is unnecessary, because transformation simply "is" the case by satisfying an interest in changing what is the case. Existence manifest as satisfaction of interest stands well on its own, and does not need a rule to exist.

The value of a rule, therefore, does not consist in its attachment to reality, but in the establishment or verification of a state of self-awareness, i.e., that one is engaged in the replacement of one existence with another. In the course of logical transformation, there is quite a difference between what one does at the outset—as in wanting something new—and the emergent realization of the change that was taking place. This, it seems, is the most favorable interpretation of Gibson's intuitive separation of explicit and implicit duality—the latter of which leads to the next level—i.e., that self-awareness is transformative and occurs through repetitive engagement.

One might ask, why doesn't implication extend beyond a single point? That question is a good one, though it represents a lack of understanding of what happens at this level. The thinker comes to this level perched on a platform of action and recollection, and his or her mind is still embedded in the mundane. One's gaze casts proximally in one direction—from here to there. Hence, the term "serial processing" provides an accurate, though superficial description of what is going on. The question is not whether one perceives or senses a consequence to the task at hand, but whether the magnitude of what one senses is useful within a given environment, and whether their senses are trustworthy. If he was stretched to his capacity and engaged at Level II, he will be fully engaged at Level III to effectively anticipate one and only one "other" in a given moment.

Level IV—Parallel processing. The step that involves the anticipation of many comes in part through the realization that anticipation is an act of assertion that never achieves the certainty of "knowledge" and therefore arises through progressive approximation. This awareness thus allows someone to devise theories linking two or more places (not just one) exterior to one's location—theory being a species of intelligent arbitrariness, imagining an ordered pattern and seeking feedback from the environment over whether the imagined pattern is complete and accurate. This has been labeled by some the "scientific method."

Here there is a perceptible difference between the risk one associates with an outward extension to other, and the identification of multiple others as places or locations within a pattern. Again, we encounter an array of four ideas.

[. ← (.) →.]…+. Disorder Symmetrical

→ ← Order Anti-symmetrical

[.← (.)→.]…+. To [.← (→…←)→.]+. Transitive

To [(→…….+.←)] Theory

Order cancels disorder Reflexive

There are significant and obvious similarities between the two groups, and some that are not so obvious. That anti-symmetry describes a relational characteristic used to define "order" is well accepted. Whether and to what extent they reflect true equivalents engages us in unnecessary nuance, as the choice of words is, in each column subject in part to creative license, and there does not appear yet to be a reason to introduce further refinements.

Less obvious, and perhaps worthy of more attention, is that what mathematicians refer to as a "transitive" relation may serve, at its core, a transformative purpose, i.e., to bring binary relations of symmetry into order relations, or perhaps, linear (serial) intimations into patterned complexes discernible within a single moment—[.←(.)→+] to [→..+←)]. A process of transformation thus allows us to appreciate an essential difference between an act of outreach and an act of consolidation—both of which are active in the formation of wholes out of parts, and strongly suggests that intimative processes are foundation to and included in the development of systemic theory.

The term "parallel" processing, though consistent with its use in the cognitive sciences—the favored example of which is how a face differs from the collection of its parts—may mislead slightly insofar as it encourages one to think of this transformation as naught but the aggregation of serial processes. Here it is presented as a process of deconstruction and reconstruction that proceeds to the point of exhaustion in a given field of possibilities. Indeed, it is the fact that we are examining logic within prescribed limits—limits of capacity, interest, object complexity, and field extension (all related)—that enhances appreciation of logic as an organizational process.

Level V—New declarative. Having alluded above to the limits of the organizational subject matter—a limited field of possibilities—we now consider how a field is separated from others, and is absorbed into a higher order. The separation of one field of possibilities from among others occurs in accord with what we want from it—interest. It isn't until we arrive at a fifth level of logic that an important ambiguity over interest appears.

At Level IV we examined a process in which interest ( ) was actually expanding its range of accommodation. It is difficult to say whether interest expanded or whether the parts of the system under observation shrank—in a manner of speaking. We were, however, immersed in a state of secondary interest, as the interest in order derived from the interest that attracted us to the field in the first place. Theoretical expansion is enabled by capability, and has limits that extend outward in accord with it. Such boundaries are real, but are somewhat porous, as they represent intentional rather than conceptual limits. So, the use of a new symbol to express the idea that organizational consolidation functions within a radius defined by interest and capability would be a circle "O", and replaces a bit "." as a space within a larger field-- OOOOOO⧧O. In order to navigate this field, a new interest emerges {} seeking a new reward within a higher "order" of complexity.

The ambiguity over interest consists in the following. On the one hand, a new interest serves to activate engagement in a higher order, while on the other hand, it serves to limit and/or complete the extension of the lower order field. Effectively, a higher order interest serves to terminate and endorse expansion in a lower order—identifying its purpose and state of satisfaction—while activating engagement in a new field. The use of these symbols—and their underlying assumptions—allows for the depiction of a much more convincing transition from one order to another than propositional logic allowed.

| | |
|---|---|
| O Object | Term (Universe) |
| { } Interest | Predicate (Universal Quantifier) |
| O to {⧧} Distinction | Negation (Existential Quantifier) |
| Interest cancels neutrality | Assignment (either, but not both) |
| | (Solution to Russell's paradox) |

The terms in the right side are arranged, in part, to make a point. Quantifiers are a way of indicating whether an expectancy (interest) is in its conception applicable to all (Universal Quantifier—predicate applicable to all members) or at least one (Existential Quantifier—predicate applicable to at least one individual member) of a given field of possibilities. These two quantifiers thus show the difference between an activating interest (predicate) identified as a principle of selection applicable to all and an act of intervention (negation) that selects an individual out of a field. Presented this way, it appears as though a "predicate calculus" invented as a language to address confusion wrought by contextual ambiguity, redefined logic as an information processing function—fields of data (universes) subject to the selective power of interest. Since the most essential principle of exclusion (difference) is that between the force of intervention (value/interest/predicate) and its subject matter (objects or term within a universe), we have a solution to self-referential paradoxes, such as Russell's paradox. Sets (as defining principle) cannot have themselves as members for the same reason that "P" cannot equal "-P"—as the intervention which selects or distinguishes an object is a different kind of thing than object.

As noted previously, the solution to self-referential paradox is more important as conceptual systems become more complex, as there is a tendency to have objects place value on objects, rules to place value on rules, processes on processes, etc. Being connected to value, however, is as important to an organization as a predicate is to the formation of a proposition.

In order to complete this exercise, it may be useful to refer back to the descriptors we extracted earlier from a background article on Requisite organization. Now, however, we graft a more detailed work level description from another author, at People Fit –Australasia, Level of Work and Role Complexity, www.peoplefit.com., 2008.(PFA)

Level I: lead self. (AO)

Follow predefined procedures. When an obstacle is encountered, seek help, no anticipation of problems is expected. (PFA)

Level II: lead team. (AO)

Accumulate bits of information to diagnose and anticipate problems. Proactivity appears. Trends are noticed. (PFA)

Level III: lead others who lead team. (AO)

Plan and carry out sequential projects while considering contingencies and alternatives. (PFA)

Level IV: lead multiple functions/processes. (AO)

Manage multiple, interdependent serial projects. Balance resources among a number of departments. (PFA)

Level V: lead business. (AO)

Optimize the function of a single business unit or corporate support staff. (PFA)

With the juxtaposition offered above, we have the opportunity to appreciate how the introduction of information processing imagery/logic might influence one's use and interpretation of words such as "lead." People Fit—Australasia has clearly internalized the processing vocabulary endorsed by Requisite in the mid 1980s—Declaratory ("predefined "), Cumulative ("accumulate"), Serial ("sequential"), Parallel ("interdependent serial"), New Declaratory ("optimize single business unit"). It also appears that the interest in leaders has shifted to an interest in problem solving—no anticipation of problems, anticipate problems, consider contingencies and alternatives, balance resources (problems redefined as resource limitation issues), optimize function (problem solving redefined optimization of imperfect solutions).

The question at hand (as these suggest) is whether there is an underlying logic guiding these descriptions, and it appears as if they correspond quite well to the logic explained above. It is necessary, however, to begin with the assumption that a field of objects is redefined as an assembly of tasks, and that this field is organized well if each task has a productive relation to an organizational purpose, such that instead of identifying a field in which only one among many operations satisfies an expectancy, all satisfy. An organized field thus appears as

++++++++ and interest ( )

brought to bear when an individual is in each instance productive. We thus have a description of levels of work as follows.

Level I. One is ( ) expected to do one of an organized whole of jobs, and is not expected to identify and solve a problem, i.e., ++++++(+)+. Interest ( ) refers to an orientation (a form) theoretically adapted to a range of activities.

Level II. One is [ ] expected to determine or adjudicate whether another person ( ) is in compliance with predetermined work system, and thus ranges over an assembly of workers in order to assess and record compliance. Problem is defined as failure to perform, ++++++(.)+, and is addressed through corrections in worker performance. This person therefore "leads" a group of others.

Level III. One is → expected to evaluate the implications that one job has relative to another job, and thus to determine whether to make changes in a work process. The move is from compliance into the assessment of whether compliance expectations are feasible or appropriate. This person uses that understanding to modify and communicate modifications of a work system to compliance directors.

Level IV. One is →← expected to integrate or consolidate diverse processes into a functional whole, and thus to balance those processes in a way that optimizes the use of limited resources. In the case of job redesign, this person would press for feasible alternatives and choose among them in a way to assure system wide performance. This individual would also examine budgets designed to effectuate processes and evaluate trade-offs of cost (or cost risk) associated with anticipated deficiencies related to resource failure.

Level V. One is { } expected to set a system wide performance standard within a universe of possibilities that is not organized— OOOOOO≠O, but where at least one option is presumed productive—thereby effectively expressing "interest" as a common expectancy, girded by expectancy of real implementation. While this interest functions as an activating expectancy within a larger universe, it serves as ruling principle to a business unit, and thus allows for selections which optimize performance within that unit. This platform thus allows not merely an integration, but a blending of processes and interests into a single business identity in which all baseline activities are productive—++++++++.

This analysis is possible because the logic of developmental processes contributing to the formation of wholes provides a theoretical backdrop for the insertion of descriptive terms and phrases, and more importantly a basis in which to compare and translate formal expectancies into context—thereby proving that an awareness of logic does, in fact, have a salutary and productive effect on one's examination and understanding of organizations in context. It also has a number of beneficial implications, which include:

1. Team building and cross training to avoid organizational bottlenecks are generally more feasible than many might otherwise suspect because of logical similarity between many tasks within a given level.

2. Development of sensitive and performable expectations of a given individual working on a given task or project, and the avoidance of mismatch between task and capability.

3. The potential for lateral transfer between organizational contexts involving comparable acquired management and/or leadership skills, and the assessment of contextual orientation needed for retraining.

4. A determination of whether diverse processes are amenable to organization or otherwise at what level organization needs to occur in order to achieve desired results.

With the development of confidence that there are laws influencing the content of organizational structures, and that these laws are experienced as motivational states among the participants in organization, we are well positioned to move from (and between) the structure of a given institution and the emergence of structure in larger socio-economic settings such as, industries, markets, governments, disciplines, etc. That natural order of human collectives is not chaos, but oppositely, a movement toward order within expectancies experienced by real people. Within a "logic" we are able to discern that these expectancies are not only transpersonal, but transcontextual, inasmuch as context is a work product of logical processes.

# Author Biography

Peter Friesen received his Bachelor of Arts from Williams College in 1978, majoring in Philosophy. He continued to pursue his philosophical interests in Public Administration at the University of Southern California, and a Juris Doctorate at the University of California, Hastings, awarded in 1982. While a student at the University of Southern California, he studied with Elliott Jaques, and developed the first logical descriptors for cognitive development utilizing an information processing model. Following his J.D., he continued to work under a grant from the Mead Foundation in 1983, producing a manuscript identifying symmetries between levels of logic, morality, language and politics. This manuscript leaned heavily on the work of R.O. Gibson in the formulation of "levels" in first order logic (who was then a collaborator with Jaques) and notational system formulated by G. Spencer Brown in his ground breaking work, Laws of Form.

At the same time, Friesen developed a law practice focused at first on criminal trial work, and then moved to civil trials in cases against corporate and governmental institutions. His casework included lead roles in employment cases, police misconduct, defamation and unfair competition; he was recognized with four San Diego Outstanding Trial Lawyer awards and named on the list of America's Best Lawyers.

In 2000, he took three years away from his law practice to finish the work he started with Jaques in 1979, producing a manuscript entitled On Freedom. As a result of the manuscript, Friesen was invited to serve on the Board of Advisors of Requisite Organization International, Inc, (ROII). He has since been working on the completion of works suitable for publication and various applications of the theory of organization they represent. He has continued to practice law on matters related to employment, business organization and the management of policy.

This current work, *Law and Economic Order: A Theory of Requisite Economy* is his second of three, his first being *On Freedom: Organizational Science Examined Philosophically* published in 2016 by PM Library (an imprint of Poetic Matrix Press). Friesen sees his role as one that can assist in the development of productive communication between Logical, Psychological, Legal and Economic disciplines, and as part of this role, to assist in the marginalization of influences that are interested in disrupting this communication. The third book will be about the use of organizational science in the clarification of issues pertaining to AI, propaganda and the philosophical problem of certainty, all in application to unresolved political controversies.

www.ingramcontent.com/pod-product-compliance
Lightning Source LLC
Chambersburg PA
CBHW051119160426
43195CB00014B/2256